Women and the Italian Resistance

Women and Modern Revolution Series

*Series Editors*

Jane Slaughter                  Richard Stites
University of New Mexico         Georgetown University

# WOMEN AND THE ITALIAN RESISTANCE

## 1943-1945

by
Jane Slaughter

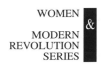

WOMEN & MODERN REVOLUTION SERIES

ARDEN PRESS, INC.
Denver, Colorado

**Library of Congress Cataloging-in-Publication Data**

Slaughter, Jane, 1941-
    Women and the Italian resistance, 1943-1945 / by Jane Slaughter.
        p.    cm. -- (Women and modern revolution series)
    Includes bibliographical references and index.
    ISBN 0-912869-13-5 (cloth), -- ISBN 0-912869-14-3 (paper)
    1. World War, 1939-1945--Underground movements--Italy.   2. World
War, 1939-1945--Participation, Female.   3. Women--Italy-
-History--20th century.   I. Title.   II. Series.
D802.I8S53   1997
940.53'45--dc21                                                                97-4937
                                                                                    CIP

Typography and design by AK Graphics, Inc.
Published in the United States of America
Arden Press, Inc.
P. O. Box 418
Denver, Colorado 80201

# Contents

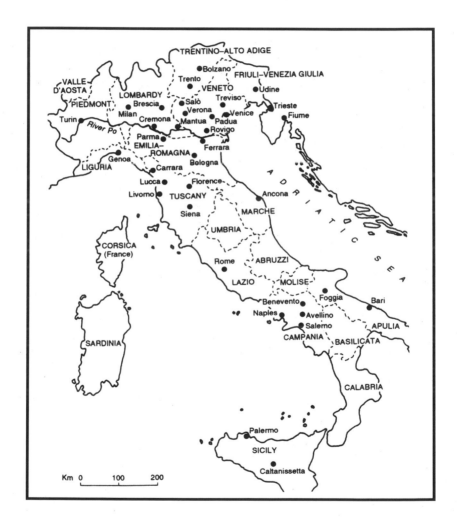

# Editors' Introduction to the Series

The history of the twentieth century has been marked by frequent revolutions and mass popular resistance to oppressive, dictatorial regimes. Few segments of the globe have remained untouched by these conflicts, which have sparked the interest of historians, political scientists, sociologists, and others who seek to understand the unique character of each conflict as well as the themes common to all. An ever-growing body of literature explains the causes or pre-conditions for these mass mobilizations and collective rebellions, examines the role of ideology in the revolutionary process, analyzes leaders and insurgent organizations, and assesses the results of the social conflict. The scope of the scholarship on the topic is impressive, but with rare exceptions, until quite recently the actors considered in each drama have been almost exclusively male and the sexual politics of revolutions have remained in obscurity.

Marie Mullaney, in her work *Revolutionary Women*, begins with a review of existing analysis and notes that "the biggest problem with the available literature...is neither its unscientific quality nor its reductionist nature, but rather its unstated assumptions regarding the gender of revolutionary participants."[1] In other words, revolutionaries are assumed to be men. The need for innovative approaches to the study of revolutions thus seems obvious. It is our intent in this series to meet this demand by uncovering women's previously hidden experiences and perceptions and by analyzing and interpreting revolutionary events and processes in creative ways.

These goals fit within the more general frameworks developed by recent work in women's history, new social and cultural history, and women's studies. This scholarship has recognized and sought to redress imbalances in our historical perspectives, first by retrieving the experiences of women in the past and then by using gender itself as a category of historical analysis. The implications of this approach were clearly stated by Natalie Zemon Davis in her 1975 address to the Berkshire Conference on Women's History. "Our goal is to understand the significance of the sexes, of gender groups, in the historical past. Our goal is to discover the range in sex roles and sexual symbolism in different societies and periods, to find out what meaning they had and how they functioned to maintain the social order or to promote its change."[2]

Though the focus of history in this series is on women and the female experience, the authors recognize that one gender does not stand alone, but is embedded in relationships with the opposite sex and conditioned by class, ethnicity, and age, among other factors. The sex/gender system as defined by Gayle Rubin is a "set of arrangements by which a society transforms biological sexuality into products of human activity."[3] All societies have such a set of arrangements, but their particular function in social organization and their relative importance in determining the course of human history vary. The multiple and complex set of relationships arising from gender and the connections among these relationships and other fundamental forces in history provide the framework for our studies.

In this series we are examining the function of sex/gender systems in the revolutionary process. Our authors will ask the usual questions about revolutions: what are their causes, social components, ideologies, organizations, goals, and results? But they are also asking whether revolutions mean different things to men and women, and if so, why? We need to know, therefore, what motivates women to become involved in collective rebellions, what women contribute, and what happens to women objectively and subjectively as a result of this involvement. Such a quest forces us to include in the political arena points of struggle that exist outside "the formal legal institutions and the public sphere."[4]

Additionally, we should consider how women judged their own actions and articulated their goals. To do this we must listen, as scholar Shirley Mangini has suggested, to "how women [tell] their stories of war and repression…and what they [tell], in order to understand what was of utmost importance to them."[5] We recognize that the most complete historical record includes the cultural forms and processes by which individuals express and interpret their experiences and assign meanings to them. Such widely divergent "cultural productions" as demonstrations, newspapers, and cartoons serve as the bridges between experience, imagination, and eventual political consciousness.[6]

The study of revolutions can be informed and improved by testing the models and considering the challenges posed in recent works in political and cultural history. For example, numerous scholars recognize the value of erasing lines traditionally drawn between consent and dissent, support and opposition, while others see "heroic" actions of both men and women as the results of catastrophic situations in which none of the choices open to them are either desired or expected.[7] Especially useful in providing comparative models are the increasing numbers of studies that describe state-building and nationalism as practices and ideology that rely on gender structures and incorporate the rhetoric of gender norms.[8]

A common theme that links the volumes in this series is the understanding of how individual actions and reactions coalesce in movements and organizations with specified goals, but equally important is the analysis of "the political institutions and state structures through which [they] must operate if their agenda is to be realized."[9] On this latter point it is important to examine the relationship of women and their organizations to what Jane Jenson has described as "the universe of political discourse," which "defines politics, or establishes the parameters of political action."[10]

These common themes are set within the diverse conditions of discrete national histories, and here it is important to emphasize the significance of comparative studies. General questions are addressed in all the volumes of the series, but specific processes and outcomes vary. Comparative studies must consider the particular political and economic characteristics of each national history, as well as the singular forms of national cultural expression. Simultaneously, we must recognize those places where national experiences overlap and individual histories co-exist comfortably. Although the history we share may not be identical, understanding its complexities may help us to define acceptable human standards of social justice for men and women.

1. Marie Marmo Mullaney, *Revolutionary Women: Gender and the Socialist Revolutionary Role* (New York: Praeger, 1983), p. 3.

2. Cited in Joan Kelly-Gadol, "The Social Relations of the Sexes," *Signs* 1:4 (Summer 1976), p. 817.

3. Gayle Rubin, "The Traffic in Women," in Rayna R. Reiter (ed.), *Toward an Anthropology of Women* (New York: Monthly Review Press, 1975), p. 159.

4. Barbara Seitz, Linda Lobao, and Ellen Treadway, "No Going Back: Women's Participation in the Nicaraguan Revolution and in Postrevolutionary Movements," in Ruth Howes and Michael Stevenson (eds.), *Women and the Use of Military Force* (Boulder, CO: Lynne Rienner Publishers, 1993), p. 168.

5. Shirley Mangini, *Memories of Resistance: Women's Voices from the Spanish Civil War* (New Haven, CT: Yale University Press, 1995), p. 59.

6. Sonya Rose, *Limited Livelihoods: Gender and Class in Nineteenth-Century England* (Berkeley, CA: University of California Press, 1992), pp. 8-13 describes these "cultural productions" and the relationships between experience, meaning, and consciousness.

7. For the former see the essays in Paul Thompson and Natasha Burchardt (eds.), *Our Common History: The Transformation of Europe* (London: Pluto Press, 1982); an example of the latter is Claudio Pavone, *Una guerra civile: Saggio storico sulla moralitá nella Resistenza* (Turin: Bollati Boringhieri Editore, 1991), p. 23.

8. See, for example, articles in the special issue, "Nationalisms and National Identities," *Feminist Review*, No. 44 (1993).

9. For these two approaches, see, respectively, Janet Saltzman Chafetz and Anthony Gary Dworkin, *Female Revolt: Women's Movements in World and Historical Perspective* (Totowa, NJ: Rowman and Allanheld, 1987); and Mary F. Katzenstein and Carol M. Mueller (eds.), *The Women's Movements of the U.S. and Western Europe* (Philadelphia, PA: Temple University Press, 1987).

10. Jane Jenson, "Struggling for Identity: The Women's Movement and the State in Western Europe," in Sylvia Bashevkin (ed.), *Women and Politics in Western Europe* (London: Frank Cass and Co., 1985), p. 7.

# Acknowledgments

This volume is dedicated to the Italian women of the Resistance who sacrificed and gained "a sense of themselves" during that struggle. It is also dedicated to my parents, whose example and encouragement enabled me to develop a sense of myself.

A number of individuals were instrumental in the conception, development, and production of this volume. In particular, without the information, critique, and hospitality of Giuliana Beltrami, I might have lost my way in the process (and certainly wouldn't have enjoyed it nearly as much). My dear friend Margherita Repetto Alaia always backed the work with greatest enthusiasm and provided me with valuable research suggestions, helpful interpretive models, and access to sources and individuals in Italy. Cinzia Donadelli, Gisela Floreanini, Maria Michetti, Emiliana Noether, and Agnes Peterson all provided critical support at various stages in the work. I also have had the pleasure of working with Susan Conley, who qualifies as the ideal editor. Her attention to detail, astute questions, almost intuitive grasp of historical significance and constant encouragement are evident on every page of this volume in either form or spirit.

The research for the volume began during an NEH Summer Seminar directed by Joseph Palombara held in Rome in 1980. The University of New Mexico subsequently provided several travel grants to help me to complete the research. I would like to thank colleagues Charles Delzell and Alexander De Grand, who read early drafts of appropriate chapters; my co-editor, Richard Stites, who carefully read the first draft of the manuscript; and my colleague Melissa Bokovoy, who pushed me for clarity as she reviewed the near-final drafts of key portions of the book. University colleagues such as she, Steven Kramer, Jonathan Porter, and Virginia Scharff consistently provided moral support, intellectual jostlings, laughter, and friendship, for which I am most grateful.

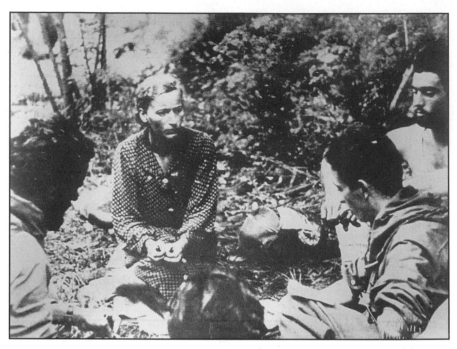

A woman talks with partisans about joining a mountain brigade. From private collection of Margherita Repetto Alaia.

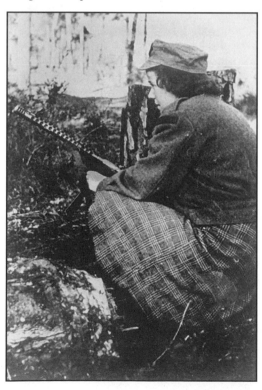

A woman partisan. From the collection of Giuliana Beltrami.

# Chronology of Events

| Date | Event |
|---|---|
| 1919 | |
| March 23 | Founding of Fascist movement |
| 1921 | |
| January | Communist Party established |
| 1922 | |
| October | Mussolini forms his first government |
| 1926 | |
| November | The government assumes "exceptional powers" |
| 1929 | |
| February | Lateran Accords signed by Catholic church and the government |
| 1935 | |
| October | Italy invades Ethiopia |
| 1936 | |
| July | Spanish Civil War begins |
| 1938 | |
| July-November | Racial laws enacted |
| 1939 | |
| May | Italy and Germany sign Pact of Steel |

1940

    June                      Italy enters World War II

1942

    July                        Action Party founded

1943

| | |
|---|---|
| March | Industrial strikes in northern Italy |
| July | Christian Democratic Party founded |
| July 10 | Allies invade Sicily |
| July 24-25 | Fascist Grand Council votes no confidence in Mussolini; Badoglio head of a new government |
| September 3 | Allies invade southern Italy |
| September 8-9 | Armistice between Italy and Allies is announced; Badoglio and King move to southern Italy; CLN issues call for resistance |
| September 10 | Germans occupy Rome |
| October 13 | Italy declares war on Germany |
| November | GDD formed in Milan |

1944

| | |
|---|---|
| January | CLNAI formally constituted |
| Spring | MFDC is organized |
| June 4 | Rome is liberated |
| June 8 | Badoglio government is replaced by that of Bonomi in cooperation with CLN parties |
| June 9 | CVL unites partisan forces |
| August 22 | Florence is liberated |
| September 15 | Organizing committee of the Union of Italian Women meets in Rome |
| Fall | MFGL is formed and organizing for CIF begins |
| October 16 | CLNAI accepts the GDD as the organization representing the masses of women |
| November | Cadorno is named commander of resistance forces |
| December | Allies recognize the CVL |
| December | CLNAI is recognized as representative of the government in occupied Italy |

1945

| | |
|---|---|
| February | Women are granted the vote |
| February | DC proclaims its women not to be members of GDD |

| | |
|---|---|
| March-April | Strikes in Milan and Turin |
| April 19-25 | Insurrection and liberation of northern cities |
| April 28 | Mussolini shot |
| September 25 | Consultative Assembly meets |
| October 22-23 | GDD-UDI hold national meeting in Florence |
| December | First De Gasperi government formed |

1946

| | |
|---|---|
| January 1 | Allied Military Government hands over administration of Italy to new government |
| June 2 | Referendum on the monarchy and election of members for the Constituent Assembly; Italy proclaimed a republic |

1947

| | |
|---|---|
| December | Constituent Assembly approves new constitution |

1948

| | |
|---|---|
| April | General elections held under new constitution; 41 women elected to government |

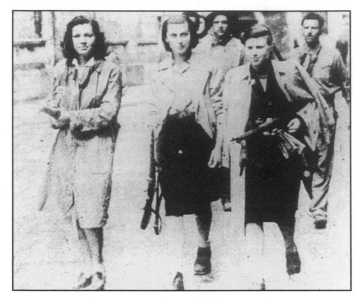

The newspaper caption reads, "Beautiful and proud young women of Milan." From *Noi Donne* 2:6 [15 May 1945].

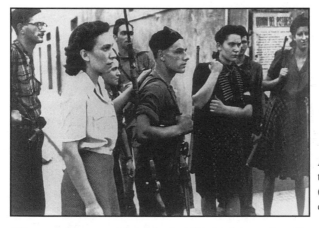

A group of partisans at the time of liberation, Pistoia (Tuscany). From Beltrami collection.

Women volunteers with the Garibaldi Brigades march at liberation. Beltrami collection.

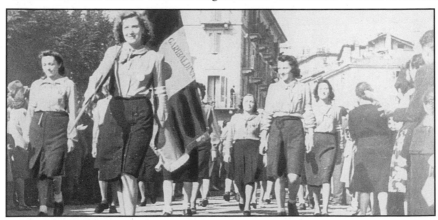

# Abbreviations

| | |
|---|---|
| AC | Azione Cattolica (Catholic Action) |
| AMG | Allied Military Government |
| CIF | Centro Italiano Femminile (Center of Italian Women) |
| CLN | Comitato di Liberazione Nazionale (Committee of National Liberation) |
| CLNAI | Comitato di Liberazione Nazionale per l'Alta Italia (Committee of National Liberation for Northern Italy) |
| CVL | Corpo Volontari della Libertá (Corps of Volunteers for Freedom) |
| DC | Democrazia Cristiana (Christian Democratic Party) |
| FUCI | Federazione Universitaria Cattolica Italiane (University Federation of Italian Catholics) |
| GAP | Gruppi di Azione Patriottica (Groups of Patriotic Action) |
| GDD | Gruppi di Difesa della Donna (Women's Defense Groups) |
| G&L | Giustizia e Libertá (Justice and Liberty Movement) |

GFCI                        Gioventú Femminile Cattolica Italiana (Young Italian
                            Catholic Women; sometimes GFdiAC Young Women
                            of Catholic Action)

MFDC                        Movimento Femminile della DC (Women's Movement
                            of Christian Democracy)

PCI                         Partito Comunista Italiano (Italian Communist Party)

Pd'A                        Partito d'Azione (Action Party)

PNF                         Partito Nazionale Fascista (National Fascist Party)

PSI                         Partito Socialista Italiano (Italian Socialist Party)

SAP                         Squadre di Azione Patriottica (Patriotic Action Squads)

UDCI                        Unione Donne Cattoliche Italiane (Union of Italian
                            Catholic Women; sometimes UDACI, Union of Women
                            of Catholic Action)

UDI                         Unione Donne Italiane (Union of Italian Women)

# Introduction:
# The Study of Revolution and the Case of Italian Women of the Resistance

Giovanna Zangrandi, a former partisan, observed that the Italian resistance struggle during the Second World War was a war "nested in kitchens." In her autobiography, Zangrandi noted the many hours she and her comrades-in-arms spent in "kitchens, all different from one another," but all presided over by the "mother" who fussed over them.[1] Zangrandi's words reflect some crucial dimensions of Italian women's place in the Resistance. First, clandestine meetings of underground political groups, partisan leaders, and their couriers often *were* held in ordinary houses, around ordinary kitchen tables. Though locations and physical structures would vary, these spaces usually were identified with an unnamed "mama" of one of the partisans. Second, women, both individually and in organized groups, provided food, clothing, and medical supplies for the partisan units. Kitchens thus had both productive and political significance during the Resistance. Bruna Betti's first memory of collaboration was of herself as a teenager carrying to the partisans "a lovely plate of *pastasciutta* (macaroni and cheese) prepared by [her] mother."

Gender scripts and symbols mark the Resistance in other ways as well. Resistance activists often used stereotypes of feminine behavior in both offensive and defensive ways. Would "foolish girls" be suspected of stealing weapons from Fascist or Nazi soldiers? Even if a woman were suspected of partisan activity, might not a mundane or silly remark convince officials that she was not political or a serious threat? A year after beginning work with the partisans, Betti and her sister were arrested by the Germans. Bruna remembered acting "a little stupid, pretending to be frivolous and not interested in politics." When they asked her what she most wanted at the moment—of course all partisans wanted an end to war and fascism?—she answered, "a piece of cake with whipped cream."

Contrasting the maternal reflections, the domestic connections, and the manipulation of femininity in these accounts are other records of the Resistance that describe the "unwomanly" behavior of women partisans who shot and killed the enemy, that depict the need for women to "act like men" in the struggle, and that demonstrate the vulnerability and danger of being a woman, wife, daughter, or mother in those years of conflict and contest. Zangrandi herself reflected that as a result of suffering the hardships and dangers of the partisan struggle in the northern mountains she almost forgot what it meant to be a woman. And young Anna Cinanni, as she prepared to join the Resistance forces, was admonished by her brother to remember that "you are not a woman; you are a communist and you are fighting in the Resistance."[2]

This volume tells a story of women in the Italian Resistance that is replete with such contradictory experiences and understandings. It is the author's purpose to place these experiences in the broader history of Italian anti-fascism, war, and resistance by detailing the nature and assessing the meanings of women's participation in these events. The material that follows also incorporates and provides a measure for testing various theoretical frameworks developed by other scholars who have studied collective rebellions, the emergence of political consciousness, and the nature of feminist politics. But, whatever the topic at hand might be, it is crucial to listen to women's own voices as they remember events and assign significance to their activities.

The following chapters describe what motivated women to join the Resistance and the nature of their contributions to that effort. The political dimensions and results of women's participation are also key features of this history. On a less concrete and tangible level, the ways in which gender ideology and expectations were either reinforced or altered by the events, organizations, and individuals of the Resistance will be considered. And finally, this book focuses on *women's* acts of resistance. In many cases, women's responses to hardships, danger, and repression are not much different from men's. But because the sometimes mundane events of everyday experience serve as motivations for actions and may well be transformed into resistance itself, there often will be as many differences between men and women in their resistance as there are separate spheres in the social worlds they inhabit. For women, gender can sometimes be an advantage, but it can be a major liability as well. At times being both a woman, particularly a mother, and a revolutionary seems quite natural and unquestioned. In other instances these two roles appear contradictory and create internal anguish and turmoil.

In recent years, the study of women, war, and revolution has provoked heated debates and produced varied interpretations regarding the importance of gender in conflict and combat and the degree to which war and revolution alter the social relations of men and women. Questions commonly raised are: To what degree does war "emancipate" women? Does women's participation affect the course of revolutions and wars? How do individuals and society interpret and respond to this participation? To answer these questions is to understand the relationships among women's activities on all fronts in war and revolution as well as the broader meanings and structures of gender that define our lives. As historian Joan Scott argues, "War must be understood as a *gendering* activity," during which women's status and representation are characterized by both progress and regress.[3] The examination of specific historical cases and women's experiences provides the information with which to build models and test our knowledge.

This volume focuses on women's involvement in the Italian Resistance between September 1943 and May 1945. In those years a mass-based and well-organized movement in Italy sought to overthrow the existing Fascist regime, expel the Nazi-German occupation forces, and bring an end to the war. It also sought to transform Italian society and government, to create a "new," democratic, and progressively modern Italy. Women played a significant role in this resistance. Thousands of women were mobilized to fight the oppressors and to end the war, the first mass women's organizations were created, and women gained the vote and assumed public roles to an unprecedented degree.

Many American and British scholars have produced excellent studies of Italy during World War II; though these describe and assess the partisan Resistance, they rarely mention women. By contrast, in Italy there is a large body of literature written by former partisans and scholars that focuses on women and the Resistance. Many of these works are regionally or topically focused, have a political purpose, and, while their preservation of records and memories is invaluable, are narrative rather than analytical. In these writings one frequently reads of the Resistance as "the decisive moment in the process of female emancipation"[4] and that "it is in the Resistance that women broke traditional schemes, and emerged from their traditional isolation."[5] Many authors assert that a "new" woman emerged in Italy in 1945.

The purpose of this work is to assess the truth of these contentions, to determine what steps toward emancipation were taken, and whether fundamental structures of women's lives did in fact change. The most important questions are: To what degree was the Resistance epoch a revolution for women? Was the high level of female activism accompanied by corresponding changes in female experience? These questions can be answered by considering a variety of factors such as women's motives for activism, forms of their mobilization, and other forces and changes in Italian life that affected women's activity. To what extent did a changed consciousness emerge in this process, and how might this be related to a more fundamental transformation of the sex/gender system? Ultimately, this approach seeks the links between female experience, mobilization, expectations, and results.

The study begins in Chapter 1 with an examination of the two decades of Fascist rule after Benito Mussolini was appointed prime minister in 1922. Only by understanding what it was like to be a woman in Italy during those years and the significance of gender to the Fascist regime can we understand the factors that impelled women to act. Historian Temma Kaplan has argued that "women's consciousness of broader political issues emerged in their defense of rights due them according to the division of labor."[6] Changes in such things as labor force participation, fertility patterns, and marital stability often precede active public involvement because "they may force women to confront what it means to be female outside the context of traditional values."[7]

Chapter 2 provides a profile of Resistance women and discusses the various motives for their activism. It is here that the lines between private, individual experience and collective public rebellion are drawn. The paths leading to resistance varied considerably. During the Fascist era, some women already had a political consciousness and a social vision that transcended the specifics of gender. They had been involved in labor groups or political parties that had broadened their expectations, and they in turn faced additional prospects of arrest, imprisonment, or the option of exile as the regime eliminated its opposition. These women would emerge as leaders during the years of the Resistance, but their number was fairly small. For the masses of women, it was their ties to conventional social roles that ultimately led them to act in unconventional ways.

Though the Fascist regime emphasized women's traditional roles as wives and mothers, the crises of the regime, particularly its increasing militarism in the 1930s, helped to disrupt these roles. As economic conditions worsened and threats of death and destruction became more immediate, it was increasingly difficult for women to protect and care for their families and raise happy, healthy children. They began to rebel, creating what sociologist Maxine Molyneux has termed "combative motherhood."[8] But choosing to dissent was not necessarily easy. Acting aggressively in public in either a military or civilian capacity would have much different meanings for women than for men, for whom such actions would be "natural" and expected.

Women were not just victims or martyrs; their own positive identification with female roles, their own perception of how these roles *should* be fulfilled, and their own notions of rights due them as females pushed them to act. Traditional roles did not dissolve but rather expanded, assumed new value, or became politicized. Women were not simply defending what was, but what they thought should be, the female experience.

Once women had taken the first steps to resist, what were their major contributions to the overall effort? Chapter 3 details the variety of roles assumed by women during the Resistance, pointing especially to those areas where women were most visible and had the greatest impact. Historians of the Resistance often note, with some surprise, the degree to which women's activities deviated from the norms and stereotypes of female behavior. Women led demonstrations and carried and used arms, often risking or losing their lives in the process. But women also made use of "less orthodox tactics of disorder," utilizing existing, informal networks to recruit more and more women, to build their own organizations, and, ultimately, to give form and substance to a female voice and perspective.[9]

At this point, it becomes crucial to place women's activism and their emerging organizations in the broader context of Italian Resistance politics. How did formal Resistance structures and political parties and their leaders respond to this mass mobilization of women, and how did the women feel about these political entities? Chapter 4 considers men's attitudes toward women's social roles and the ways in which female expectations were shaped by more general political forces and agendas. Male political leaders and their parties recognized the need to involve women in the struggle against fascism and the war, but how they solicited women's support, responded to women's demands, and envisioned women's social roles was another story.

Of particular interest are the ways in which the two major parties, the Communists (PCI) and the Christian Democrats (DC), dealt with women's issues. Were there significant differences in their approaches, or was it true that there was "limited conflict between the male political elites on the 'woman question'," making it difficult to raise questions about traditional gender relations?[10] It is important to determine the degree to which women were accepted as legitimate political actors and their issues considered an important part of political debate. We must also consider possible contradictions between theory and prevailing practical, political needs and, in the long run, what happened to the women who had been mobilized and unified against the Fascist threat once the regime was defeated.[11]

One of the central purposes of this work is to explain the links between mobilization and organization and the emergence of political consciousness. Chapter 5 focuses more specifically on women's expectations, how goals were set, and the degree to which these can be described as feminist. This topic is complex and contradictory and must incorporate a variety of interpretive models.

Various authors in the volume *What Is Feminism?* have suggested that "all actions and campaigns prompted or led by women" are not necessarily feminist.[12] General collective actions by women must be distinguished from specific actions that have as their focus some aspect of gender inequity. Explaining the variations in women's motivations and expectations, Maxine Molyneux has developed the useful distinction between practical and strategic goals for women.[13] The former "arise from concrete conditions,…are usually a response to an immediate perceived need [e.g., daily welfare], and they do not generally entail a strategic goal." The latter "are derived…from the analysis of women's subordination and from the formulation of an alternative, more satisfactory set of arrangements to those which exist…. These demands are usually termed 'feminist'."

The key to making these differentiations is in how the women themselves saw their conditions and interpreted their actions. If Italian women sensed their oppression and rebelled against it, how did they explain their reactions? Did women's individual conflicts and frustrations push them to question their position as *women* within society, or to promote solidarity with other women to solve their problems? Political scientist Ethel Klein has pointed out that "personal problems become political demands only when they are seen as a consequence of social institutions and social inequality....Feminism is learning where to put the blame."[14]

Were the Italian women of the Resistance feminists or feminist sympathizers? As we attempt to answer this question, it becomes clear that feminism is never absolute because it is an emotional, intellectual, and practical response to particular conditions, and not simply a matter of choosing equality and justice for all. Solutions eventually proposed by feminist activists are tied to concrete conditions and problems, and their causes. Fascism and the war it had begun provoked rebellion and were considered the universal enemies, and this perception in turn shaped the character of Italian feminism as it emerged during the Resistance.

Female participants in the Resistance were keenly aware of how fascism disrupted their lives as women, and they eventually fought back aggressively and militantly. At the same time, because the proximate problem was so easily defined, they failed to analyze the ways in which gender inequities were embedded in more fundamental social structures. As an Italian work on women in the Resistance points out, women "felt, like all the oppressed, that they fought against fascism, but also above all against inequality and injustice: nevertheless, *compagni* (comrades) who would talk of the specific oppression of women were rarely found."[15] If fascism were the "first cause," then problems of gender would be subsumed in it, affecting both practical and strategic goals and producing an often conscious avoidance of any discussion of sex antagonism. The unwillingness to consider gender oppression was tied to another, more general concern in the Resistance—a desire to maintain unity at all costs.

The success of the struggle was linked to an insistence on the homogeneity of goals and interests of all Italian citizens. Though there were fairly frequent conflicts and practical divisions in the movement, political leaders always spoke of unity in the face of adversity and outwardly used the rhetoric of cooperation and compromise. Historian Claudia Pavone has noted that among the partisans there was a sense that "they were all in agreement" in their willingness "to risk their lives for a particular political battle that was also a battle of the people."[16] For women, loyalty to the movement and the commonality of certain features of female experience served them well during the Resistance, and challenging these by bringing up conflicts among men and women, or differences among the women themselves, would have threatened a precarious harmony seen as necessary for victory and then reconstruction. Thus, there were real and necessary reasons for downplaying problems and stressing harmony. Mussolini and his regime, the Germans, and the war were common enemies, while the Resistance goal of a reborn, democratic Italy offered similar promises to all, regardless of class or gender. Thus, on one level, the women of the Resistance were "gender blind." On other levels, however, they were keenly aware of gender difference, illustrating what historian Nancy Cott has shown to be a major paradox of contemporary feminism: that its goals and visions may simultaneously seek the elimination of gender roles *and* "the valorization of female being."[17]

When explaining their actions, in building their organizations, and in formulating their goals, Italian women emphasized both similarities and differences between men and women. In justifying their engagement in the Resistance movement and arguing for women's advancement, they could claim that women "had the same intellectual and spiritual endowment as men...and therefore deserved equal or the same opportunities men had." Or they could assert that "their sex differed from the male—that whether through natural endowment, environment or training, human females were moral, nurturant, pacific and philosophically disinterested." Thus, equal opportunities were necessary for women "in order to represent themselves and to balance society with their characteristic contribution."[18] During the Resistance, women were both "moral mothers" and equal citizens. The inherent difficulties in resolving this paradox had a profound impact on decisions regarding the nature and extent of women's political activity and the strategic goals they ultimately set.

The contradictions in defining women's "nature" not only affected the characteristics of women's emerging consciousness and their expectations but were reflected quite practically in organizational strategies. During the course of the Resistance, separate and autonomous, mass-based women's organizations built upon a common female experience, solidified the ties of female networks, fostered the growth of confidence and political awareness of many women, and encouraged the articulation of women's needs and concerns.

Such separatism also could be the source of problems if it hindered women in their ability to influence the decision-making bodies of the political parties and the government, or if it placed women in ineffective female ghettos. The opposite strategy, abandoning their separate status and integrating into other political groups, was equally problematic, as within the broader structures women risked becoming second-class citizens and losing the cohesion necessary to promote their own interests. During the Resistance and in the immediate postwar years, the leaders of women's organizations and political parties struggled with these questions. The lessons of their dilemmas illustrate the values of women's culture and autonomous politics as well as the possible pitfalls that accompany an affirmation of female separatism both practically and theoretically.[19]

The concluding chapter returns to the initial question: whether, indeed, the Resistance was "the decisive moment in the process of female emancipation." Though, without doubt, many women in the Resistance saw politics as the avenue for solving problems emanating from the private sphere, and some women did see themselves as political beings with political rights and responsibilities, whether they wanted to enter the arena of public politics or could do so was another story. The realities of much more fundamental change must be examined in order to determine whether the Resistance did alter or transform the sex/gender system and to understand what lay ahead for Italian women. As we travel through the events of these years with the women of Italy, we are reminded of the complexity of historic forces that lead to visions of equality and justice, as well as the immensity of the task of realizing these goals.

I was fortunate enough to meet and work with Giuliana Beltrami in Milan in 1981. She had been a participant in the Resistance and had just completed a manuscript on women's participation, the basis for which was a series of extensive interviews with ex-partisans. Not only did she give me guidance in interpretation, but she provided me access to all the typed transcripts of her interviews. It is this friendship and those sources that allowed me to gain a personal connection to the women of the Resistance, which otherwise would have been impossible. This immersion in women's own words has allowed me to relive, in a sense, the events of those years so carefully documented in the other kinds of sources and to balance historical judgments or significance with the meanings the women themselves attribute to their experiences.

# ▪ 1 ▪

# The Sources of Discontent: Women's Service to the State and to the Family

The years from 1919 to 1939 were decades of crisis for Europe. Between the disastrous legacies of World War I and the pressures and tensions created by the preparation for the Second World War, the populations of Europe lived in an atmosphere of insecurity and threats of social, economic, and political disruption. In this setting, Fascist regimes arose in Italy and Germany, while in other nations Fascist parties at least played a role on the national scene. While the primary focus of this chapter is the Fascist experience in Italy, this experience must be considered as a particular national response to conditions that were often international in character. Because there were common problems, and similarities as well as differences in political reactions to these, fascism should not be viewed in isolation but instead as situated at one end of the continuum of European political developments in the interwar years.[1]

When examining the impact of fascism on women, it should be noted that gender-related Fascist policies had their more pallid counterparts in all the nations of the West. The Fascist regimes were not completely unique or aberrant in this regard, though their reactions were much more extreme, programs more oppressive, and controls more violent than those of the non-Fascist states.

In order to place fascism in its proper perspective, it is important to understand general conditions in Europe as well as the position of women in these years. There is no doubt that the First World War created massive problems for the nations of Europe, but it should also be remembered that many of the difficulties had their roots in prewar society. It was almost as if, coming out of the war, Europeans were suddenly forced to confront the tensions and complexities of a "modern," technological world that often did not play by the rules many had assumed to be operating in their lives. After 1919, Western Europe faced large government debts, inflation, and unemployment. The fumbling attempts to solve these problems were frequently superficial or ineffective as the crises culminated in a worldwide depression beginning in 1929 in the United States and affecting Europe by 1931-32. Since the mid-nineteenth century, birth rates of the nations of Europe had gradually fallen, and even before 1914, political leaders had expressed alarm as to how this would affect national strength and vigor. The war added to this set of problems, not only with immediate population losses but with threats to future population growth as well.

Before World War I the nations of Europe had moved in the direction of political democracy, most of them granting men the vote at least by the time of the war. This extension of suffrage did not, however, signal greater harmony in the political sphere. Older nineteenth-century liberalism was either diluted or in many ways proved to be unsuitable as a solution to the problems and structuring of modern industrial societies. As new social groups gained the vote and entered the political arena, they often turned to workplace organizations and Socialist parties as mechanisms for political expression. The outbreak of war increased political controversies while the beginning of a revolution and the establishment of the Bolshevik regime in Russia in 1917 added fuel to political fires. For some, the October Revolution was welcomed as the symbol of a new era; for others it was evil incarnate, and Western politics were often colored by the red brush of pro-Socialist fervor or anti-Bolshevik fears. In general, then, indecision and crisis marked European politics as the nations entered the twenties.

Though historians generally comment on the fact that fears of disorder and disillusionment with traditional values and attitudes marked the end of the war, signs of these were evident prior to 1914. Certainly by the end of the nineteenth century a veneer of optimism and a belief in evolutionary progress and the ability of human reason to cope with human problems were characteristic of most of European society. However, beneath this lay a degree of uncertainty about the future, fears of change and shifting values, and ideological currents that stressed the irrational or called for a new definition of human behavior and values.

The war itself brought these tensions to the surface. On the one hand, "the menace to bourgeois society and to the nation seemed to increase after the war, [provoking the desire] to fight against the so-called rising tide of immorality."[2] On the other hand, a generation of young men and women came of age, practically and symbolically emphasizing an individualism and freedom in personal behavior that challenged older Victorian notions of morality and order. Increasingly, social welfare professionals, sexologists, demographers, sociologists, and those in the medical field sought to bridge the gap of generational differences. While many applauded the new freedom as a sign of progressive civilization, they also sought to channel it so as not to threaten the stability and harmonious functioning of society.

The anxiety about family, sexuality, and morality that pervaded Western Europe in the interwar years frequently centered on women and women's proper place.[3] There was, indeed, a "new" woman in the twentieth century, though not exactly modeled on the well-publicized and free-wheeling American flapper. Increased female employment and a rise in the numbers of working married women; the use of contraception, especially among middle-class women; increased access to legal divorce in some countries; improved education; and publicly active women's rights organizations all marked a major shift in women's social status. Though most women's lives were still defined by home and family, the boundaries for acceptable female behavior were less clear and women's access to the public world had expanded. Public institutions such as schools, hospitals, and social welfare agencies had taken over some traditional family activities and were interfering more directly in private behaviors. Men and women felt the pressures of changing gender roles and family functions, often reacting with dismay to what they saw as challenges to social order and stability.

When veterans returned from the war seeking employment and a place in their societies, the anxieties and discontent intensified. The most extreme fears resulted in a backlash of antifeminism that blamed the "new" woman for social disorder and insisted that a sexual division of labor was both natural and necessary to a smoothly functioning society. The depression exacerbated these tensions, as working women were often seen as the cause of the economic crisis and debates arose around "married women's right to work and the future of family life."[4] Desires to "create peace and order in the public sphere by imposing peace and order on the private sphere" combined easily with the efforts of "government and welfare institutions…to shape marriage to conform to the state's needs for population control and consumption."[5]

It was not uncommon in these years for governments to pass laws to either restrict or control reproduction and to limit women's spheres of work. Legislation in France in 1920 restricted use of birth control and abortion, the latter now becoming a major crime; in the same year, the "Medals of the French Family" were awarded and a "Mother Holiday" proclaimed. In Britain, political parties and commercial interests encouraged marriage, motherhood, and domesticity as ideals for women, and eventually, during World War II, as birthrates continued to fall, the newly appointed Royal Commission on Population recognized that "women required encouragement from the state to remain at home and rear children."[6] Both the "carrot and the stick" were used to promote marriage and fertility. Family allowances, housing projects for families, higher wages for married men, subsidies to poor mothers, and clinics for prenatal and postpartum care were among the practical methods adopted to support population increases. More punitively, women were discouraged or prevented from working by reductions in pay and benefits, denial of access to some jobs, and outright removal from others. For both Fascist and non-Fascist governments, "women and the family" became a significant target of public policy as modern welfare statism combined with social conservatism to consolidate women's traditional roles.[7]

The Fascists resembled political leaders in the rest of Europe by asserting the social desirability and political necessity of "natural," separate spheres. Fascism emphasized "the home, family, restraint and discipline,…promised to support respectability against the chaos of the modern age, [and pledged] to restore the traditional family and relieve women of their double burden [of waged and family work]."[8] However, there were some significant differences between the Fascist regimes and other political systems as to the clarity and severity of their ideologies and actions. The Fascists rigidly defined desired "natural" roles for men and women and attempted to enforce these through extensive, restrictive legislation and harsh punishment for noncompliance. Persuasion and coercion were used to recreate social order, women were consistently denied a public role, and there was a "heavy emphasis on the masculine principle and male dominance…[as the Fascists worshipped] masculinity and the community of men as the ruling elite."[9]

Among the general characteristics of fascism was a fundamental ideological concensus on the "woman question." Emphasis on "natural" gender differences and rigid divisions of labor was not a trivial or peripheral matter but essential to both the immediate social stability and the future grandeur and strength of the nation that the Fascists promised. However, beneath this broad umbrella of similarities there were significant differences among the regimes. Fascism was, after all, a response to national problems, built on particular historical traditions and heavily dependent on national conditions and resources in developing and carrying out its programs. Not only were there differences in what a national, Fascist movement could accomplish, but the response or resistance to the regimes differed in degree and kind. Germany certainly did not experience the partisan warfare that characterized Italy after 1943, and the visibility of Italian women in resistance activity was equalled only by that of women in the partisan movement of Yugoslavia after 1941.[10] In order to determine what moved significant numbers of Italian women to actively oppose the Fascists, we must understand the various starting points from which resistance began. The eventual decision to rebel was determined by women's experience and expectations under an evolving Fascist dictatorship.

## Italy Between the Wars

At the close of World War I, Italy was not, in the most basic terms, a highly industrialized society. Agriculture still contributed slightly more than 38 percent of national income, industry 31.4 percent, and services 30.4 percent.[11] But the economy was shifting, bringing with it substantial dislocations as rural workers sought employment or land; urban workers fought for improved wages, working conditions, and social services; and newly trained, skilled technicians sought upward mobility. Poverty, "primitive" health care, and widespread illiteracy were additional burdens to a nation coming out of the war with a large national debt and massive inflation. Above it all was a government that was both unresponsive and often unable to deal with these conditions and crises.

## *The Fascist Rise to Power*

Italy was essentially a nation divided along the lines of competing interest groups with differing expectations and fears: rural versus urban sectors and forces pushing toward modernity and technological advance versus those tied to a traditional economy and values. Whatever their specific complaints and goals, these disparate groups found conditions unsatisfactory or even threatening, and they were willing to consider and support the promises and solutions offered by an emerging Fascist movement.

In its infancy in 1919, the Fascist party was made up of a peculiar mix of "students, professionals and shopkeepers [and] provincial lower middle classes and landowners."[12] Ideologically eclectic, the movement emphasized nationalism, elitism, authoritarianism, and collectivism, and simultaneously promised orderly change to modernize Italy while stressing cultural and social continuity. As its popular base grew, established political, economic, and military leaders began to see in the Fascist movement a possible answer to postwar demands for reform and a solution for Italy's social and economic problems. In October 1922, the Fascists accelerated their plans to assume political power through the "March on Rome." By mobilizing Fascist squads to seize provincial power centers and eventually move to Rome, the leaders hoped "to use the threat of civil war to force King Victor Emmanuel III and conservative politicians to bring the Fascists into the government."[13] Armed with the support of political leaders and the neutrality of the army, the king offered Benito Mussolini the position of prime minister on October 28. Thus, according to constitutional guidelines and abetted by the threat of violence, the Fascists had "seized" power.

## *The Fascist Regime*

Though legitimately at the head of government, Mussolini and the Fascists were hardly in control of a cohesive political apparatus or a homogeneous society. The support of different and often conflicting groups had underwritten the rise to power, and now special interests and concerns had to be dealt with. Though Italian women were neither homogeneous nor powerful enough to be considered one of these special groups, because they were part of the social fabric the Fascists were trying to hold together, the regime made specific promises to them. The ultimate effects on women were mixed, as in some cases the regime altered characteristics of social life; in others it reinforced or solidified previous traditions. Historian Victoria De Grazia has pointed out that there was always a tension in the Fascist state "between the demands of modernity and the desire to reimpose traditional authority" or between needing to modernize women in some respects, while not emancipating them.[14]

Because of the range of problems it faced and the needs and solutions proposed by competing social and political groups, the Fascist government often shifted policies and priorities. Thus, fascism must be looked at as having different "phases." The period from 1922 to 1925 is sometimes referred to as the "liberal" phase because the trappings of constitutional, representative government were maintained and there was still open opposition to Mussolini and diversity among the Fascists themselves. Between 1925 and 1929, institutional structures were created and a dictatorship consolidated, which "increased the power of the state over public life through monopoly of the Fascist Party, establishment of press censorship, and control over labor organizations."[15] While Mussolini gradually assumed control of the party and incorporated it into the operations of the state, external controls were also extended. Through acts of terror, the creation of a secret police, and a special system of courts to prosecute those "disloyal" to the regime, opponents were arrested or driven underground and into exile.

During the years 1929 to 1935, termed the "corporative" phase, the regime launched a number of economic "experiments" intended to stabilize the troubled economy and to encourage growth and development through centralization and state subsidy, thereby satisfying the needs of the various interest groups that had underwritten the regime. Additionally, efforts were made to reach the masses of Italians in new ways which, even if they did not build enthusiastic loyalty, would build a "culture of consent."[16] This process included founding new youth groups and organizations for the rural population as well as establishing recreation and leisure programs. The year 1935 marked the beginning of what historian Alexander De Grand terms a "downward spiral," during which there were fewer internal policy innovations and more focus on foreign affairs and the dream of "empire." Preparations for war escalated into overt acts of aggression as Italy invaded Ethiopia in 1935, intervened in the Spanish Civil War in 1936, and eventually entered the Second World War on the side of its German ally in the summer of 1940.

None of these chronological divisions should be seen as rigid, as characteristics of one often blurred with another; nevertheless, they are helpful in determining which groups and individuals were most affected by particular policies and how they reacted to those policies. Certainly the nature of women's experiences was affected by the shifts in the regime's priorities, and among women there were differences in how they perceived fascism and responded to its ideas and programs. During the period of the movement's emergence, and then between 1922 and 1929, the years of political institution-building and elimination of the opposition, the women most obviously affected were those already organized or connected to political groups.

## Women and the Fascist Movement

At the close of the First World War, Italian women did not have the vote, and although there existed a liberal democratic suffrage movement with international connections, its numbers were quite small. In its infancy in 1919 and 1920, the

Fascist movement had promised women the vote and social equality, and the ten women who belonged to the original group in Milan were ardent suffragists.[17] If dreams of "emancipation" brought some women to fascism, glorification of female virtues and idealization of gender differences were appealing to others. In a different vein, militant action and imperial expansion attracted nationalist women or those who sought to demonstrate their physical courage as women soldiers in Fascist "action squads." For very different reasons, then, some women became enthusiastic supporters of fascism; they ranged from wealthy, aristocratic women who created a feminized elitism in their own image, to young, educated, progressive women who saw in fascism an opportunity to join the "modern" world.

Mussolini put little energy into organizing women, but he did continue to play to their interests, particularly in the promise of the right to vote. Once in power, in fact, a bill was introduced in the Chamber that gave women of the age of twenty-five or older the vote in local administrative elections. Mussolini urged his colleagues to support this legislation, referring vaguely to the "extensive" place of women in modern society and reminding his listeners that should it be necessary to mobilize the nation for war, such mobilization would involve all citizens, male and female, and thus women's administrative activity on the local level could be useful.[18] The law eventually was passed in November 1925, but within a year Fascist restructuring of elections and government itself eliminated democratic local administration so that the newly gained right to vote for women was meaningless. Women's Clubs (Fasci Femminili) were organized to connect women to the regime, though these auxiliaries to the party lacked financial and even moral support from the leadership, and initially their membership was quite small (40,000 in 1924).[19] During fascism's rise to power and its first phase of government, variety and autonomy characterized the women's groups affiliated with the movement or regime, but this was largely the result of ideological ambiguity or indifference rather than developed policy.

## Women's Early Opposition to Fascism

For the political women who were members of the established parties that constituted the opposition, fascism had an entirely different meaning. The development of the dictatorship obviously interrupted their political evolution, but even when they were imprisoned or driven underground or into exile, it did not destroy their political consciousness or erase what they had learned of ideology and organization. The Fascist "seizure" of power did help to establish their priorities and shape their political philosophy. If fascism was the cause of all oppression and misery, and if unity in the face of the enemy was paramount, there would be little room for discussion of different problems and needs stemming from gender.

By the beginning of World War I, in Italy as in other European countries, Socialist parties and working-class organizations had begun to recruit women and to recognize specific problems of working women. In the Italian Socialist Party (PSI), women leaders such as Anna Kuliscioff, Argentina Altobelli, and Anna Maria Mozzoni raised women's issues, including suffrage, working conditions, and wages, and organized separate women's sections within the party. By mid-1916 there were seventy of these sections, but feminist leaders often had difficulty in convincing male party members of the significance of "the woman question" and in gaining support for women's issues.[20]

The war swept many young Socialist women into anti-war and workers' demonstrations, and in 1919 and 1920 they joined workers' strikes and the movement, led by Antonio Gramsci, to occupy factories in the north. The early activism of Rita Montagnana, Teresa Noce, and Rina Picolato was typical of this pattern. All three were born in Turin and began work in the textile and clothing industries at an early age. As teenagers they participated in strikes, opposed the war, and affiliated with the Young Socialist movement. After the war, their militancy continued as they organized and even led factory occupations and fought against the first Fascist bands. When the Italian Communist Party (PCI) was founded in 1921, many of the younger militant women became charter members. This practical and ideological experience helped to forge a dedication to political, economic, and social change that would remain a constant in the next two decades. As Teresa Noce put it, "We began to understand the need for a true revolutionary party, a party of the proletariat."[21]

In the twenties, ongoing female activism in both the Socialist and Communist parties produced a small group of seasoned leaders with a political consciousness, knowledge about organizing, and a growing awareness of the threat posed by the emerging Fascist movement. The Communist party, dedicated to organizing the working class, also emphasized the importance of recruiting working-class women, and by early 1922 it had established a national committee for work among women and had begun to publish a woman's journal, *Compagna*.

However, problems continued in the leftist approach to the "woman question" on both practical and theoretical levels. In 1922, of the 43,211 members of the PCI, fewer than one percent were female, and since class consciousness and unity were the focus of the party, little was done to develop an understanding of the role of gender in social relations. The Left clearly recognized the "double burden" that working women carried and discussed the social functions of family, but in general, though directed to the overthrow of bourgeois society, it "retained bourgeois morality and respectability."[22] The place of women in the party, particularly after Mussolini's assumption of power in 1922, was clearly stated by Ruggero Grieco, the director of the women's committee: "Human society is grouped into two classes—not those of men and women, but those of the bourgeoisie and the proletariat.... The woman worker and the peasant woman fight on a par with the proletariat against fascism. Any other question is, for the moment, without any importance."[23] Between 1923 and 1943, the Left was occupied with the struggle against fascism. This focus had particular implications and limitations for the women in the parties during the Resistance as they inherited a mandate for unity that would limit the degree to which they could discuss problems arising from gender differences and envision feminist solutions.[24]

At the same time that leftist organizations recruited women members while sidestepping the thorniest aspects of the "woman question," women were being organized within the context of Catholic politics. "Catholic feminism" was born in the early years of the century as specifically Catholic political organizations appeared. Early Christian feminism in general emphasized women's roles as wives and mothers and sought to elevate these roles through encouragement of female moral stewardship (*sacerdotessa*), human dignity, and more equality for women within the family.[25] A slightly more radical religious perspective emerged in Milan, where in 1905 Adelaide Coari founded the Women's Federation (Federazione Femminile). The new organization was concerned with women's rights within the family and advocated married women's control of their own property but also dealt with working women. Though industrial work was seen as detrimental to women's traditional functions, the Women's Federation did support equal pay for equal work and encouraged more practical education for women. The Federation ultimately endorsed female suffrage and women's responsibility to participate in public politics, but this spark of feminism was short-lived.[26] In 1908, after a general congress of Catholic women was held, the Union of Italian Catholic Women (UDCI) was organized with much more direct clerical sponsorship. The new organization moved away from an earlier emphasis on public activism, focusing instead on women's spiritual, moral, and private roles. Under the increased weight of church influence, a more rigid hierarchy abandoned concerns about women's wages, marital rights, and suffrage.

Two other turn-of-the-century Catholic organizations, Catholic Action (AC) and the University Federation of Italian Catholics (FUCI), also had women members, though in neither group were gender-specific concerns considered significant. In 1922, Pope Pius XI directed Catholic Action to become more aggressive in civil society for the purpose of "restoring Catholic life in the family and society," particularly in the face of growing leftist activism.[27] By 1923, attempts to build membership were accompanied by a clearer separation of men and women, as organizations of young women, of female university students, and of mature women mirrored the existing men's Catholic Action groups.

A more directly secular political approach was developed by the Italian Popular Party (PP), formed in 1918. Reflecting the party's more progressive viewpoint, women's suffrage was included in the party platform and a number of women were visibly active in the organization. Angela Cingolani Guidi, born in Rome in 1886, had grown up in a progressive Catholic family and participated in young Catholic women's groups. After receiving her university degree, Angela married Cingolani, a founder of the Popular Party, joined the party in 1919, and directed the publication of *Il lavoro femminile* while continuing to work with young Catholic women.[28]

## Clandestine and Exile Politics

As the Fascists became more aggressive in eliminating their opposition, men and women active in the political groups from center to left were either forced underground or into exile, or imprisoned after conviction by special law courts created to handle those "disloyal" to the regime. Most of the parties established headquarters in exile, usually in France, and attempted to maintain contact with an underground network in Italy. The Communist Party was probably the most effective in this work, though its membership dropped and noticeable activities were limited. It was often difficult to overcome differences, but during the thirties the exiled parties did attempt to create some sort of anti-Fascist unity and to educate the entire population of Europe about the threats of fascism and the increased possibility of war.

The Communist Party continued to recruit women and by 1931 had decided it should make special appeals to women of all classes. The Women's Office of the party explained this strategy in an article appearing in the party *Bulletin* in January of that year: "Our work among women should be a mass effort—that means that we should work to gain a decisive influence over the masses of women that work in offices, in the home and among the poor peasant women."[29] The practice of organizing women separately was also clearly justified: "[Although] equality between men and women will be one of the realizations of a socialist society, since, in fact, women are more backward than men, we must take account of this situation in our work." There were those like Teresa Noce who opposed this policy, arguing that "there cannot be a party for men and one for women. If the work among the masses of women is so difficult, that is a stronger reason to do it all together, and not to give the task solely to women's sections."[30] The desirability of recruiting from all classes to oppose fascism ultimately formed the practical base for the conception of a cross-class, democratic party. At the same time, organizing women separately and challenges to the practice became a regular part of party life in the twentieth century.

For those who were connected to political organizations, activism, arrests, and exile often went hand in hand, as in the case of Communist Egle Gualdi. A textile worker in Reggio Emilia, she was first arrested in 1924 and detained briefly for distributing leaflets calling for a strike on May 1; the order for her sixth arrest in 1932 forced her to seek refuge in France, where she lived illegally (i.e., without documents) until the Second World War began. As she remembers, she was "wanted" until the Liberation. "I was told that in OVRA's book [special secret police] I was listed with a large photograph as among the most dangerous."[31] Both Communist and Socialist women such as Rita Montagnana, Giuletta (Lina) Fibbi, Virginia Tonelli, and Lina Merlin traveled in and out of Italy in these years as couriers for their parties. Others like Rina Picolato, Alma Vivoda, and Emma Turchi remained in Italy, distributing clandestine literature and working in the underground network.

In these years, Noce played an increasingly important role in the Communist Party, attending congresses in the Soviet Union, traveling in and out of Italy, and after 1936 serving as a correspondent during the Spanish Civil War. Although she opposed separate groups for women, she also had specific responsibilities in directing the women's movement in the party and in helping to create an international movement of women against fascism and war. In 1934, when 500 women attended the International Congress of Women in Paris, Noce was one of 47 Italian delegates. The meeting was dedicated to the fight against fascism, and when Noce reported on the events of the congress, she noted that it "clearly demonstrates the immense possibilities that decisive and continued agitation and propaganda among women offer to our Party. The prejudice, resistance and negligence of working among women which still exist on a large scale among our comrades and our organizations should be fought and overcome."[32]

In a series of pamphlets and articles designed to rouse women to activism, Noce pointed to the specific forms of oppression that women suffered under fascism and in turn equated women's emancipation and equal rights with resistance to the regime. She stressed that women's slavery in the home, and as breeders of cannon fodder, had to be replaced with equal pay for equal work, economic independence, and rights to divorce and legal abortion. Reflecting the party's belief that loyalty to the Catholic church was a major obstacle to organizing among women, Noce argued that the church and the priests were the natural allies of the bourgeoisie and thus could not be friends of the poor in the struggle between oppressed and oppressor. She reminded women that the church opposed their liberation from slavery in marriage and the home while supporting the Fascists' need for workers and soldiers. Noce also assured her readers that spiritual devotion and Christian values would not be destroyed by opposing fascism. The most consistent appeal was, however, more generally that "the victory which women want is the return of their sons, an end to war, peace!"[33] The formula that equated women's subjugation with fascism and women's freedom with opposition to the regime was thus articulated long before large-scale resistance began in 1943.

Catholic political groups were also affected by the Fascist dictatorship. The Popular Party was under fire and in disarray after 1922, and its most visible leaders went into hiding or exile. In the later years of the Fascist regime, there appeared other democratic, Christian-inspired, and anti-Fascist organizations with women members. Several of these came together on July 25, 1943 to create the Christian Democratic Party, described by its leader, Alcide De Gasperi, as "a lay party of the center, moving to the left."[34] Cingolani Guidi was one of the early members of this party, as was Laura Bianchini, a graduate of Milan's Catholic University, who directed the women's movement and helped publish *Il Ribelle* in that northern city.

Maria Luisa Cinciari represents a more radical Catholic tradition. In 1939, as a student at the University of Rome, she joined with a circle of students who hoped to build a Christian Left and to fight actively against fascism. Though they did meet with other Catholic groups, including De Gasperi and his supporters, they desired more direct, militant action, and in 1942 Franco Rodano (Maria Luisa's future spouse) wrote the program for the Movement of Catholic Communists. Shortly thereafter, the authorities "clamped down on them and the only real connections were maintained by women students," among them Cinciari and Marisa Musu. Active during the Resistance, this Catholic political alternative eventually merged with the Italian Communist Party.[35]

Catholic organizations that adhered to more specifically spiritual, non-political goals were recognized and given legal status by Mussolini, who came to terms with the Roman Catholic church in the 1929 Lateran Accords. In essence, the church agreed not to oppose the regime and, in return, maintained influence in education and was able to establish a "semi-autonomous sphere and develop its own political subculture" in groups such as Catholic Action, the University Federation of Italian Catholics, the Union of Italian Catholic Women, and the Young Catholic Women.[36] These groups, with memberships in the hundreds of thousands, refrained from direct challenges to Fascist policies and generally co-existed peacefully with the regime. However, its control over youth and its role in education brought Catholic Action into a confrontation with the state in 1931, and later, in 1938, racial laws produced additional tension in their relations. By 1943, with the regime in crisis, Catholic Action in particular became more actively oppositional, joining with leaders of other Christian groups to help found the Christian Democratic Party.

For some women, leadership of these organizations led them quite naturally into the new party and to participate in the Resistance. Both Maria Jervolino de Unterrichter and Angela Gotelli, who served as Christian Democratic legislators after the war, began their public activity as leaders of the University Federation of Italian Catholics (FUCI) in the mid-twenties. Maria, after her marriage to Popular Party member Raffaele Jervolino in 1930, also directed the national center of the Union of Italian Catholic Women.[37] When the Christian Democratic Party began recruiting women, it saw the advantages of seeking members from the ranks of existing organizations.

Though on all fronts the Fascist order interrupted the evolution of women's politics in Italy and restrained certain kinds of public activism, it could not destroy political consciousness or organized female networks in the local communities and in exile. For already active, politically conscious women, their treatment at the hands of the Fascists and the daily struggles to survive only strengthened their determination to build a new and more egalitarian Italy. Simultaneously, women organized for social and religious purposes were increasingly potential opponents to the regime as conditions worsened in Italy. Alda Micelli, head of a Catholic girls school in Milan in the 1930s and a member of several Catholic organizations, noted that after World War II began, Catholic Action provided an outlet and structure for civil and political, as well as religious, activity.[38]

## Daily Life and Popular Response to Fascism

But what about the thousands of Italian women who had never been organized and had no political identity? In their attempts to mobilize the population, the Fascists did touch sectors of the population previously uninvolved in public life. They built their own organizations, like the women's auxiliaries, which were intended to create popular support for their goals and policies. By 1939 the Fascist Party itself counted about 2.5 million members, the youth groups had expanded to 8 million, and an organization for peasant women had about 1.5 million members. But organizing did not necessarily build massive support for the regime. Comparing absolute numbers of individuals who joined the wide network of Fascist groups with those who openly resisted the regime would lead one to conclude that the Italian population backed Mussolini. However, recent scholarship cautions against an oversimplified evaluation, challenges the rigid dichotomies of consent/dissent and support/opposition, and points to the fact that the regime was "accepted in certain respects and rejected in others by the same people."[39] Historian Steven White, in writing about the attitudes of schoolteachers toward the Fascist government, concludes that their loyalty was "broad but superficial—the product less of faith than a well-developed instinct for self-preservation."[40] This assessment can probably be extended to much of the population who were uncertain or ambiguous about identifying with the regime *or* its obvious opponents.

In the rhythms of day-to-day existence, and in popular culture and expectations, the Fascists touched the lives of most Italians, regardless of their politics. Particularly between 1929 and 1935, the years of experimentation and escalating economic crises, the regime adopted economic and social policies that had significant impact on the population. Under the often mythical structure of the corporate state, the Fascists hoped to increase productivity, speed up technological progress, promote self-sufficiency, and eliminate excessive individualism and class conflict. Structurally, all social and political, as well as economic, activity was to be based on a series of corporations, or occupational groupings, which would be integrated into the hierarchy of the state. Because all citizens would participate in achieving collective goals set by the state and would share in the benefits of their successes, cooperation and harmony would also result. The new system did not work as effectively or efficiently as planned and in reality evolved into a sort of state capitalism in which monopolies and cartels were encouraged and subsidized to increase productivity.

## *Economic Conditions and Policies*

Fascist goals of technological progress, productivity, and self-sufficiency required state intervention in the economy, and, as one might expect, this activity escalated once the depression hit Italy in 1932. Whether in adopting a monetary policy that would stabilize the currency, building roads, overseeing irrigation and land reclamation projects, or investing in and assuming the debts of major industrial and banking concerns, the presence of the state in economic affairs was heightened. This presence was felt quite directly by some middle-class Italians who found employment in the expanding government bureaucracy and transportation industry. For most workers, urban and rural, the new role of the state meant management of labor relations, the outlawing of strikes, and periodic reductions in wages, cuts in hours, and job reclassifications with lower pay. More severe was the problem of unemployment, which reached over 1 million by 1933 and remained at about 700,000 for the rest of the decade.[41] Some relief for workers was attempted through expansion of fringe benefits in the form of family subsidies, sick pay, health insurance, and a system of paid national holidays, but these generally could not compensate for other economic losses.

## Demographic Patterns and Programs

Fascist economic policies were accompanied by a range of social measures intended to revitalize Italian society and pull together the Italian citizenry. In the interests of productivity and aggressive expansion, Fascist leaders scrutinized patterns of immigration, urbanization, and fertility. Equating high birth rates with national vitality, and a return to the land as crucial to both population growth and self-sufficiency, the leadership was not pleased with the demographic picture painted by the 1931 census. As of that date, the numbers of changes in residence had risen to over 1 million from a level of 600,000 in 1923, and less than 50 percent of the population resided in towns of under 1,000 inhabitants.[42] Rural to urban migration was accompanied by continuing declines in birth rates, with noticeable regional differences.

### Table 1.1 – Fertility Patterns, 1882-1981 (Births/1,000)

| 1882/91 | 1902/11 | 1912/21 | 1932/41 | 1951/61 | 1961/71 | 1971/81 |
|---------|---------|---------|---------|---------|---------|---------|
| 37.4 | 37.2 | 27.2 | 23 | 18 | 18.2 | 13.6 |

Source: F. Bettio, *The Sexual Division of Labour* (Oxford University Press, 1988), Table 3.8, p. 62. Reprinted by permission of Oxford University Press.

The relationship between economic conditions and birth and marriage rates was not lost on the Fascists as they closely analyzed the returns of the 1931 census.[43] Volume 6 of the published census was devoted to an "inquiry into fertility," and its introductory comments analyzed who was having children, in what numbers, and where they resided. Though the overall birth rate per 1,000 in 1931 was 24.8, down from 30.7 ten years earlier, there were obvious differences among regions and occupational groups. Commentators pointed out that in Turin married women on the average had 1.93 children (the national low), while for Naples the average was 3.99. It was evident that birth rates were highest in southern Italy and the islands, while in larger, northern cities the numbers of married women without children were considerable (19.8 percent in Milan and 23.6 percent in Turin). Finally, officials noted that birth rates were related to the occupation of spouses, with the highest rates among agricultural populations, and in particular among those "where the tie to the land is strongest" (those with a stake in a particular piece of property having higher rates than ordinary day workers).[44]

Given the Fascist interest in population expansion, an obvious corollary would be concern about marriage rates, and here, too, the demographic characteristics were troubling. Marital rates for those 25 to 50 years of age dropped from 130.6 per 1,000 in 1921 to 80.2 in 1931.[45] More generally, in 1931, for the entire female population over the age of 19, 25 percent were listed as single/never married. For northern Italy the figure was even higher, at 37.3 percent, and in that area 17 percent of households were registered as headed by women.

## Gender Ideology: Rhetoric and Practice

The conditions these statistics described could certainly alarm anyone who feared change in gender roles and the disintegration of the family. From the outset, as guarantees of strong family life and social order, Fascist rhetoric had provided reassuring and recognizable rules for social behavior through its masculinist ideology and a belief in the rigid separation of male and female spheres. As Mussolini stated in 1925, "The issue was not one of whether woman was superior or inferior; we assert that she is different," while an article in *Il Mare Nostro* (Our Sea), written in 1937, explained that the Fascists hoped to educate and direct women "to their sacred and natural mission of wife and mother, [with] poetry, joy and smiling at life."[46] Even when it came to empire building, women had a particular function as described in the women's magazine *Gioia* (Joy) in 1937: "[Although protection of borders and conquest of new territory] are the affairs of heroes and soldiers, it is profoundly true that the sacred custody of the spiritual and moral patrimony is the Mother's, and the conquest of new interior grandeurs is the prerogative of the woman who preserves the purity of the latin race with granite-like firmness."[47] Scholars have pointed to the tension and irony in this rhetorical stance. According to De Grazia, "The perfect fascist woman was a remarkably new hybrid: she served her family's every need, yet was also zealously responsive to the state's interests."[48]

For both practical and ideological reasons, the Fascists hoped either to return women to the home or to keep them there, as public work distracted women from their "primary responsibilities" and threatened destruction of men's egos and virility. If women *did* hold jobs, "it had to be out of family necessity or because no men would take them."[49] Ideally, under fascism, women were to learn to be better, more efficient homemakers, "mothers, morale-builders, consumers, and volunteers," while men were to serve the state energetically and patriotically as they exercised dictatorial control over wives and children as modernized Roman patriarchs.[50] Legislative intervention in the form of both the "carrot and the stick" was used as the Fascists attempted to implement their ideology.

As early as 1925, the Fascists had created a national office to coordinate and promote maternal and infant care and in 1933 initiated a series of major programs designed to discourage emigration from rural areas and to "encourage marriages and births by granting tax exemptions, job priorities, special loans and prizes for large families."[51] In a punitive fashion, the regime attempted to outlaw celibacy by taxing unmarried men, and the 1931 Penal Code, in addition to forbidding the advertisement, sale, and distribution of contraceptives, established two-to-five-year prison sentences for those convicted of obtaining or performing abortions. The effects of these measures were at best mixed. Though infant mortality did drop slightly with improved health care, marriage and birth rates continued to fall, despite Mussolini's legal and rhetorical "demographic campaign." Birth rates dropped to about 23 per 1,000 in 1936, while in the northern provinces rates were down to between 14 and 20 per 1,000. The marriage rate for the 25- to 50-year-old population fell to 75.2 in 1935, and by 1939 Italy's overall marriage rate was lower than that of either Germany or Britain.[52]

The Fascists recognized that if a woman worked outside the home she could not fulfill all her familial and maternal duties and that there were connections between female employment and low birth rates—in the extreme, women's entry into the public work force presaged the moral decline of the nation. Given these perspectives, it is understandable that the regime would enact legislation limiting where and for whom women could work. Beginning with the teaching profession in 1926, restrictions were extended to other areas of employment until eventually, in 1938, decree-law 1514 set "a quota of 10% [for women] in large and medium sized public and private enterprises and excluded them completely from offices or other business having less than ten employees."[53]

## Table 1.2 – Women and Employment

| Year | % of all Women Emp. | Women as % of Emp. Population |
|------|--------------------|-------------------------------|
| 1901 | 32.2 | 32.0 |
| 1911 | 28.8 | 29.7 |
| 1921 | 27.6 | 29.5 |
| 1931 | 24.9 | 27.9 |
| 1936 | 24.9 | 28.3 |

Source: ISTAT, *Sommario di statistiche, 1861-1965*, Table 4, p. 13.

Between 1921 and 1931 there was a decline in both the percentage of all women employed and the female proportion of the total employed population (see Table 1.2). However, this was not a new pattern but rather a sharpening of trends evident at the outbreak of the First World War. These changes are explained by overall shifts in the Italian economy: transformations in agriculture that required fewer workers, lags in industrialization, and slow growth of the service sector. In general, the issue of employment had been a concern of Italian women and men for some time. The Fascist economic policies described earlier failed to alter these conditions, and most families found little institutional relief from economic pressures.

## Table 1.3 – Employment of Women by Sector (percentage of work force)

| Employment Category | 1921 | 1931 |
|---|---|---|
| Agriculture, hunting, fishing | 30.0% | 19.0% |
| Industry/crafts | 23.7% | 23.6% |
| Commerce, Transport, Banking | 20.6% | 14.5% |
| Administration, Public and Private | 6.5% | 34.0% |
| Domestic Service | 85.4% | 88.0% |

Source: ISTAT, *Censimento 1921, Relazione Generale,* Vol. I, Prospetto 66, p. 236, and *Censimento 1931, Relazione Generale,* Vol. IV, pt. II, Table XIV, p. 274.

The unstable economy and the previously noted migration to urban centers resulted in significant regional variations in female employment. In the northern provinces, the percentage of employed females over 10 years of age was considerably larger than the national average, ranging from 40.6 percent in the Piedmont to 27.3 percent in Liguria in 1936.[54] Drops in wages, whether "natural" or mandated, hurt most workers in Italy, but women were particularly vulnerable as they earned on the average only 52 percent of the wages paid to men and were often employed in textile or agricultural work where cuts were more pronounced.[55] The depression, which increased unemployment, ongoing inflation, and further government-mandated wage cuts in the thirties, caused a decline in living standards and consumption throughout the decade.[56]

What do all these figures mean in relation to the female experience under fascism? First, regardless of its ideology and programs, the regime was unable to alter previous demographic trends; as other studies have pointed out, men and women made decisions about marriage and childbearing on the basis of their own material conditions and expectations. The Fascist regime sought to remove women from the workplace, but those plans were never successful as, in fact, the number of women in the work force (including married women) increased gradually by the end of the thirties. In the northern provinces, women went to work, had fewer children, remained single, and headed their own households more often than in other areas of Italy. Combined with greater urbanization, industrialization, and leftist political organizing, it is not surprising that in these areas the largest percentage of women joined the Resistance movement. These women had their own goals and private expectations regardless of the stated goals of fascism. No doubt many women agreed with Fascist ideals about gender, marriage, and family, but how these would be applied or followed in their lives was another matter.

Fascist policies were not only ineffective, but often contradictory as well. Ideas about women and work often directly countered labor force needs, particularly when workers were required to replace men called up for military service. Additionally, while extending a network of popular organizations to create a "culture of consent," the Fascists also clearly mobilized hitherto isolated populations.[57]

As women were organized, a mixed message was put forth; women's primary duties were in the private sphere of home and family, but motherhood, and the organizations created to foster it, had a public, patriotic role. There were more concrete problems for women who joined the Fasci Femminili (Women's Clubs) expecting to have an expanded political role in the new state. In fact, the official bulletin of the organization, *Rassegna Femminile,* established in 1925, began in semi-autonomy with the goal of educating Italian women. The journal argued that woman should not only "conserve her position as queen of the home...but modernize and accept new civil responsibilities."[58] Adopting American ideas of "domestic economy," the journal described a new sort of housewife and tended to emphasize mothers' educative rather than biological roles, even questioning "men's incompetence which reduces woman to a reproductive machine." By 1929, the Fascist Party secretary, Roberto Farinacci, began to question the function of the organization, and in 1930 publication of the *Rassegna* was halted. Simultaneously, other semi-autonomous women's organizations were pushed to affiliate with the Fasci Femminili, which lost much of their independence and served more as support groups and propaganda instruments for the regime.

## *Education*

In the arena of education, Fascist policies and their results were a web of contradictions. Many men and women seeking upward mobility and entrance into a "modern," technological world looked to education, but opportunities for professional employment were limited.[59] The Fascists hoped to channel girls and young women into maternal and homemaking careers, but, in fact, such segregation never occurred, and both the absolute number and the percentage of female students in both secondary schools and universities increased. The number of females in secondary schools almost tripled between 1930-31 and 1939-40, and the female percentage of all students in those years rose from 31.4 to 45 percent. Similar changes occurred in the universities, where women constituted only 10.5 percent of the students in 1921 but were 22 percent of the total by 1941. As historian Claudia Koonz has noted, "Fascism offered young and progressive women an escape from family life...and created a mentality and a new esprit de corps for younger, urban women that appeared to involve them in public life without giving them entry into formal politics."[60] In these ways, the regime's policies both pushed women into the private sphere and pulled them into the public one, which no doubt affected the degree to which women would consistently and enthusiastically support the regime.

### Table 1.4 – Literacy Rates

|  | Total | | Male | | Female | |
|---|---|---|---|---|---|---|
|  | 1921* | 1931** | 1921 | 1931 | 1921 | 1931 |
| All of Italy | 73 | 79 | 76 | 83 | 70 | 76 |
| Northern Area | 88 | 92 | 90 | 93 | 87 | 91 |
| Southern Area | 54 | 61 | 59 | 68 | 49 | 55 |

*(out of 100 of those over 8 years of age)
**(out of 100 of those over 6 years of age)
Source: ISTAT, *Censimento 1921, Relazione Generale*, Vol. II, Table XX, p. 142; *Censimento 1931, Relazione Generale*, Vol. XIX, p. 289

## *Popular Discontent*

Among "believers" there was potential for dissatisfaction as their expectations remained only partially fulfilled. The new order and social harmony that were to be the result of gender complementarity did not develop, no matter what the Fascists did to clearly define and legally enforce male and female roles. The material problems of daily life also created a base for resistance, as the strikes and demonstrations in 1927-28 and 1930-31 illustrate. Such activities were not entirely surprising, as Italy had a long history of both urban and rural working-class militancy. However, since the regime clearly focused on controlling the masses and eliminating autonomous workers' actions, these events assume greater importance. Strikes were carried out by both industrial and agricultural workers, and by both men and women; at times they were organized by the left-wing underground political network, but in many cases they were spontaneous, and the motives for the actions varied.

In 1927, 500 women at the Jutificio factory in Ravenna demonstrated against a mandated 15 percent wage cut, while in the same year predominantly female agricultural workers in Ferrara demanded "bread and work."[61] In 1930 in Piacenza, 2,000 women and 200 men *bottonaie* (button makers) protested against their wage cuts, while silk workers at Modena objected to an increased work day and imposition of fines in the workplace. In 1931, a partially successful strike by 30,000 women rice harvesters (*mondine*) was organized in the Po Valley to rebel against wage cuts. While workers went on strike, more general public demonstrations also occurred, usually protesting scarcity of food as well as arrests of friends and companions. During the thirties, such actions were few and far between as the masses seemed increasingly passive. But as pointed out earlier, this lack of measurable reaction cannot be simply interpreted as consent or support, but perhaps demonstrates instead a pragmatic skepticism and a "wait and see" posture.

## Fascism at War

In 1935 Mussolini's dreams of an empire became a reality as he went to war with Ethiopia in October and eight months later victoriously announced the existence of an Italian African empire. During the autumn of 1936, these actions were followed by Italian intervention in the Spanish Civil War when war materiel and military units were sent to support Francisco Franco and the Nationalists. But Italians were involved in this conflict on the other side as well. Thousands of Italian anti-Fascists went to Spain to fight for the Republic in the International Brigades, and from the start their battle cry was "Today Spain, Tomorrow Italy." On the international level, the process began that would result in a formal alliance between Italy and Germany in May 1939; simultaneously, the struggle against fascism took concrete form, and the efforts of the anti-Fascists received more publicity. Internally, the results were an end to any creative attempts to solve Italy's economic problems and the beginning of what De Grand has termed the "downward spiral" of the regime.

Though doctrines of racial purity were not central to Fascist ideology and policy, there certainly were anti-Semites in the regime, and after 1935, the conquest of black Africans gave voice to more racist viewpoints. Increased connections with Germany intensified anti-Semitism, evident initially in pamphlet and newspaper propaganda and culminating in a series of racial laws promulgated in November 1938.[62] This legislation had its major impact in the areas of employment, education, property ownership, and marriage but also went to the extremes of prohibiting Jews from publishing books and spending vacations at popular resorts. There was little Italian enthusiasm for ties with Germany, and, for many, the racial laws were seen as a foreign import, thus simply adding to the "sins" of the regime. Italy's entry into World War II in June 1940 provided the ultimate set of conditions that led to a resistance movement. The nation was ill-prepared for the conflict, and instead of great victories it suffered increased economic pressures and destruction.

During World War II, economic conditions in Italy worsened dramatically. In 1943, the price of a kilogram of bread was five times what it had been in 1938, while in the same period the cost of pasta tripled and that of oil rose over 800 percent. Wages, meanwhile, continued to slip in real value, and it was estimated that in 1943 a textile worker, "to buy a bottle of oil on the black market, would have had to work for more than a month," while by August 1943 a woman in Rome would have had to get up at three a.m. and stand in line until eleven to get half a kilogram of charcoal.[63] A single egg on the black market in 1944 cost about one-fourth of an unskilled worker's daily wage, but occupation was no protection against inflation. Moderate pay raises for teachers in the war years could not begin to match the twenty-five-fold increase in prices.

While women's magazines like *Annabella* suggested ways women could support the war effort and insisted that women could win the war by securing the homefront, in reality, protests over wages and rations accelerated, and demonstrators increasingly demanded an end to the war.[64] These issues were raised in the strike by 3,000 female workers in explosives factories in Emilia Romagna in 1941. A 1942 protest by women hosiery workers in Reggio Emilia was known as the "strike of the electricity." In order to better utilize electricity, officials had decided the workers would have Saturday off rather than Sunday; this, of course, did not coincide with the schedule of other local workers, so the women protested the fact that the newly defined work week would disrupt family and social life. In some of these cases, the protests were started by a handful of women whose arrests simply spread the action to their co-workers.

The spring of 1943 saw strikes at factories producing tobacco, shoes, matches, and salami, as well as munitions, while office workers also staged demonstrations. The strike by 100,000 workers in Turin on March 5, 1943 began a flood of protest that swept most of the country by the end of that month.[65] All of these actions centered on fundamental economic demands, but increasingly, they were also protests against particular Fascist officials, against arrests, and clearly against the war. As Virginia Tonelli, a Communist organizer in Friuli, noted, "A sense of impending catastrophe was profoundly felt by the women among whom I worked."[66] The Fascist ideal of militant motherhood became reality as women took to the streets to fight for their own survival and that of their families.

Meanwhile, opposition to Mussolini was growing among the Fascist hierarchy and in the military. When the Allies landed in Sicily in early July 1943, conspiracies coalesced. On July 25, Fascist leaders voted "no-confidence" in "Il Duce," and the king, Victor Emmanuel III, dismissed Mussolini, replacing him with Marshall Pietro Badoglio, former chief of staff of the armed forces, who began discussions with the English and Americans to end the war. These actions do not represent an outright rejection of Fascist ideology or goals but rather a reaction against Fascist failures. The final revolt was against "a system of government that no longer functioned in an orderly manner and against a leader who failed in wartime."[67] Fascism had failed the masses of Italian women as well. "Poverty, a stingy welfare system, and, finally, war-making made mothering an exceptionally arduous undertaking."[68] The regime's promise of material security through the separation of public and private spheres had not been realized.

On September 8, 1943, after invading southern Italy, the Allies moved on Salerno, and the Badoglio government announced that it had signed an armistice with the Allies. The next day, the government unceremoniously fled from Rome, heading south, while the Germans quickly moved to protect their southern flank, occupying Rome on September 10. In the midst of these shifts and maneuvers, armed resistance to fascism began, building on the already existing anti-Fascist organizations. Back in October 1942 in Turin, representatives of the Communist, Socialist, Christian Democratic, Liberal, and Action parties had formed a clandestine National Action Front committee, which issued a manifesto calling for denunciation of the alliance with Germany, a separate Italian peace, and expulsion of the Germans from Italy. Building upon increasingly intense popular opposition, Committees of National Liberation (CLNs) were formed in 1943 in communities throughout Italy, as traditional opposition parties now had the opportunity to expand their anti-fascism into a more general movement that could oppose what remained of the Fascist regime and, eventually, the forces of German occupation.

# ■ 2 ■

# The Participants: "No to the War, to Hardships, to Destruction"

## The Political and Military Setting

The beginning of formal, armed resistance occurred in a confused setting as Italy was divided geographically and administratively after September 1943. The Badoglio government and the king, having fled Rome in rather shameful haste, situated themselves at Bari in the south and, after some indecision, declared war on Germany on October 13. The British and Americans recognized Badoglio and his cabinet as the official government of Italy. The Allies, moving slowly to the north, had arrived at a point slightly to the south of Rome in early October. As they advanced, they created administrative districts under their control and in November established the Allied Control Commission (ACC), which would oversee administration of the military units and interact with the Italian government. Territories "liberated" by the Allies would eventually be handed over to the Italian government, though the influence of the ACC remained. But organization and control in Italy were not so easily achieved because there were other centers of power competing for authority.[1]

When the Italian armistice was announced, the Germans immediately sent additional troops to Italy. By early October, there were some eighteen German divisions in Italy, occupying the territory from a line slightly to the south of Rome to the northern frontiers. Mussolini, who had been imprisoned by the Badoglio government, was rescued by the Germans and, along with those Fascists remaining loyal to him, was set up in a puppet government, the Italian Social Republic, at Salo on Lake Garda. In this fashion, competing Italian governments and their supporting allies occupied and attempted to control the Italian peninsula.

Matters were made more complex when indigenous and autonomous military and administrative units quickly emerged in opposition to German occupation. A

Committee of National Liberation (CLN) took formal and public shape in Rome on September 9 under the leadership of Ivanoe Bonomi, a pre-Fascist government leader of moderate Socialist leanings. This committee, like its regional counterparts, was made up of traditional anti-Fascist political groups including the Communists, Socialists, Christian Democrats, and Liberals. Also represented on the committee was the Action Party (Pd'A), organized in 1942 as an "attempt to blend liberal values with a socialist economic system...[and to offer] a radical, interclass alternative to both the communist left and to the conservative order."[2] The differing political viewpoints on these committees quite naturally led to internal conflicts, but the Rome CLN was at least united in opposition to the government of Badoglio and its claim to be the true representative government of Italy.

In the northern provinces of Italy where the struggle against the Germans and the Fascists was most intense and of the longest duration, another committee was formed in November 1943 to direct resistance activities. Formally constituted in January 1944 in Milan as the Committee of National Liberation for Northern Italy (CLNAI), this group coordinated political and military activities in the north and put together the Corps of Volunteers for Freedom (CVL).

Throughout the period of the Resistance, which lasted until the northern territories were liberated between April 19 and April 25, 1945, there were conflicts and divisions among the royal government, the CLN of Rome, the CLNAI, and the Allied military administration, as well as among the political parties that made up the various resistance committees. What held all the groups together was a common goal—the final defeat of fascism and nazism.

In a series of political compromises, the major parties of the CLN agreed to join the Badoglio cabinet in a government of national unity on April 24, 1944. However, shortly after the liberation of Rome by the Allies in June, they forced Badoglio to withdraw in favor of Ivanoe Bonomi, whose new government lasted through the end of the war. In the meantime, the Allies acknowledged the existence of the CVL, and in several agreements in December 1944 recognized the CLNAI as both the representative of all the resistance forces and the government in German-occupied Italy. For their part, the CVL accepted General Raffaele Cadorno, a regular army career officer, as their commander, and the CLNAI agreed to disarm the partisan forces at the end of the war.

These compromises represented pragmatic, working agreements but left numerous political and constitutional questions unresolved throughout the Resistance. What exactly was the authority of the king, and would Italy remain a constitutional monarchy? What would happen to the Fascists and their collaborators at the end of the conflict, and to what degree would the resistance struggle become a mechanism for political and social revolution as well as a large-scale military operation?

# The Resistance Takes Shape

During the course of the Resistance, some 200,000 Italians were formally recognized by government and military leaders as members of the Resistance; of that number, there were 35,000 women *partigiane combattente* (partisan fighters) and 20,000 *patriote* (patriots), designated as such on the basis of the nature of their activity and the recording of it by a partisan commander. This mass mobilization was unusual among the countries of Western Europe, and therefore it is important to understand the general factors that produced such resistance and then to examine in more detail motives that can be described as gender specific.

Events and changes in national politics created a set of circumstances that encouraged the population to rise up. Especially significant was the fact that the Fascist regime had collapsed internally and that the new government eventually aligned itself with the Allies. Even though the American and British armies did not move north as quickly as expected, their presence on Italian soil certainly encouraged many Italians who hoped to expel the Germans. In June 1944, after Rome was liberated, the new Bonomi government issued a call for a constituent assembly to be held at the conclusion of hostilities in order to construct a new and permanent government for Italy. These macro-political events stimulated popular resistance to fascism by demonstrating that Italy was on a new course and by holding out the promise that the war would end and Italy would be on the winning side.

Resistance was strengthened by the fact that the remaining Fascist regime was supported and even dominated by German forces. Connections with the "foreign" Germans had never been popular in Italy, and overt occupation intensified hostile feelings. Draft decrees, harsh economic measures, deportation of workers to Germany, increased anti-Semitism, and the escalating brutality of the Fascists and Nazis in the final months of the war were clearly major factors provoking mass reactions.

## *Political Origins of the Resistance*

Another factor of considerable importance was that an Italian anti-Fascist movement had existed for some time. Though the movement was small in numbers, and its members were in exile or underground, it could quickly surface to provide leadership and direction for mass activities. From the outset the anti-Fascist parties were determined to create an "organized army that would fight a war of liberation."[3] Unlike bands of a strictly military origin, these units were "organized in political form and politically inspired" and gave the Resistance its ideological character.[4] The Italian Communist Party, which had the most extensive underground network, directed between 40 and 50 percent of the Resistance forces. The newly formed Action Party (Pd'A) commanded the second largest fighting component. Resistance forces were also organized by the recently constituted Christian Democrats, the Socialists, and the Liberals, all of which were represented in the CLNs and CLNAI. Each group had its own military units, the partisan brigades, as well as smaller sabotage or guerrilla groups, called Patriotic Action groups or squads (GAP or SAP), which usually operated in urban areas.[5]

The leaders of these Resistance groups sought not only to end the war but to create a democratic and progressive Italy. They claimed to represent the people of Italy and, as a result, to have the right to a decisive role in the functioning of any nationally recognized government. Their message to the populace was that in the struggle for liberation, Italy would be "reborn." Since all of the parties were committed to electoral democracy and had an eye to the future, they also consciously developed a mass base to ensure their place in postwar Italy. In this activity the groups were highly competitive, as their visions of the transformation of Italian society often differed. In many cases, the political leadership in the north advocated solutions to Italy's problems that were more radical than those of the southern government. These political differences often provoked controversies and dissension among the various groups directing the war effort and ultimately had significant impact on postwar Italian politics. However, in terms of mobilizing the population, the important fact is that experienced leaders and existing parties provided an organizational base and had plans and programs that appealed to the general population.[6]

## *From Anti-Fascism to Resistance*

During the summer of 1943, when the regime began to disintegrate, anti-Fascist leaders returned from exile, political prisoners were set free, and shadowy underground structures and clandestine activists came out into the open. The dreams of many men and women were finally realized as their often dangerous and hidden journeys of opposition led to direct, militant resistance.

Vittoria Guadagnini was typical of these individuals; she had joined the PCI in Imola in 1929 while her husband was in prison for anti-Fascist activity. As she explains, "At the moment of my husband's arrest I had a month and a half old son and couldn't go to look for work; all I could do was weep out of desperation."[7] She remembered that her husband Roberto had said, "If we were all organized there would be a force sufficient to fight fascism," so she went to talk to a friend whose father was also imprisoned, with her help joined the party, and together with three other women formed the first women's "cell" in Imola. "From that moment onward our spirit changed completely: we set out on our work with faith in our strength, even if we were politically illiterate and our numbers small." That work consisted of distributing literature they received from the party provincial federation, meeting with party leaders (often at Vittoria's home), and organizing demonstrations of community women to demand "bread and work" or to protest arrests and imprisonment of neighbors and comrades.

In 1934, after Roberto had served his time and was released from prison, Vittoria and her husband left Italy for the Soviet Union, where she learned to type and was employed at the international Leninist School. When Roberto and other exiles left the USSR to fight in the Spanish Civil War, Vittoria went to work with the European anti-Fascist radio network. With the start of the Second World War, she began planning her return to Italy. Eventually, in 1942, carrying outlawed literature in two suitcases with false bottoms, she crossed the Italian-French border and made her way back to Imola. There she resumed underground activities, was arrested but then released when the regime collapsed, and by September 1943 was organizing women in the area of Bologna.

Virginia Tonelli, born in 1903 in Castelnuovo (Friuli), had dreamed of an education and training as a nurse. However, when her father died, she went to work as a dressmaker at a young age to help support her large family. In the twenties, through friends and workplace acquaintances, Tonelli became familiar with anti-fascism and the work of the PCI. In 1933 she moved to France, where she married party activist Pietro Zampollo and then joined the exiled Communist organization in 1935. When Zampollo went to fight in the Spanish Civil War, their home in France became a "safe house" for various party leaders. Like many of his comrades, Zampollo was imprisoned in 1940, but Virginia continued her work and in May 1943 the party sent her back to Italy, where in June she organized women's demonstrations in Castelnuovo.[8]

Lina Fibbi grew up in exile after her family emigrated to Lyon, France in 1923 when she was three years old. By the time she was a teenager she was doing textile work in Lyon and had joined the local Communist youth league, becoming its head in 1937. She was arrested in 1939, along with many others (e.g., Teresa Noce), and was in and out of prison, both in France and in Italy, until July 1943. Upon her release, Lina immediately resumed party work and eventually participated in the war as attaché to the General Command of the Communist Party's Garibaldi Brigades. Ada Gobetti, who later worked with Fibbi in organizing women, had collaborated with her husband Piero on an anti-Fascist journal in the early twenties. When Piero left for France, Ada remained in Turin, where she taught English and did translating. While her home became a center for clandestine opposition to the regime, she maintained communication with exiled leaders. In 1942 she was one of the founders of the Pd'A and a logical nucleus for a resistance network that evolved in Turin in late 1943.[9] These small but enduring networks of clandestine opposition, either in exile or underground, provided a crucial basis for early resistance organizing.

A common prison experience also connected many individuals. The various courts of the Fascist government had sentenced more than 300 women to prison or confinement between 1926 and 1943. Communist Lucia Scarpone Bianciotto was in and out of prison between 1932 and the summer of 1943 but always resumed political activity when not incarcerated and thus, like many others, logically moved into formal resistance work after September 1943. Socialist

Angelina Merlin was another detainee, who was first arrested for anti-Fascist activity in 1924, spent five years in prison, and until 1943 was under Fascist surveillance. At the time of her first arrest, the police chief had told her father: "Your daughter is uncompromising...." In May 1943, when she was once again brought to Fascist district headquarters for questioning, she was asked why she was not a member of the Fascist Party. She responded, "Do you know the date of the origin of fascism? I do, March 23, 1919. Today is May 18, 1943. If I am not a member it is because I am not a fascist."[10] Though not always wise or prudent, such consistency in convictions and continuity in activities on the part of politically conscious men and women provided a strong core of leadership for the resistance struggle.

Other individuals with less formal or longstanding party connections were also obvious candidates for leadership in building resistance organizations either because of family political backgrounds or participation in well-publicized acts of opposition. For example, both Rosanna Rolanda in Turin and Gina Vanoli in Bergamo came from longtime anti-Fascist families and had led factory strikes in March 1943. After September 8, they were recruited by the PCI as organizers in their workplaces and communities. Maria Luigia Guaita, a student in Florence, had been distributing anti-Fascist literature since 1941, and as the Pd'A organized she was contacted, joined the party, and went to work for its resistance organization in Tuscany.

The newly formed Christian Democratic Party (DC) had its own pool of active women from which to recruit partisans, party members, and leaders for its women's organization. Young Women of Catholic Action had served an important function during the Fascist years, "breaking many of the passive aspects of the home-church connection, to offer forms of militancy, initiative, and organizing responsibility which represented in fact the stimulus for women's entry into history."[11] From this group the DC would draw women like Ines Boffardi of Genoa, who became active in a Patriotic Action Squad (SAP) and eventually joined the party by the end of the war. Lucia Banti perhaps best represents the experience of Catholic Action women. In Florence, in 1943, she was one of the leaders of the young women's organization. She admits she paid little attention to political parties though she had heard of the clandestine opposition, and she and her associates talked about it in their meetings. In the spring of 1944, Maria Giubbi, who headed the senior women's association in the area, approached her, saying a DC representative from the CLN had come to her looking for women to act as couriers for the movement. Both Banti and Giubbi thus encouraged women of their respective organizations to participate in the Resistance.[12]

The organization of Catholic university students, which became increasingly anti-Fascist by 1943, provided proportionately high numbers of volunteers for resistance work. Experienced Catholic political women such as Maria Jervolino de Unterrichter and Angela Gotelli, already established as leaders of the University Federation of Italian Catholics (FUCI), were joined by a younger generation of university women. In particular, the Catholic University of Milan produced many new activists, among them Tina Anselmi and Lidia Menapace, who joined the Resistance and served in DC politics. Like their counterparts on the Left, some Catholic women also spent a portion of the Fascist years away from their homeland. During the regime, teacher Maria Federici and her husband Mario first lived in Egypt, then moved to Paris. In 1939 they returned to Italy, where Maria was active in the Roman Resistance, and at the end of the war represented the DC in the Constituent Assembly.[13]

Thus a variety of existing organizations, ranging from the barely political Union of Catholic Women to the small but determined clandestine networks of the political parties, served as logical recruiting grounds for partisan activists. The political upheavals of 1943 provided both stimulus and opportunity to pull together the various strands of opposition into an effective Resistance movement. But this is only a part of the story. There was no automatic connection between membership in one of the organizations mentioned and willingness to risk one's life in open conflict. And what of the thousands of Italians who had no prior political affiliation yet participated in the Resistance? A full understanding of the movement must include consideration of the quite specific conditions and motives that impelled individuals to act.

## Becoming a Partisan

The male population of Italy followed several roads into the Resistance. One identifiable and instrumental group was composed of men who were exiled in France and had begun to fight fascism in 1936 in the Spanish Civil War. When that conflict ended, most of them were deported to Italy and imprisoned there until the "fall" of Mussolini. These men utilized their previous experience as they carried out initial acts of sabotage and began to organize partisan bands. Shifting to this sort of fighting in the setting of their own hometowns was not always easy. Giovanni Pesce describes his experience after returning to his native Turin in September 1943: "I feared being alone, because I had no comrades rushing with me to the assault. I had missed the fierce shouting from hundreds of throats. In this new war, silence reigned. No banners fluttered, no friends or enemies stared at deeds of valor. Yet, war was the same in all places."[14] With that realization and the recognition that they could fight a different sort of war in Italy, he and other Spanish Civil War veterans or ex-prison colleagues formed the first GAP (Gruppo di Azione Patriottica) in Turin.

Often men who joined the Resistance were recruited after November 1943 from already existing Italian army units. A variety of sources confirm the uncertainty many soldiers felt in the summer and early fall of 1943 due to Italy's governmental and diplomatic shifts. Claudia Pavone reports the words of a soldier returning from France, who asked his commander: "But, basically, sir, Colonel, what should we do now?"[15] Similar sentiments are eloquently described by Nuto

Revelli, a young army officer who returned from the Russian front in March 1943 after most of his unit had been lost. After September 8, Revelli rejoined his Alpine unit, assuming they would have to fight the Germans, but the army was in such disarray that there was no organization or action so he returned to his home. There he prepared to resist with a group of friends. "We know that soon we will have to shoot, that the war will be long. We know we are alone on the plains, that a few groups are forming in the mountains.... We don't want to hear talk of politics.... [W]e are still soldiers." By December his group and others were organizing seriously even though according to Revelli, "many joined the partisan brigade of necessity, simply to find a temporary refuge; the decisions to fight were few."[16]

These political and military veterans were joined by a younger generation of men just coming of age who were targets of a conscription decree issued by the "new" Fascist/German government, which affected all men born in 1924-25. Fascist terror and reprisals in January and February 1944 plus a second conscription increased the number of men who joined the opposition. By March 1944 there were between 20,000 and 30,000 men in the partisan bands; among them were "professional soldiers faithful to their oath of loyalty, Catholics whose Christian conscience had been stirred, students and intellectuals whose ethical code abhorred violence, and 'common people' who perceived instinctively that they could not obtain peace except by resisting the Nazis and Fascists."[17]

Women had no prior military experience and were not threatened by the "draft"; though many undoubtedly shared men's "crisis of conscience" and recognized that they would have to fight to end the war, determining the specific factors that led to women's involvement is complicated. Who were these women, and what motivated them to participate in the Resistance? At first glance, one could answer that they were heroines, some already active opponents of the regime, such as those mentioned above, or they were women of unusual personal courage, swept into the Resistance almost accidentally, who performed extraordinary feats of bravery. Many of the women served in prominent political positions after 1945, and they are the focus of much of the existing literature.[18] However, an examination of documents and reports in various archives, newspapers, and countless personal testimonies, as well as the author's interviews with women who were a part of the Resistance, revealed two signficant facts. First, the "heroines" were only the tip of the iceberg; after all, 55,000 women participated in the Resistance, though their names usually appear in impersonal lists of partisans or as casual references in accounts of specific actions or events. Second, explanations for women's participation in the Resistance were often superficial or romantically ahistorical. There were gaps that needed to be filled in order to gain a broader picture of Resistance women and establish some general explanations for their activity and its impact on their lives.

# The Profile of Women Activists

In order to place in a broader context individual women's subjective statements of motives for joining the Resistance and their experiences once engaged in the struggle, the author created a profile of women activists. Each time an individual name was encountered it was recorded, and then from all possible sources bits and pieces of information were added. Eventually this produced 936 women for whom there was comparable descriptive data on such things as age in 1943, occupation, and political affiliation. The accumulated data were then mechanically analyzed and the results compared to personal expressions and accounts. In each case where the author's calculations and the personal records seemed to point to some conclusions, an attempt was made to check them against the impressions of the women interviewed who were familiar with the subject. The importance of these discussions cannot be overestimated; although the research for this book was not intended to produce an oral history of women in the Resistance, the author's connections with women like Giuliana Beltrami, Gisella Floreanini, and Maria Michetti added a dimension of personal understanding that has been invaluable.[19]

## Age and Occupation

Analysis of the data indicates that there was nothing unusual about the women who became partisans. They were typical of the overall female population in age, occupation, and lack of prior political experience. Almost 50 percent of the sample were born between 1920 and 1927. In 1943, 27.4 percent were 19 years of age or younger; 42.4 percent were between the ages of 20 and 29; and 15.4 percent were in the 30 to 39 age group. Thus, an overwhelming majority of these women were born and raised under fascism, with expectations and motives shaped by that experience. As one might expect, though their number was smaller, of women 40 years of age and older, a fairly high percentage had been involved in anti-Fascist activities before 1943 (50.8 percent of those aged 40 to 49, and 30 percent of those 50 to 59).

The occupational distribution of the participants was also what one might expect and mirrored fairly accurately the employment picture of the time. Some 203 women (21.7 percent) were housewives, though it should be noted that this census category included very young women not yet employed and may have included women who worked part-time or in the home. A total of 182 (19.4 percent) were agricultural workers of some sort, 140 (15 percent) were in industry, and 120 (12.8 percent) were in commercial activity, mostly retail or clerical workers.

In some regions certain occupation categories are over-represented among participants, but this probably reflects the nature of the sources and reporting rather than actual contrasts. For example, in Liguria, though only 7 percent of all employed women were in industry, 45 percent of the region's partisans in the sample were in that occupational group, and in Lombardy, while teachers/ professors and other professionals were only 2 percent of the female work force (fairly typical for all regions), 39.5 percent of the region's activists came from these groups. These differences can be explained by the fact that the reporting for these areas focused on women who were often leaders or individuals who came to some prominence, and such women were more likely to be factory workers and professionals than agricultural workers or housewives.

## Party Membership and Political Background

As pointed out earlier, few Italian women were members of political parties, and this is borne out in the characteristics of the sample. Only 75 of the women were known party members by 1943 (49 of those in the PCI), and while another 156 had joined a party by 1945, this means that for the vast majority, 705 women or 75.3 percent of the total, there was no known party affiliation. Though these figures probably underestimate exact membership because of the imprecise nature of records, it nevertheless would be safe to conclude that party membership was not a general pre-condition for involvement in the Resistance.[20]

If one distinguishes between a background of protests or public anti-Fascist activity that took place prior to September 1943 and joining the Resistance after that date, one of the most important conclusions of this study is obvious. The Resistance brought new groups of women into the public forum and for a time changed the face of women's political activity in Italy. Of the 936 women, 168 had been active in some fashion before 1943, 705 after that, and the year in which 63 became active is unknown. Of the 168, 65 percent were either industrial workers (45), in commerce or clerical work (25), teachers/professors (20), or other professionals (20). These same occupations comprised only 31 percent of the 705 who joined after September 1943. Agricultural workers, domestics, and housewives made up 11 percent of the 168 who were active prior to 1943, and 58 percent of the 705 who became active after 1943.

Of the 168 women active before 1943, 101 clearly indicated that family or personal connections had influenced their decisions to demonstrate, distribute literature, or assume some other political stance. Their experiences support Willson's argument that "women who did get politically involved almost invariably formed their ideas at home, learning from other members of their families."[21] Sixty-nine of the 168 were party members before 1943, and another 62 joined a party during the Resistance. Characteristics of the 705 who became active after September 1943 are quite different. Only 102 cited the importance of a family or personal connection, only 3 listed a party before 1943, and 59 joined thereafter. Traditional examinations of women's mobilization and militancy often point to their work experience, family influence, and political loyalty or ideology as the factors that explain raised consciousness and willingness to act. While for the early group there are direct correlations between these factors and public activism, such obvious connections do not exist to explain the Resistance activity of the vast majority of women who were newcomers to the public arena.

## Family/Personal Relationships

Earlier studies have explained women's part in the Resistance as an extension of male participation, motivated by personal connections, and as acts of selfless and unconscious devotion to loved ones. In quite typical fashion, a commemorative pamphlet published in March 1953 was dedicated to the thousands of women in the Resistance "who found the means to express traditional female virtues," while two decades later, a study of Catholics in the Resistance was entitled *Rebels for Love*.[22] Certainly some women became active because husbands, companions, or other male relatives and friends were partisans. For example, Leda Orlandi Bastia, who became a partisan in the Bologna sector, recalls, "I found myself joining the Resistance gradually, almost without understanding, working at the side of my husband Mario." Maria Dal Pozzo of Imola insists that she began to help the partisans and continued to do so without knowing much about the Resistance because her son Giovanni asked her to go to someone's house to pick up "things." He told her there was no need to talk—"Only tell them you are Giovanni's mamma." In this fashion she carried food and arms for a PCI brigade without knowing any of the particulars. Gina Borellini of the PCI, who became a brigade officer and was awarded a gold medal for her activities, stated in a 1950 interview that her motives were not political but "simply for love of [my] husband and brother." And it was certainly Mila Malvestiti's partisan father, a former member of the Popular Party and then the DC, who enlisted her services as a *staffetta* (courier) for the CLN in Lombardy.[23]

Brothers often influenced their sisters' behaviors, though not necessarily in intended ways. In September 1943, factory worker Alberta Rossi in Reggio Emilia was aware of Mussolini's fall and the arrival of the Germans. Her brother, a soldier, returned home, but the war continued, and when he began to hold meetings with other men in their house, Alberta eavesdropped. "Mine was not simply curiosity; I wanted to do something." Eventually she approached her brother to tell him she had heard their planning and wanted to help. He initially answered that they had not received orders to make use of women. However, he did give her some printed material to distribute, and by September 1944 she was asked to work as a *staffetta* for the regional military command.[24]

Eighteen-year-old Delia Covina of Imola had a similar experience. She, too, witnessed gatherings her brother had in their house and when she offered to help was told it was too dangerous and that she shouldn't do anything. One morning, however, a regular courier who was supposed to bring them arms failed to show up and Delia offered to go. The men reluctantly agreed, and that began her resistance activity.

The initial curiosity of younger sisters Lina Magri and Edera Parenti caused them to observe their brothers' comings and goings and to pester them for explanations. As Parenti recounts, "At first he refused to answer me, but because...I gave him no rest, he confided that partisan activity was developing, [and] that I shouldn't tell our mother so as not to worry her." Shortly thereafter, her brother joined a partisan formation, and though she saw him rarely, when she did, "he spoke to me with enthusiasm of the crucial work the *staffette* did, without asking me to do anything. Finally, the desire to be near my brother, and his words exalting the partisan struggle brought me to tell him of my decision to enter the partisan organization."

Rita Bazzanini Comoglio, from a Socialist family in Turin, attributes her raised political consciousness to her brother, who had participated in the workers' occupation of the factories after World War I and constantly talked to her about justice and injustice. In the early thirties, Rita attended a commercial school and worked at home as an accountant. "In that period, naturally, I went out with other girls, and curiously, spontaneous sympathy always led me to friends who were anti-Fascist." At the home of one of her friends whose family was very religious, she met her future husband, Luigi, a Communist and dedicated anti-Fascist. "Naturally he was not open to tell me who he was, and I, seeing that he associated with a family of that sort, did not suspect it." Luigi eventually persuaded her to carry banned books and political letters for him. "I did not know the content; he had not yet told me." Gradually through these personal associations, Rita's political awareness and activities increased to the point that she was arrested and jailed from May to August 1943 and went on to serve as a *staffetta* for one of the PCI divisions.[25]

It is important to see personal ties not only as motivation for women's activism but one of the few possible entrances to the political and military worlds that a typically gender-segregated society defined as male. How else would a woman connect with a partisan brigade or military commanders? Eventually women created their own autonomous organizations and avenues into the struggle, but for many women, at least at the outset, men were their link to the conflict, and men thus determined the roles they would initially play. Beginning with individual acts of devotion and support, such as hiding a deserter or providing food and clothing for a loved one, women's contributions often expanded into formally recognized duties for entire brigades as the scope and organization of the Resistance grew.

Clara Dragoni, a young woman from Ferrara who was eventually arrested and sent to the Ravensbruck concentration camp, recites: "I was very young during the war, and because my father was a partisan, I also wanted to enter the Resistance. I became a *staffetta* and had contact with the partisan groups in Ferrara and the command in Emilia Romagna."[26] Maria Donadio explains rather romantically, "I became a partisan in the most simple and human way...pushed by patriotism, by an unbounded love of peace and freedom," but then goes on to describe the gradual evolution of her involvement, at first providing supplies for men hiding out in the mountains (usually people she already knew), then, when units organized, supplying them and eventually becoming a *staffetta*.[27] Elsa Oliva, a twenty-two-year-old clerical worker from Novara, recounts that she had gone to the commander of a local unit thinking he could assist her in locating her brother and because she wanted to help in any way she could. Insisting that she could both nurse the wounded and handle arms, she finally convinced the commander to give her guard duty. At that point she felt tremendous pride "in having become at last a real partisan."[28]

A sense of whether or not these individual cases were indeed typical can be gained by comparing them to the experiences of the women in the larger sample. For the vast majority of women (707 out of 936), the sources or records do not document clear personal connections to individuals associated with Resistance activity. Family connections were most often cited by older women: 42.4 percent of the women aged 40 to 49 and 30 percent of those over 50 listed a family connection of some sort, while this was true for only 15.6 percent of those 19 years of age or younger, and for 21.2 and 29.2 percent of those in the 20 to 29 and 30 to 39 age groups, respectively. It seems appropriate, therefore, to consider factors other than family loyalties or personal devotion as the explanations for women's decisions to resist. Supporting this argument is the statement of Fidalma Garosi, who was twenty three years old in 1943 and whose husband was a partisan: "[Joining the Resistance] was a collective and anonymous act, but political, not out of piety, nor in the train of husbands and sweethearts."[29]

## Daily Life and the Struggle To Survive

A father's membership in a political party, a husband's anti-Fascist sentiments, or a brother's military experiences might have made it easier for women to actively participate in the Resistance. But women responsible for their own day-to-day survival and that of their families acted spontaneously, regardless of what husbands, brothers, or fathers were doing. Events of these years profoundly affected women's lives and, as pointed out earlier, often conflicted with their own notions about female roles. Even within the spheres assigned to them, women had agency, and their responses were "more complex than attitudes commonly ascribed to them."[30] Gisella Floreanini, a major figure in Resistance activity and postwar Italian politics, denied that women joined the Resistance "only for love of our families." Women had their own vision of their role and believed they were fighting for a "new motherhood" that society would finally recognize as socially valuable, politically influential, and therefore worthy of public support.[31] Bombings, hunger, unemployment, wage reductions, Fascist requisitioning and rationing of food supplies, and forced transportation of workers to Germany all provoked reactions from masses of women.

The multiplicity of motives for resistance is illustrated by the experiences of a number of women from distinctly different backgrounds. Twenty-one-year-old Diana Sabbi, a garment worker from Bologna, came from an anti-Fascist family with two uncles who were PCI members, both of whom were arrested in 1933. Sabbi grew up hearing discussions about socialism and anti-fascism, but it was only during the war, when her family was under constant surveillance and she had no job and no money, that she finally took action. On September 15, 1943, she joined the Resistance, first with a PCI brigade, then the 7th GAP, and finally as a *staffetta* for the command in Emilia Romagna.[32]

The experience of agricultural worker Vittorina Rifredi is a good example of the material difficulties and Fascist brutality that pushed many women to act. At the time the Resistance began, Rifredi, along with others, had to go to Fascist headquarters in Modena to obtain "coupons" necessary to buy supplies like milk and fuel. Usually this required several trips because they were told the "coupons" were not ready. As she remembers, by early 1944 "I was in a particularly delicate period. I was in a state of advanced pregnancy, had two young children and couldn't work because I had to take care of my husband who was ill and confined to bed. I couldn't turn to my family for help because my brother Vasco had been deported to Germany and Giancarlo was a prisoner of war in Russia."[33] After several futile trips to Fascist headquarters, her frustration and humiliation built to the point that she hid a rolling pin in her shopping basket, and when her turn came to ask for the "coupons," she pulled it out and threatened to use it on the official in charge. Suddenly the "coupons" appeared, but additionally, Rifredi acquired a political reputation and shortly thereafter was approached and asked to work with the local Women's Defense Group (GDD). For many women, like Rifredi, specific incidents provoked their anger and then action; for others, more general resentment toward the Fascists accumulated over a period of time and cannot be attributed to a targeted event.

Elvira Fae, a Fiat worker in Turin who had been helping to support her family since she was fourteen, expresses this kind of sentiment: "I was against the Fascists, but not because I had a clear idea; I saw the Fascists around here, they had no professions, were without work, without the ability, little desire to work, 'loafers' in the true sense of the word. I couldn't stand to see it."[34] Seventeen-year-old Teresa Costa, a clerk from a firm in Turin who worked with both a Garibaldi Brigade and a G&L group, was asked in an interview why she had joined the Resistance. She answered: "I don't know…not because at that moment I knew anything about the parties, because for us [she and her friends] the parties didn't exist….We did what had to be done against the fascists, and—enough!—against the Germans."[35]

This same sort of diffused opposition is apparent in the experience of Nelia Benissone Costa, who had joined the PCI in Turin in 1938, largely through contact with her husband's friends. Costa reflected that in 1943 neither she nor her female friends had very clear political ideas. On the other hand, "We were discontented with the war, the cold, the hardships. Propaganda work could be done best in the lines in front of the shops. There we talked, discussed and began to understand that it was fascism that wanted war and now we should end it. It was time the women organized because on us there was, perhaps, the greatest burden."[36] The war, accompanied by the collapse of the institutional structure of fascism and the emergence of a public and formal opposition, opened the floodgates of women's dissatisfaction and channeled women's activism.

Women employed in factory work had a history of protest, and for many the strikes in March 1943 were only the beginning of a series of demonstrations and organizing activities in the workplace. An anonymous factory worker in Emilia Romagna explained: "Life in the factory had become impossible; the intensity of the work, the low salary, the lack of food, the black market, the war, constituted the motive for our rebellion."[37] Fiorina Friziero, a twenty-three-year-old Fiat worker in Turin whose husband was in the army, stated that though their actions were "so-called economic, they still had a political color."[38] Economic motives combined with general anti-war sentiments and family needs and experiences, sometimes in an almost accidental fashion. Irma Bandiera, who became one of the heroines of the Resistance, could not specify an immediate reason for joining, while Laura Polizzi, who came from an anti-Fascist family in Parma, had no consciousness of the role she could play until Lucia Sarzi, a PCI organizer, came to her home. "It was for me a great revelation to see a young woman who was in the movement, to hear her discuss political problems with great competence, to see how she was listened to and respected by her comrades. She was the first person who asked me to collaborate."[39]

Even for longtime leftist women like Irene Castagneris, the step into partisan activity was not necessarily planned. Castagneris had been an associate of Rina Picolato and Teresa Noce in the Young Socialist organization and had moved with them into the Communist Party in 1921. In the 1930s, she had distributed anti-Fascist literature at the textiles factory where she worked, and then in September 1943 as the PCI was forming its squads, she was asked to work as a courier. "If the party thought I was capable of carrying out that task, well, good, and I accepted."[40]

## Private Ideals and Personal Rebellion

Vague ideals, private rebellions, and personal aspirations and desires also served as motives, particularly among the younger women. According to historian Tracy Koon, "When the young learned that their hopes would not be realized, the long voyage began. The disillusionment meant only passive resistance for some; it led others into open opposition outside and against the regime, [and this opposition was] a pre-political stance, a prevalently moral one."[41] The universities provided a particularly fertile ground for the growth of resistance. The Fascists never gained complete control of curriculum or ideas at these institutions, which were also the sites of mass organizations of young people, such as the University Federation of Italian Catholics (FUCI) and the Fascist University Group (GUF). The majority of university students were in the GUF and probably had "joined the movement not because they were dedicated Fascists, but rather because membership enhanced their chances of employment after graduation."[42] At the same time, this sort of association promoted connections among the students that could lead to collective rebellion. Luciana Viviani, who was a student in Naples, attests, "If attending the meetings of the GUF at the university I had not had contact with a group of young students who were also in the clandestine organization of the PCI, perhaps my life would have been completely different."[43] Viviani married one of her colleagues and in 1943 moved to Rome, where she joined the Communist Party and became a partisan with the rank of second lieutenant.

Between 1940 and 1943, universities in Italy became the scene of protests in which young women participated. It was often the enforcement of racial laws, increased Italian ties to Germany, and the war itself that provoked a crisis of conscience and then revolt. Laura Conti, a medical student in 1939, maintains that among the students, largely lower middle class in origin, anti-fascism was in many ways altruistic, but more likely based on personal desires for freedom and individual rebellion or "because they saw the obstacles which fascism put up to their development." In her own case, the response was both intellectual and emotional. During the course of her education she disliked the Fascist vision of women and was even more repelled by racial doctrines. But it was in the context of the war that Conti developed the sense that "the world was too small to accommodate the Nazis and me, that it was even necessary to die....Thus I participated in the military actions in the city....[N]othing else interested me. I had become a war machine: I wanted only to get rid of the Germans."[44]

Similar sentiments were expressed by Carla Capponi, who later became one of the heroines of the Roman Resistance. As a student, Capponi was exposed to anti-Fascist ideas, and in 1940, at the age of nineteen, she joined the PCI. "We were young, and young people are affected by injustice. They possess qualities such as generosity and feel sympathy towards their fellow men. That is what drove us to organize against fascism and later to fight." Capponi's future comrade in arms, Marisa Musu, came from a family of leftist liberal activists, but when she joined the PCI in 1941, "it wasn't an ideological or theoretical choice but rather a childish one, due to the fact that it was only the Communists who were doing anything about fascism."[45]

Lisetta Giua was born in 1923. Her father, a teacher and a Socialist, was arrested for his political activity, and her brother Renzo was killed in the Spanish Civil War. Giua worked with Red Aid, a PCI auxiliary or front organization dedicated to helping the families of opposition leaders and political emigrants, and in 1941, as a law student in Turin, she began to organize students, creating the nucleus of what would become a section of the PCI's Youth Front (Fronte della Gioventú).[46]

As anger and frustration mounted, an overwhelming sense that they should act in some way motivated many young women such as Matilde Di Pietrantonio. Attending the university in Turin, she had contact with other students associated with the G&L movement, and she joined the Resistance after September 1943, ending up as a brigade commander. Pietrantonio stated that "the popular revolt meant for me concrete and immediate action,...above all of a military sort."[47]

The situation for teachers in primary and secondary schools was somewhat different. Fascist intervention and control were much greater at these levels than at the universities. The regime was particularly disturbed by the fact that the teaching force was increasingly female and by 1928 had introduced a range of discriminatory measures to "keep more women at home and place more men in the classroom."[48] Though these restrictions had the potential to produce resentment on the part of women teachers, most accounts indicate that in the face of fascism, teachers were neutral, or apolitical. Education alone was an insufficient criterion for anti-fascism or resistance. Even someone like Bianca Montale, who eventually became a partisan, recognized that "when I joined the ranks of the Resistance, I knew Greek and Latin well, but I ignored the existence of parties in the CLN; I had...even forgotten that [Giuseppe] Mazzini was a republican."[49] After September 1943, teachers were asked to take an oath of loyalty to Mussolini's puppet regime, and that, combined with wartime conditions, helped to draw more schoolteachers into the Resistance. But even then, political maturity came slowly, as teacher Lydia Guarnaschelli in Milan remembers. "Our anti-Fascism was more impulsive than based on profound reasons; it was mostly the anti-Fascism of 'no' to this or that, no to the war, to the hardships, to death, to the German power, to the destruction....[From there] we had to teach ourselves."

For the very young who were educated solely under the influence of fascism, and who were often enrolled by their parents in Fascist youth groups, the road to resistance would be longer. Iste Cagossi, who eventually became a partisan, started out as a proud young Fascist. Not until the war began did she recognize the failures of the regime, and the hypocrisy of its promises.[50] For some, childhood experiences could produce the glimmerings of an awareness that all was not right with the world. Annita Malavasi, who later became the commander of a partisan detachment in Reggio Emilia, remembers an emerging sense of injustice when in her school she was denied a prize because she was not a member of the Fascist young girls association. That feeling was reinforced when a friend had to leave school to support his family after his father was shot.[51] At the age of eleven, Laura Polizzi's studies were interrupted because her family could not afford to have her in school; to continue to study, "my father would have had to ask the 'Duce' for support, something he would not do." Silvana Guazzaloca was not even a teenager when she first rebelled against the Fascists. From a family of hired agricultural workers, Silvana grew up with her grandfather and uncle, both of whom were Communists. She learned dissent from them. As a youngster in school, she refused to shout "Long Live Il Duce" and usually hid when Fascist officials visited the school to avoid having to acknowledge them.

Outside the confines of the schools, many young women commented on their growing resistance to a variety of forces that oppressed and tyrannized them. According to Cecilia Pron, her rebellion and that of the other young women she worked with in a textile factory occurred "because we were young, because we wanted to go to dances and we couldn't because there was a war; we had many dreams and desires that made us detest fascism without really knowing the reasons."[52] Maria Beltrami, who was seventeen years old in 1943, states: "I rebelled against being a woman first, and I wanted to show that I could do the same things as a man, get involved in the same way and fight with arms…to demonstrate that I wasn't inferior, but in fact braver, more intelligent, more capable, more everything than the men." Similar sentiments were expressed by twenty-five-year-old Rosina Becchi in July 1943 when she wrote: "The first symptoms of a reaction began to manifest themselves, and I, who for some time had felt new confusions boiling up in me, joined several other young people who sought to find the way to free us from those who oppressed us."[53]

These feelings of rebellion, frustration, and even desperation were not confined to just the young women; for older women as well, the need to act and to participate in the movement, even without specific ideological direction and goals, brought them into the Resistance. Maria Baroncini, forty years old in 1943, was no doubt representative of many of these women. In Ravenna, "after September 8, I went to a partisan leader and told him that women also wanted to work for the Resistance and wanted to be organized. He directed me to make contact with the women. At first we were only five; then our numbers grew."[54] Thus the seed of one woman's spontaneous reaction could grow to create a network in her neighborhood, workplace, school, or community as she found others who were sympathetic and ready to follow her lead.

Connections among female kin were often important in drawing women into the Resistance. One of the most notable examples of this is the experience of sisters Vera and Libera Arduino. Their father, an anti-Fascist, was arrested eighteen times for political activity. In 1943 Libera was only fourteen, and Vera, seventeen, was a factory worker in Turin, where she took part in the March 1943 strikes. Vera persuaded Libera to join the action, and when her older sister became a *staffetta* for one of the nearby mountain brigades, Libera provided her with support and assistance. Both sisters were eventually captured and shot by the Fascists on March 13, 1945, and their funeral became the occasion for a mass demonstration organized by the Women's Defense Group (GDD).[55]

Among other such teams were the Guerrini sisters from Siena, who worked with the Pd'A, and Luigia Ercoli and her sister Antonietta, who were members of the women's branch of Catholic Action and served with the command of the Christian Democratic brigades in Lombardy. Finally, Cesarina Bracco and her cousin Neva, both workers from anti-Fascist families, eventually joined the PCI and worked with their brigades in the Turin area, where Cesarina served as a *staffetta* with the rank of lieutenant. These specific examples illustrate the more general importance of female kin networks in the mobilization of women in the Resistance.[56]

## Conclusion

Personal testimony and objective data demonstrate that there was no single motive for women's participation in the Resistance. Nevertheless, what appears as a widely diverse cast of characters with a multiplicity of reasons for joining the struggle can be grouped together by common experiences and goals, and set into the broader context of Italian wartime politics and society. It is certainly clear that political uncertainty and the shift in military fortunes after the summer of 1943 created new hopes and fears for both men and women, as well as the possibility to take action. The existence of prior clandestine opposition and seasoned military and political leaders helped to shape compelling appeals for support and provided an organizational skeleton for partisan activity. If these were the magnets pulling individuals into the Resistance, it was ultimately the nature of daily life and personal experience that pushed the masses of the population in that direction. For most women (and probably men as well), political ideology and identification had little to do with their initial activity; neither are personal devotion or "natural" female altruism sufficient explanations for women's mobilization. Family connections and individual loyalties were important, but for reasons other than those traditionally offered. The Resistance was a military and political drama whose actors were usually men, and thus it was often ties to brothers, husbands, and fathers that enabled women to step onto the public stage, frequently whether their male relatives encouraged and approved of their behavior or not. But family was important in other ways as well.

As is usually the case in wartime, women crossed the lines between private and public worlds as social necessity demanded that they act in unusual ways. In addition to the universal function of food preparation, women were increasingly responsible for either producing some income or providing food by bargaining with neighbors or on the black market, standing in long lines for meagre rations, and threatening those responsible for controlling food and other supplies. The same extension of functions applied to providing clothing, medical goods and care, or, in fact, any of the material resources necessary for survival. The pressures created by these broadened roles helped to increase frustration and discontent. It also became obvious that if women were capable of finding and commandeering these basic supplies, then why not paper and typewriters, or even rifles, ammunition, and hand grenades?

Women's own expectations and identities, hopes, and goals, whether conscious and stated or not, led them to resist. The minority of women who were part of the opposition political community or "family" prior to 1943 were driven by personal loyalties and party ideologies and platforms, and some were specifically concerned with social and political reforms that could benefit women. As already indicated, the vast majority of women did not share these concrete political motives; nevertheless, they, too, had expectations and goals and would eventually fight for them. Women who struggled to feed their children, lived through bombings, watched neighbors and loved ones being deported to Germany, and bore the brunt of Nazi and Fascist abuse and brutality were keenly aware of immediate threats to survival and fearful of future perils. Young women moved to act because they were denied education, dubious about their futures (whether as wives and mothers or workers and professionals), disappointed that they were being denied the pleasures and carefree experiences of youth, and surprised or even shocked by social injustices. If, at a later time, many women stated they did not know exactly why they became partisans, they also remembered that there did not seem to be any other choice.

As women joined the Resistance, they no doubt had a vague sense of who the enemy was and what they hoped to change, but their goals can best be described as practical and immediate rather than strategic and long-term. It is important to remember the degree of spontaneity and lack of political consciousness that characterized women's initial involvement. These would be decisive factors in determining how women organized, their functions in the Resistance, the leadership of their movement, and the ultimate results of their activity. To weld together this almost accidental and highly personal resistance would take a great deal of energy; to transform it into a movement that could fight for women's rights would be more difficult. Understanding that fascism and the war were not solely responsible for women's problems and that gender inequities were embedded in their society were even greater challenges. The creation of feminist consciousness was a monumental task and one that would be only partially accomplished.

# ■ 3 ■

# Gender and Women's Functions in the Resistance: "I Would Do It All Again"

## The General Structure of the Resistance

In 1944 the Allied Military Command distinguished between four types of resistance activity: (1) military operations in which partisans engaged enemy troops, (2) military intelligence service, (3) sabotage and seizure of enemy materiel, and (4) creation of civil disorder and passive resistance.[1] The Command also acknowledged the significance of the activity, admitting that at times "the resistance forces have been so powerful that the Germans have had to employ mechanized troops against them. [Specifically in northwest Italy], if they [the partisans] are obliged to cease this activity, through lack of food and equipment, four enemy divisions may become available to the enemy for employment on the front of the Allied Armies in Italy."[2] In fact, the scope of resistance activity ultimately became a problem for the Allies, who were disturbed by the strength of leftist parties in the organizations.[3] On the other side, Nazi and Fascist officials were particularly concerned with the increasing acts of sabotage and public demonstrations and were impressed by the excellent and extensive information and communication network that the partisans created on a significant popular base.[4]

Women were visible in all areas of resistance activity, especially as *staffette* (couriers) and partisans with both the Brigades and smaller assault groups (the GAP/SAP), or with command units such as the CLNs, or in Emilia Romagna, the CUMER (Unified Military Command of Emilia Romagna). They created and staffed medical services, recruited and organized the populace, arranged demonstrations, distributed anti-Fascist literature, worked in the information services, or simply collaborated by supplying provisions, hiding partisans, and aiding Jews and other deportees and their families. In many cases, women had multiple functions or moved from one activity to another.

51

It is important to remember that this was a war in which there were no clear lines between battlefront and homefront. Both the sites and the nature of the conflict shifted constantly. Some confrontations were planned and well-directed; others were spontaneous and almost without leadership. Because of the character of the fighting, it often made little difference whether one was a man or a woman. When involved in mortal combat, while blowing up bridges or buildings, and when arrested and tortured, both men and women showed courage and fear. Determining the extent to which women and men were "equal" in Resistance activity requires further consideration. Luciano Bergonzini, in his monumental study of the Resistance in Bologna, concludes that with regard to the experiences of women in the GAP and partisan brigades, "no operative distinctions are evident: the duties, the activities, the risks, the problems are exactly equal to those of the men."[5]

The problem is in agreeing on what criteria should be used to assess equality, as is evident in the following statement by Nori Pesce Brambilla, wife of legendary GAP leader Giovanni Pesce and herself an experienced partisan:

> In that moment no one felt discriminated against: because those who commanded and those who did the simplest things felt equal there, because there was the struggle and we were all in danger, no one dreamed of valuing themselves more than anyone else....All of us, from the commander to the private, found ourselves in situations in which we had to decide. Thus we were all leaders. Each one had to make their own choice....How many times even the most humble courier very simply had to make her own decisions![6]

This sense of equality in battle should not be over-romanticized or generalized to conclude that gender differences and the usual accompanying inequities disappeared. Pesce herself admits that she did not fire on the Fascists, and, although she did participate in sabotage activity and was always with the *gappisti* (members of the GAP), she generally brought them materiel and carried their arms so that if they were stopped it would be less dangerous for them. Young Bruna Betti, a *staffetta* in central Italy, assessed her experience in a similar fashion. When asked if she ever felt inferior to the male partisans, she responded:

> I would say actually no. But there is one thing: I would never be capable of shooting. I don't know if you mean inferior in that sense....In effect, we never handled arms. Perhaps in northern Italy, where the Resistance lasted longer, the women did fight, but in our zone, women had other duties.[7]

A study of women's activities in the countryside and mountainous regions of Liguria perhaps provides a more accurate general picture. After noting that women's treatment and functions varied from command to command, and that most of the women interviewed emphasized "the respect, fraternity, and solidarity which linked men and women in the mountains," the author also recognizes that there were relatively few women in brigade detachments and that most commanders were averse to having women in the bands. This would duplicate the conclusion in Barbara Jancar's study of the Yugoslav resistance that "the sense of togetherness achieved in participation in a common cause is not the same as equality."[8]

In the Italian case, men did have particular views (which they were able to enforce) about appropriate female roles, and the women were aware of these, knowing clearly when they had "stepped over the line." Additionally, in the broad sum of resistance activities, women and men were concentrated in different sectors and often were organized separately. Finally, gender differences often served useful purposes during the Resistance, as customary activities like food shopping and child care and feminine stereotypes of weakness and flirtation either hid or supported partisan activity. Thus, through the course of the conflict, the pre-existing sex/gender system remained intact, although the significance of "women's work" and the value of "women's nature" were reshaped as the lines between private and public worlds blurred.

## Women and the Organized Resistance

### The Staffette

The functions of the *staffette* were among the most crucial as well as difficult and dangerous activities undertaken by men and women alike—to maintain communication among the units and their command, to transport arms and documents, and occasionally to engage in combat. Most units had between four and ten *staffette* serving them. In the historical memory of the Resistance, the *staffetta* on her bicycle became the symbolic heroine, fearlessly passing Nazi and Fascist checkpoints or eluding pursuit and capture. There was certainly danger in this activity, and mobility and willingness to take risks were preconditions for the work. In October 1944, the Communist Party distributed a list of rules that *staffette* should observe and included the warning that "your work because it is confidential and valuable is also dangerous. You can fall into the hands of the enemy and be arrested as a result." If that were to happen, the courier was admonished, "Never talk!...You should choose any other fate; even death is preferable to doing harm to your Party."[9]

Luisa Terziani, a young student from Florence who began her work as a *staffetta* in 1944, remembered that "there was certainly no monotony in that work. An excessive presence of Germans, an inopportune encounter, an improvised German or Fascist blockade, anything unexpected could be dangerous because hidden in your purse or in some other part of your clothing was the secret message."[10] An experience recounted by Lina Merlin graphically illustrates the danger involved in the work of the *staffetta*. She was riding on a tram in Milan, carrying a package of sticks of dynamite, when several German soldiers boarded and began to search the passengers. "I had the package on my knees; could I hide it? How or where? Who was sitting nearby and wouldn't they begin to suspect me? I remained immobile while I looked out the window and thought: 'Soon they will come to me, they will find the dynamite, they will make me get off the tram and they will shoot me tied to that tree out there. Patience, thus it will be over!' Instead it ended well." The Germans only looked at her and left without doing a search.

Being a *staffetta* was dangerous and often "nomadic" work. Because the courier usually knew a great deal about resistance personnel and plans, unquestioned loyalty was demanded and some sort of political "references" would be required. For these reasons, only a small proportion of the women were formally engaged as *staffette*. In the author's sample, there were 113 women so listed, or only 12 percent of the total. The profile of these women shows some distinct characteristics: 66 percent of them were under 30 years of age during the Resistance, 40.7 percent had been engaged in anti-Fascist activities before 1943, 53 percent had a party affiliation, and the largest single occupational group represented was that of industrial workers. In all, 60 percent were either factory workers, in commerce or clerical work, or students or teachers/professors. Very few agricultural workers, housewives, or domestic workers served as *staffette*.

Because of the visibility, danger, and need for tight security, it appears that the ability to travel, proven loyalty, and familiarity with anti-Fascist leadership were pre-conditions for becoming a courier. Often women were gradually introduced into this activity, first carrying a few letters, or passwords, then being given more responsibility. In this regard, twenty-year-old Lidia Valeriani's experience is probably quite typical. As a worker in Reggio Emilia, she had started her anti-Fascist activity with the Red Cross helping the families of those persecuted by the Fascists and, after September 8, fleeing Italian soldiers. By early 1944 she was distributing clandestine literature and helping to organize demonstrations and strikes. She then became a target for arrest, and the local partisan leadership helped her to get out of the area and move to Modena, where she eventually was attached to a GAP unit as secretary and *staffetta*. The unit command was constantly on the move from house to house, business to public square, city to surrounding countryside, and Valeriani moved with them, as well as making several bicycle trips to Bologna to contact GAP in that city. On several occasions she also exchanged fire with the enemy, and for her dedication, courage, and even "audacity," she was awarded a bronze medal for military valor.[11]

## The Partigiane with Brigades and Action Squads

By far the vast majority of women formally associated with the Resistance were listed as *partigiane* (partisans). In that category, functions ranged from combat and military command (including formal rank) to serving as guides and cooking and sewing for a mountain partisan brigade. Some 648 women, or 69.2 percent of the sample, served in that capacity, and their profile is somewhat different from that of the *staffetta* described above. Few *partigiane* had a record of pre-1943 activity, only 8.8 percent had a party affiliation, and most agricultural workers (92 percent) and housewives (88.7 percent) were listed in this category.

It was fairly unusual for women to be attached to the formal Brigades, which engaged enemy units on the largest scale, most closely resembled traditional military organizations, and were quartered in a segregated fashion, often in the mountains. Only 161 women in the sample were with such units, constituting only 17.2 percent of the total sample and 24.8 percent of the women listed generally as partisans.

Women were not welcomed or equally integrated into the mountain Brigade units. In 1944, when nineteen-year-old Antonia Maggioni asked to join a partisan formation, she was told: "No thank you. We have had enough of women who give away secrets. It is better that you stay at home and wait until it is over."[12] Several general studies of the Resistance conclude that commanders of those units "preferred not to have women under foot. Women in the bands were trouble, too great a responsibility." It was feared that "the co-habitation of men and women would harm the solidarity of the units. The few women accepted in normal periods looked after the laundry or worked in the kitchen....[I]n difficult times they shared the experiences of the formation and sometimes were involved in armed actions."[13]

For many of the women, the process of becoming attached to a brigade was circumstantial or expedient. Because their homes were suspected of being meeting places or because they had contact with known partisans, they often came under surveillance or were arrested. When it appeared that they might be picked up by the police, or after release from custody or possible escape from the authorities, they had no choice but to head for a mountain unit. Even in such circumstances, male partisans were not anxious to have women join them.

Teacher Giovanna Zangrandi recorded in her diary that in the summer of 1944 a raid on her home forced her to flee from Cadore (Bolzano). But where could she go? Approaching a male companion, she was told, "In the bands they don't want women, even if they are less of a nuisance than most young students and clerks...[but] he would do the best he could for me."[14] Zangrandi became a *staffetta* for a mountain brigade and, later on, part of a small ski patrol band. Another teacher, Ideale Cannella, whose home was a meeting place for partisans, was arrested for a brief period of time, then fled to join a mountain division. Teresa Testa had joined the Resistance in Turin in September 1943 and worked to recruit and organize women; she, too, was arrested, but the partisans won her freedom by returning a Fascist they had captured. After her release, Testa joined a Garibaldi Brigade, where she was "a political commissar, cook, laundress, and *staffetta* until the liberation." Elsa Oliva, a twenty-two-year-old domestic work-er in Novara, was arrested for anti-Fascist activity in 1943; she was to be trans-ferred to a prison camp in Germany but escaped and then joined the division in which her brother fought and in which she eventually held the rank of lieutenant. Anna Maria Vignolini was a *staffetta* for a CLN but in the summer of 1944, after being recognized by the Fascists, was transferred to a brigade. Iste Cagossi was also forced to join a brigade after she came to the attention of Fascist authorities in Genoa.[15]

Gina Borellini, a recipient of the gold medal for military valor, had joined the Resistance in Modena because of her husband and brother. Initially she trans-ported arms and materiel and carried orders. She and her spouse were arrested and "three times brought before a firing squad [but] continued to remain silent." When Gina was unexpectedly released, she refused to hide herself in the moun-tains because she wanted to remain near her husband, who was still detained. After he was shot, and her brother arrested, she joined a partisan unit. Borellini was wounded in action and lost a leg as a result.[16] There were other women noted for their courageous actions in the Brigades, and some units pointed with pride to their female members. *Il Pionere,* a newspaper for several Pd'A units in the north, reported romantically on the exploits of an unnamed young woman in an alpine formation. With "initiative" and "audacity," she engaged in gathering supplies and arms and on one occasion escaped capture by "fording a river while under machine gun fire," after which "with serene simplicity she shares the hardships and danger of the group of partisans."[17]

The general and most typical attitude toward women in brigades was ambiva-lent, at best. When those leading the Resistance appealed to women for their sup-port, they were quite specific. Women were to love their men and help when they could by nursing the wounded, hiding refugees, providing information, and "sewing with your own loving hands the clothing that will protect [your loved ones] from the cold." Above all, women were advised not to keep their men at home: "Open the door and let him go."[18] When seeking volunteers, women's groups took a slightly different tack. In Bologna it was reported that "some young women have asked to go and fight in the ranks of the partisans, and this is an ini-tiative which we enthusiastically support; already some women are fighting courageously at the side of the partisans, but this is not within everyone's reach." Instead, all women were encouraged to provide support, gather supplies, and aid the wounded.[19]

Given these attitudes, and the ways in which the Resistance was organized, and the population mobilized, it is understandable that the majority of women partisans joined GAP and SAP units. Of the author's sample, 402 of the 648 women listed as partisans were with the GAP or SAP. These units were small, usually detachments of five or six people attached to a larger squad, and often operated in an area close to the residences of the participants. In some cases when groups went underground, members left their homes and lived "on the run." Carla

Capponi, one of the most noted women of the Roman resistance and a recipient of the gold medal for military valor, describes her life underground. She had left her family's apartment and moved back and forth from the center of Rome to one of its suburbs.

> This was the most difficult period of time for me. It was very stressful because of the constant travelling in the incredible cold, inadequately dressed, inadequately fed. I slept very little and was constantly hunted. In Rome I slept in a cellar, and at Centocelle I slept on a floor without a mattress....[T]his kind of life left a scar. It was very, very hard, sleeping on cellar floors with fifteen to sixteen men, dirty, cold, infested with lice. I suffered from scabies and other diseases that eventually resulted in the loss of one of my lungs.[20]

More commonly, individuals could remain in their own homes, unless identified and sought by the police. The squads had diverse functions, from sabotage and single-strike activity to serving as auxiliaries for the Brigades to recruiting, educating, and defending the population. Twenty-year-old Edera de Giovanni came from a poor family in the Bologna area, where she had worked as a servant but also distributed anti-Fascist literature. When the Resistance began, she helped organize a squad that on one occasion cut telephone and telegraph lines running from Rome to the Brenner Pass to Berlin. On March 6, 1944, Edera and six others were arrested and shot "as an example."[21]

The Roman resistance, in which Capponi participated, was largely the work of small sabotage and terrorist groups. In September 1943 when the Italian government fled south, the city was left in chaos with no structured defense. As the Germans moved into the area, a division of the Italian army under General Raffaele Cadorno and several thousand volunteers attempted to prevent German occupation of the city. Both Capponi and Marisa Musu were among the largely unprepared participants in this fighting. As Musu states, "I didn't get any training. I was given a revolver and simply shown how to load and fire it. With explosives I was told to try and throw myself forward, not backwards but nothing more specific."[22]

The Germans took control of the city fairly easily, and partisan activity was organized in GAP squads designed to harass and disrupt the occupying authorities. A central group of some thirty members was eventually extended to a network of zone units, usually mixed groups of five or six people that engaged in acts of sabotage, assassination, and strikes on German strongholds.[23] Both Capponi and Musu joined the GAP. As Marisa explains, "I asked to be armed. I wanted to participate. I thought armed resistance was the best and simplest solution." Capponi became a vice-commander of one of the squads and was described by a comrade as "this young blonde woman who went out at night to shoot Germans....[W]ith arms in hand, first among the first, she participated in dozens of actions, distinguishing herself in a superb way."[24]

In the broader scope of the Resistance, some GAP and SAP had unusually high female participation, and a few of these were all female and were led by women. In Emilia Romagna, the 7th GAP Gianni had 200 members, 80 of them women, led by Novella Albertazzi (Vanda). Albertazzi, who had been a furrier in Bologna, joined the GAP as a *staffetta* in December 1943 after one of her brothers had been shot and another imprisoned. "It seemed absurd and impossible to stay bent over a table ten hours a day, to gossip with friends, while the Germans walked in the streets, while the Fascists arrested young men who avoided service."[25] Regarding her sabotage activity, it is said that she "fought like a man, was wounded, arrested, released and returned to fight."[26] In November 1944, Vanda led the women of her unit in a major battle at their partisan base in the ruins of Ospedal Maggiore, where they fought against cannon, tanks, and armored cars.

## Command and Combat

Though certainly never in the majority, women throughout the Resistance did hold positions of command, engaged in combat, and attained political and military rank. Typical of these individuals was Clarice Boniburini, a worker who joined the 76th SAP in Bologna in January 1944 as an inspector-intendant responsible for recruiting, organizing, and helping to train and feed the unit. In August 1944 she was assigned more direct combat command responsibilities and given the rank of lieutenant.[27] In the sample, most of the 33 women with designated rank were under 30 years of age at the time (58 percent); were factory or commercial workers or students; by comparison to the total sample, more often cited a family connection; were affiliated with a party (particularly the PCI, which claimed 15 of them); and had been active before 1943.

Though many male commanders were reluctant to send women into combat or to integrate them into the Brigades, and both Christian Democratic and Liberal leaders took the position that women should not be used militarily, the reality was clearly different. In the last days of fighting when Florence was being liberated, 300 women saw action, including Maria Luigia Guaita, previously mentioned as one of the emerging leaders of the Resistance women.[28] Women wanted to participate in military actions and, when allowed to do so, functioned much like their male comrades. Communist Laura Polizzi had entered the Resistance in her hometown of Parma in autumn 1943; in January 1944, after being informed on by a female co-worker, she went "underground" and in March was sent to Reggio to organize women. By June she was a known collaborator there, too, and joined a mountain Brigade. However, as she recorded, "Resolving the problem of how I would be used in the mountains was not a simple thing, also because of my stubborn insistence to be used militarily in whatever unit. Finally, in early July...with the approval of the commander I was given the responsibility of vice commisar of the Brigades. My work was mostly political."[29] After several months she returned to work in an urban setting and by the time the war ended had been named lieutenant.

Elsa Oliva, who joined the Second Brigade of the Beltrami Division in Novara in May 1944, reflected, "I could have served the Resistance well as a *staffetta,* staying in the office. Instead I knew that I wanted to fight with arms in hand." She had been with the Brigade several days when she told the commander and the rest of the men, "I am not here to find a lover. I am here to fight and I will remain here if I am given a weapon and placed in the sector of those who do guard duty and take action." The result? "I was given a weapon...and in the first combat demonstrated that I could fight like they and that the rifle was not just for show."[30]

Maria Gaudino's account of her initiation into partisan activity in September 1943 clearly contradicts stereotypes of female passivity and non-violence. When shooting broke out in the piazza one day as she was on her way to fetch water, she picked up a rifle from one who had fallen. "I fired for more than two hours! I wanted to shoot them all; it had been a year of torment, of bombings, hunger and thirst, and thus that day I was possessed by a great anger. I was seventeen years old, not involved in politics, but I understood very well what the Fascists and Germans against whom I fought represented."[31] Diana Sabbi also quickly became aware that the lessons of war could be learned equally by men and women. With two uncles who were partisans in Bologna, Diana had begun to work in the Resistance in the fall of 1943. In June 1944 she joined a Garibaldi Brigade, which by October faced tremendous hardships. Sabbi and her comrades were constantly on the move in rain and fog, had no supplies and were living on chestnuts, and were either attacked by German patrols or under bombardment by the Allies. The commander decided they should leave the area, and Diana was sent to reconnoiter a new location. For her, this mission was especially memorable.

> After a few kilometres I heard a shout; two Germans with their guns levelled, forced me and the local guide, to halt. Partisan warfare has hard laws: the person who survives is the one who succeeds in shooting or striking first. And we struck first. It happened in a flash; there was no need for agreement with my companion. That event produced such profound distress in me that at first I almost wanted to turn back; but I quickly remembered the importance of the mission given me, and continued.[32]

Carla Capponi also learned the hard way and remembered the emotional turmoil she felt when she first killed a man. She had been given the task of assassinating a German officer as he left the Hotel Excelsior in Rome carrying in his briefcase important documents on the defense of the city.

> It was a traumatic experience. I almost wanted to call to him, to make him turn around...but I knew he was armed. It seemed impossible that with

my peaceful disposition, against any form of violence, I should hold the gun, point it at him and shoot him in the back. I took his briefcase. I was in shock....I began running down the street with the gun still in my hand....It was raining and tears were streaming down my face....After getting over the initial shock, especially since many of our comrades were being arrested and tortured, all our scruples were replaced by sheer determination to fight for our cause.[33]

In March 1944, both Capponi and Marisa Musu took part in the ambush of a German patrol on Via Rasella in downtown Rome. Thirty-three S.S. men were killed in the attack, and the Germans retaliated by executing 335 Romans in a massacre at the Ardeantine Caves. The event became controversial as many, even in the Resistance movement, questioned whether the assault was worth it in light of the reprisals. Later, when Capponi was questioned about it she responded, "If I had to, I would kill again every German I killed. I still believe it was the right thing to do. My opinion has not changed." Judith Hicks Stiehm's study of women's political and military mobilization has illustrated that although women are not socialized to use force themselves, and may see it as "men's business," they also do not "necessarily question force as efficacious," and when "criminals or enemies appear to be winning...may try to mobilize more force [or contribute directly] by joining the military or a resistance organization."[34] Innate or rigid linkages between gender and violence are not borne out by the experience of the Resistance.

Paola Del Din's record is another example of the diversity of female activism, and she, too, was awarded the gold medal for heroism. She had just graduated from the University of Padua when she joined the Resistance in Veneto as a *staffetta*. Her role was unusual, as she trained as a parachutist and took part in eleven air missions in which she carried information to the Allies. On one of these, she was air-dropped into the area of Friuli and though she broke her ankle on landing still delivered her documents to the allied mission.[35]

Some women who participated in the Resistance quite consciously had to confront gender stereotypes of appropriate or decorous behaviors. Irma Marchiani, a decorated partisan, is such a case. She was a thirty-two-year-old housewife who joined the partisans in the Modena area first as a *staffetta,* then as a commissar for the Roveda Brigade, one of the units of the Socialist "Matteotti" battalions. After participating in the fighting at Montefiorini, she was arrested, sent to a camp near Bologna, and condemned to death, but she managed to escape. She rejoined her unit, was made a vice-commander, and again participated in combat. Arrested again in November 1944, Marchiani was shot and killed in prison. She had been well aware of popular attitudes about women in combat and the taint of sexual impropriety that accompanied such behavior. During her first arrest, she had written to her brother from prison, stating:

I am part of a formation and I will tell you my commander has great esteem and faith in me. I hope to be useful, not to disappoint my superiors.... Believe me, I have done nothing that could offend our name.[36]

Similar concerns color the account of Anna Cinanni, who joined her brother Paolo as a partisan. Their mother remonstrated against the danger of having the young woman "thrown in the arms of the young men [of the brigades]." Paolo assured his mother that there was no cause for worry or shame and told Anna: "Remember that you are not a woman: you are a communist, and you are fighting in the Resistance."[37]

## All-Female Units

In addition to their activities in mixed units, women also formed all-female detachments, which increased in number and were formally recognized as the war progressed. It is probable that the PCI encouraged creation of these units and that the general women's organizations—the Gruppi di Difesa della Donna (GDD), or Women's Defense Groups—served as their recruitment and directing centers. The earliest of these groups, officially recognized by the CLNAI in June 1944 as the Corpo Volontarie della Libertá (Corps of Volunteers for Liberty), saw action that summer. The units were small (usually from five to twenty members), normally attached to already existing Brigades or SAP, and were commanded by women. Made up of women already active as *staffette,* nurses, or collaborators, they were, in essence, the vanguard of women activists, and duties varied from active combat to organizing demonstrations and distributing food to the populace.

The units receiving the most publicity were the thirty-eight women attached to the 19th "Eusebio Giambone" Assault Brigade, organized by the PCI in the Piedmont and officially recognized in September 1944, and the "Alice Noli" unit that became part of the Garibaldi Brigade "Nedo" in Genoa in November 1944. Though appeals for volunteers emphasized the glorious and heroic nature of women's activities in these units, it is apparent that the formations had a pragmatic base. Like the individual women integrated into brigades, these detachments consisted of wives, mothers, and sisters of partisans, many of whom had to abandon their homes when Fascist reprisals intensified and they were sought by the Fascist police. In the case of the "Giambone" group, the women participants worked nine hours a day ironing, washing, and cooking for the men.[38]

In the last six months of the war, as Resistance activities increased and Italians prepared for their liberation, two other all-female units were organized. The first of these was the Gabriella degli Esposti detachment formed in Modena in April 1945. The fifty-five women in the unit (divided into five squads) had been serving as *staffette,* nurses, and partisans. As a reward for patriotic actions, they were formally recognized as part of the first Division Modena M by the division commander. This unit was basically a GDD formation, more civilian and political than military, and concerned not only with the immediate liberation but with the future structure of Italian society and politics.[39]

Also in April, after several months of negotiation and discussion, the Allied Military Command and the Italian Minister of War recognized the formation of the Corpi di Assistenza Femminile (CAF). The CAF was made up of small groups, each attached to army divisions for the purpose of running canteens for the soldiers, providing education, and raising funds. Women who participated in the negotiations admitted they had difficulty convincing military commanders of the usefulness and appropriateness of this work, for many officers "felt the only business of women was that of staying at home and knitting."[40] Actually, the image of the woman at home knitting had a practical base, as since the first days of the conflict individual women had been relied upon to knit wool socks and articles of clothing for the partisans.

## Women in Communication and Information Services

Though transporting information and maintaining personal communication among all the Resistance forces were primary functions of *staffette* and partisans alike, women also served in the organized technical or electronic information service in Italy. In Rome, prior to liberation, women helped maintain crucial communication links with the Allies. Giorgina Madia, with a physics degree from the University of Naples, had engaged in research at scientific institutes in Germany and Italy and at the start of the war was employed in Milan's inter-city telephone office. There she joined the clandestine Pd'A and in 1942 moved to assume a position in the Department of Electrical Communications at the University of Rome. After September 1943, Madia helped set up a radio transmitting station that served to connect Rome with southern Italy.[41] Another radio transmitter located in Rome's Torre Argentina was run by Socialist Antonia Colucci, who had experience as an aeronautical radio and telegraph operator. Colucci later was transferred north to the foothills of the Alps, where she worked on communications with the Socialist partisans in Milan.

There were 34 women in a group of 173 people who operated an information-radio network connecting central Italy with the Piedmont, Veneto, and Emilia Romagna.[42] By 1945 the information/spy organization of cells in northern Italy was restructured as the SIMNI-SIP (Servizio Informazioni Militari Nord Italia-Servizio Informazioni Patrioti), which included 55 women. One individual who stands out in this service was Silvia Rota. Rota was a student at the Catholic University in Milan in October 1943 when her family, including her Jewish mother, was arrested. She fled to Switzerland, where, with her English language and secretarial skills, she found a position at the American consulate in Lugano. The consulate became the base for OSS operations, and Rota, working with another exile, Antonietta Reale, served as the conduit for all information coming out of the Resistance network in Italy.[43]

## Women's "Nature" and "Roles" Become Political

As already indicated, regardless of the determination, commitment, and even remarkable experiences of some women, the social reality of a sexual division of labor in both private and public sectors, as well as stereotypes of appropriate female behavior, could segregate women or limit their activities in the Resistance. However, this very segregation also served more positive ends and, in some instances, became a resource that women used and leaders relied upon in their struggle. To begin with, the Fascists and Nazis did not usually perceive women as assassins or combatants. Their eyes would more often be on men, thus giving women greater freedom of action, and rank and file soldiers were probably more inclined to view women as wives, mothers, or potential companions rather than as political enemies. This is not to ignore the violence and brutality with which women were treated if they were suspected and discovered. Nevertheless, age-old sexual assumptions gave women a "cover" men did not have.

Carrying bombs became a female activity; they could be hidden in baby carriages or shopping bags, and women could also carry food, small arms, and dispatches in their underclothes, purses, and packages.[44] In Bologna, a young woman member of the 7th GAP was stopped by a Fascist patrol. "An officer looked her squarely in the face, and noting the closed bag she was carrying, asked what it contained. She returned his look, and with a smile said, 'bombs.' The officer, amused and reassured, let her pass." Antonietta Panciroli, a SAP *staffetta* in Reggio Emilia, had a similar experience. Transporting arms on her bicycle, she had to cross a narrow footbridge guarded by a German soldier. She approached him with a smile and asked for help to cross over with the heavy burden. Without the least suspicion, he approached and, with one hand on the handlebars and the other on the bicycle seat, helped her reach the opposite street.[45]

The usefulness of "feminine" charm is also recognized in the following excerpt from a 1944 issue of a partisan newspaper that reported an interview with Lelia Sarti, a *staffeta* responsible for communication between the partisan command in the Marches and that of Bologna and Forli.

> And the Germans? Did they ever stop you?
> The Germans? But it was they who took me from one place to another on their trucks.
> And that was Lelia's speciality: getting the Germans to transport her. And weren't you afraid to travel with the Germans? What if they had opened your bag?
> But what was there to fear! You only had to give them a few smiles. They all squinted at me. And I looked at them and laughed. And that was enough.

Apparently Lelia's smile was enough to calm even the teutonic beast.[46]

Matilde Palmerini Steardo, an eighteen-year-old vice-commander for a GAP in Genoa, described an incident in which she and two other women disarmed two members of the Fascist militia on a tram and escaped with their weapons. "The men did not suspect they were being surrounded or that young women would steal their weapons." Such audacity utilizing sex/gender stereotypes was also characteristic of Cesarina Bracco, who remembers going to pick up a rifle to take to a unit and carrying it in a sack across the piazza in front of the Fascist barracks. Her female companion was nervous, saying it was fairly obvious what she was carrying. Bracco responded, "If it were really a rifle, two young women would not go out in the street this way in plain daylight. Exactly because it was [sic] absurd we will do it."[47]

Certain kinds of women's work also provided opportunities for groups to gather and for women to visit each other's homes without suspicion. Being a seamstress or laundress had certain advantages when it came to courier or transport work, as it was normal for clients to visit for fittings or for bundles of laundry to be delivered on bicycle. In the course of these transactions, messages and materiel could be exchanged.[48] If, in general, women were perceived as less dangerous than men, and if their work was largely invisible or ignored, then stereotypes of motherhood were even more reified and mothers with their children even less suspicious.

As noted in previous chapters, women's role as mothers was an important part in the puzzle of Fascist policy and ideology. Similarly, the pressures on women to feed and protect their children helped move them to protest the war and eventually the regime itself. During the years of resistance, women were still the caregivers, and motherhood was a fairly onerous responsibility. Joyce Lussu, while in exile in France, had a clandestine abortion because she felt it impossible to "make a defenseless creature run the risks we ran,…the vicissitudes of clandestine life, the constant, exhausting movement, the need to remain mobile to escape the OVRA [Fascist secret police] and the Gestapo." But the event remained with her "like a reoccurring nightmare; I was able to not think about it for periods of time; console myself, never." Back in Italy in 1944 Lussu became pregnant again. This time she decided to have the child. "We would fight the war together.…I felt myself strong and capable of protecting the child as I protected myself against danger, exhaustion and hunger.…Peasant women worked in the fields almost up to the last day. Why should I do less than they?"[49]

Lina Fibbi, also in exile and in and out of prison in the 1930s, returned to Italy to work in the Resistance in August 1943. She was assigned as a *staffetta* for the general command of the Communist brigades and helped organize women in the area of Genoa. Fibbi married a fellow partisan and was pregnant when her husband was shot in the liberation of Genoa; she gave birth to a daughter in June 1945. In Parma, twenty-one-year-old Ave Meglioli had joined a mountain brigade to avoid capture. She married a detachment leader and served as a guide for the mountain unit; when she was shot in a confrontation with the Germans, she was seven or eight months pregnant. Noemi Brunetti's husband was a partisan, and because of its isolation, their house in the countryside was a refuge and meeting place for a partisan battalion. Noemi functioned as the *staffetta* for the battalion, carrying arms, orders, and information. At one point in the autumn of 1944 when she was several months pregnant she transported a machine gun by hiding it in a small milk cart that she pulled behind her bicycle.[50]

Ave Albertini's account touches on the variety of ways in which gender shaped women's experiences during the Resistance. Born in 1918, Albertini lived in the area of Modena where, by early 1944, her husband was a partisan and she a *staffetta.*

> My work was made easier by the fact that I could travel freely because I was pregnant. After a period of time however, I had to stay with the Brigade because I could not return home; I was sought by the Fascists. In the Brigade, because of my condition, they gave me the job of seamstress. With my bundles I followed the movement of the Brigade from place to place....We were in the middle of a woods when the Germans began to fire on us with mortars; it was August 4, 1944. I was terrified, and immediately gave birth to a premature baby, at the seventh month....You can imagine, in the middle of a forest, what help there would be!...I stayed with the Brigade command for ten days and there my little Olimpia received her first care.

Albertini decided to return to her home, which the Germans had wrecked. They "had destroyed everything they could not carry with them....The first few days I was desperate. In that house, with no light, no fire, with a baby I was nursing, if I had not had the precious help of neighbors I would not have survived.... Certainly, in those conditions, raising a little girl was a great sacrifice."[51] Albertini's testimony points to the fact that in the Resistance being female could be both an asset and a considerable liability.

This same contradiction applies to women whose children accompanied them in their work. The presence of a child might disarm Fascist soldiers, or children's movements might pass unnoticed, but simultaneously mothers lived with the knowledge that they were risking their children's lives as well as their own. Adriana Rumori, a *staffetta* in the Ancona region who worked with Lelia Sarti, remembered "when I had to meet with someone to deliver orders I took my six-year-old daughter with me and sewed the orders in the hem of her skirt; and I told her 'if they threaten mamma with their weapons, make a game of it; you must stay in the game. However, you must never talk.' Certainly we were always greatly afraid."[52] Dorina Storchi, who worked as a *staffetta* for the regional command in Reggio Emilia, was arrested and imprisoned for three months in early 1944. During her imprisonment the authorities allowed visits from her five-year-old daughter Simona, and Dorina used her to carry information in and out of prison. As she stated, "No one can imagine my state of mind, the terror provoked when my daughter left with those notes." Ten-year-old Laura Cristina, whose father was a battalion commander and mother a laundress and a *staffetta,* often delivered the laundry on her bicycle and along with it carried letters, fliers, and even small weapons and hand grenades. Later she reflected, "Perhaps because of my young age, when I went through the street blocks of the Germans and the Fascists, they considered me only a snot-nosed kid. They stopped me and asked what I had in the basket. Frankly, I answered that I had clothes to wash and iron [and they let me pass]."

## Women Organizing Women: The GDD

As the foregoing makes clear, women participated in and were often crucial to the operations of the regular and recognized military as well as the sabotage organizations of the Resistance. The particular circumstances of their lives pushed women into public activism, but this spontaneous reaction to intolerable conditions might have remained individual and fragmented if there had not been a concentrated effort to recruit women and a structure that provided direction, support, and purpose. Of singular importance in the shaping of women's resistance activity were the GDD, which gave form to spontaneous rebellion, launched recruitment drives, encouraged all women to act, and channeled women into many resistance functions but also sponsored major civilian resistance and above all connected women to the broader social and political goals of the Resistance.

There is no doubt that the organizers of the GDD were women who had been politically active for some time. The groups with which they were politically affiliated encouraged them to recruit and to provide structure for women's activities, and they themselves believed that women could and should act in the public sphere. The first group was organized in Milan in November 1943 by Lina Fibbi and Gina Bianchi of the PCI, Pina Palumbo for the Socialists (PSIUP), Elena Dreher and Ada Gobetti of the Pd'A, and Lucia Corti for the Catholic Left (a group that eventually joined the PCI).[53] These women, and other prominent GDD activists, were somewhat different from the overall profile of the Resistance woman. They were more likely to be workers or professionals; to have anti-Fascist experience before 1943, either personally or through family connections; to have spent some time in a Fascist camp or prison; and to have a history of party membership. In the sample, 136 women were cited as working for the GDD. Of these, 33.1 percent were industrial workers, while few were housewives (only 4.4 percent); 54.4 percent indicated a family connection with anti-fascism or partisan activity; 20 percent spent time in prison; 47.8 percent were involved in anti-Fascist activities before September 1943; and 59.6 percent were affiliated with a party. Ada Gobetti described these women as *ragionata,* or women with a strong feminist or class consciousness that provided the basic motivation for their activities. For these women, individual personal experience had already become "political."[54]

The ultimately successful pattern for GDD organizing included the arrival in an area of a woman with an established anti-Fascist background and connections to a national political network. She would usually make contact with local women who had already engaged in some act of rebellion or resistance. For example, in late 1943 and the spring of 1944, Laura Polizzi was assigned to organize women in the area surrounding Reggio Emilia, and in December 1944 longtime Communist and ex-political prisoner Lucia Scarpone was sent from Turin to assist in the work. They, in turn, found likely recruits in people such as Idea del Monte, who had led strikes in the area, and Vittorina Rifredi, whose threat to Fascist officials with her rolling pin had established her political reputation. Zelinda Rossi, who worked with Polizzi, described traveling through the region, making contact with small groups of women, and meeting, usually on Sundays, in gardens behind hedges, in attics, and even in a cemetery.[55]

Activity in the area of Bologna followed a similar course. Longtime Communist activist Vittoria Guadagnini returned from exile and was sent by the PCI to organize women in the area. Covering mile after mile on her bicycle, she succeeded in establishing numerous groups, and by the end of the war there were some 9,000 members of the GDD in the province. Among the local people she contacted was Ermelinda Bersani, a worker and PCI member since 1929 who had spent some time in prison for protests prior to 1943. Another worker, Gemma Bergonzoni, was instrumental in reaching agricultural workers, as she helped to organize several strikes by *mondine* (rice workers), which raised their political consciousness and made it easy to bring them into the GDD.[56]

The basic unit of GDD organization was a nucleus or cell, usually made up of five or six women who already knew each other and had worked together in some way. In Liguria, Anna Maria Vignolini had been distributing literature since the summer of 1943 and in September organized a group of women she knew to provide money and food for the partisans as well as to discuss their own circumstances and aspirations. Eventually, Vignolini was contacted by the GDD, and from there her activities expanded to founding and directing GDD groups in other areas. In another case, Anna Melaga's home in Bologna had been a partisan meeting place since September 1943, and Anna had been recruited to distribute clandestine newspapers. In February 1944 she learned of the GDD, made contact, and "her work thereafter became much more precise [particularly as she] helped to organize demonstrations."[57]

When asked in an interview about the process of GDD organizing, Lucia Corti stated that "the women's groups frequently were already formed in a spontaneous, autonomous, and unitarian way, and the GDD only had to incorporate them into a basic political scheme."[58] These units, organized in neighborhoods, the workplace, schools, and hospitals, were then grouped into sectors, zones, and provincial groups with directing committees at each level, all overseen by the central committee in Milan. GDD membership grew rapidly in 1944 and 1945. The Milan-Lombardy organization listed 2,274 members and

6,719 *collegati* (associates with status determined by dues paid and functions) in November 1944, and 3,398 and 9,823, respectively, by March 1945, while for the entire northern area (Piedmont, Lombardy, Emilia Romagna, Liguria, and Veneto), there were 24,028 members and 15,823 associates in April 1945.[59]

Through the GDD, women were channeled into partisan activity. They gathered food, supplies, and money for the Resistance; published a variety of newspapers; and distributed clandestine literature. Communist Rita Martini describes the crucial, but not terribly glamorous, day-to-day activities of a network of GDD women in the northern area of Cuneo in 1944. In October of that year a group of partisans had moved into the mountains of the region, and the local PCI leader came to her for help. The men in the unit were without shoes and warm clothing; others were sick or wounded. Martini contacted the head of her neighborhood GDD, who in turn sent several women to pharmacies in the area to obtain medicines. Then the women of the GDD collected used clothing, which they washed, mended, sewed, and brought to Martini's home. "At times I did not know where to put the clothing....There was so much piled on my divan. [It was in such good shape] that whoever gave it would not recognize it. I thought, 'If someone comes to my house, I will have to say that I sell used clothing door-to-door or I don't know what will happen.' But everything went well. The clothing was sent and always reached the partisans."[60]

The GDD were also instrumental in civil disorders, demonstrations, and passive resistance, which, though much more difficult to measure, probably characterized the function of many of the women in the Resistance and continued a tradition begun in the decade before the war. Funerals for fallen comrades were often occasions for expressions of opposition to the regime. A prime example of this sort of action came after two sisters, sixteen-year-old Libera and nineteen-year-old Vera Arduino, and their father were shot by the Fascists on March 13, 1945. Both young women had worked with their neighborhood GDD group in Turin and had become the targets of a special anti-partisan police unit. The day after the shooting, their comrades organized a strike in factories where the employees were women and then planned a large funeral parade and demonstration at the cemetery where the young women were to be buried. The authorities attempted to disperse the crowds that gathered, and although numerous women were arrested, in jail they continued to sing political songs and hymns of protest.[61]

Almost universally, women are associated with food gathering and preparation. During the war, as already discussed, women struggled to feed their families and then became the major providers for partisan units. Giovanna Zangrandi, quite poetically, described this as a war that was "nested in kitchens."[62] Acquiring food became more clearly political when women acted to prevent the Germans and the Fascists from acquiring supplies and then redistributed the goods. Carolina Generali remembers her first action, which was the assault on a grain warehouse to prevent the supply from falling into the hands of the Germans.

Instead, the women took the stored grain and distributed it to families in the region. Maria Tagliavini, whose husband was a partisan, knew that local dairies were setting aside butter and cheese to be sent to Germany. One day she and about one hundred other women went to one such dairy known to have large reserves on hand. They demanded of the owner that he give them the butter and cheese; at first he resisted but then was convinced it would be wise to hand over the produce rather than have his house and dairy "invaded." They did pay him for the supplies, which were then sent to the mountains.

Public demonstrations often occurred to protest food rationing and the lack of basic supplies. In April 1944, such a protest in Imola turned into a major confrontation when the Fascists called in the fire department to hose down the women; the women, in response, attacked and turned the hose on the Black Shirts. Reinforcements were brought in, and this time, shots were fired, killing two of the protestors. However, the demonstrators stood their ground, and the officials eventually sought refuge in the town hall.[63]

Agricultural workers also protested conditions by destroying products the Germans and Fascists could have used, while the regime's decision to deport workers to Germany helped to raise considerable popular opposition. March 1944 saw the first of a series of general strikes in factories in Bologna, Ravenna, Milan, and Genoa, which almost paralyzed industrial activity in those areas and marked the beginning of a series of organized and highly disruptive protests.[64] By November 1944, such actions were more coordinated geographically and directed specifically against the war and fascism. For example, the GDD-organized "Week of the Partisans" not only recruited supporters, gathered supplies, and raised money but also included protests against the war and the authorities.[65] The increased militancy and numbers of protestors involved in another round of general strikes in March 1945 signaled the reality of imminent liberation, particularly in cities like Turin, or in Bologna, where in April 1945 16,000 women participated in a major demonstration.[66] The success of these actions varied, though without question they were disruptive to the Nazi-Fascist regime and required the diversion of police and military units from defense against partisan and allied attacks.

As the major impetus behind many of these actions, the GDD gained strength and visibility but also were transformed. Begun modestly as auxiliary and assistance groups, they increasingly gained their own identity and expanded their purposes so that by the spring of 1945 their stated goals were "to direct the masses of women to an active and conscious participation in the war of liberation; to raise women to a level of parity with men, legally, economically and politically; to study women's problems and develop national solutions for these."[67] There can be no doubt that it was the GDD that built connections among thousands of anonymous women, transformed individual despair and frustration into public activism, and became the symbol of the contribution of women to the Italian Resistance. The development of the GDD program and its success in achieving stated goals are the subjects of the chapters that follow.

## Assessing the Impact and Meaning of Women's Actions

What conclusions are to be drawn concerning the relationship between women's experience and functions in the Resistance and the overall significance of this participation? First of all, without the formal apparatus of a supply system, the effectiveness of the Resistance depended on the material support of large numbers of civilians; women's traditional functions in the home were thus transformed into work that had public and political value. But, as we have seen, women served in much broader capacities than provisioning, maintaining, and nursing the partisans. The second point, then, is that women wanted to do something—to act, to fight, to take risks. Unlike the men, for whom this was prescribed behavior, the women often had to challenge social stereotypes as they carried and used weapons, engaged in sabotage, and led resistance units.

By far the most important function of women in the Resistance was, in fact, neither the provisioning of partisan brigades nor combat and military leadership but rather the creation of an information network that connected the civilian and military populations. Their social placement gave women "natural" disguises, information about their neighbors, and a tradition of collective activity that enabled them to tap community resources for recruits, demonstrators, money, and hiding and meeting places and to spread the word that Italy was to be liberated and all citizens should join the cause. Informal, grassroots groups engaged in spontaneous actions were given different shape by the influence of seasoned political women. The result was the emergence of women's organizations such as the autonomous GDD and other bodies attached to political parties, which are the subjects of the remaining chapters. The importance of the GDD in the overall struggle is evident in the fact that on October 16, 1944 they were formally recognized by the CLNAI and given representation in the decision-making bodies of the Resistance.

However, strengthening their organizational structure and gaining public political recognition raised other issues for the women of the Resistance. Short-lived, spontaneous rebellion carried out for immediate, practical goals now had the possibility of shifting to a program for long-term, strategic changes in women's lives. To realize this transformation, women would have to confront not only the force of their Fascist enemies but the power of male comrades and their political organizations. Additionally, they would have to grapple with questions of self and social identity as well as their vision of Italy's future. What would it mean to be a woman in a world without fascism and war?

Giovanna Zangrandi records that in the last winter of the war, living in extreme hardship with a mountain ski patrol, one of the comrades told her, "You can't continue to live this life; it is not for a woman." For her, after all she had been through, it was very strange to think of herself as a woman, and her thoughts were only of some "far off nostalgia of unreachable childhood."[68] Whether one sought the meanings of womanhood in memory, or in dreams of the future, simply beginning to think of what women wanted would be a challenge.

# ■ 4 ■

# Political Parties and Women: "Old Prejudices Live On"

As previous chapters have demonstrated, during the course of the Resistance, women were pushed or pulled into a political world traditionally reserved for men, and many were eager to assume places of responsibility in that sphere. Spontaneous, local acts of rebellion against the Nazi-Fascist regime increased in number and intensity and were given a broader, national meaning as the network of Resistance organizations assessed the significance of the actions and planned strategy. Attacks on dairies supplying food to the enemy or funeral demonstrations increasingly were described as political events that would bring not only the defeat of fascism and an end to the war but the rebirth of a democratic and progressive Italy. Early appeals for support had called on women to push their menfolk to act and to assist male partisans in whatever ways they could. As resistance expanded, expectations for women grew and female activism became more visible. By spring 1945, with victory nearing, the message was clear—women were citizens of the nation and should assist in setting the course for a "new" Italy.

Various factors determined the meaning of citizenship for women and whether women's hopes for the future would be realized. How women saw themselves, what they expected, and what they thought they could and should do are of primary importance, but these cannot be viewed in a vacuum, as they are intertwined with the broader forces of politics. Historian Joan Scott has argued that "the realization of the radical potential of women's history comes in the writing of histories that focus on women's experiences *and* analyze the ways in which politics construct gender and gender constructs politics."[1] Thus it is crucial to discuss Italian politics in these years and to look at the ways in which the major political parties of the Resistance used gender and reflected explicit male-female relationships in their development of ideology, programs, and actions that led to the defeat of fascism and the construction of a new political order for Italy.

The various political parties that directed resistance activity were all committed to democratic, representative government and, at least abstractly, to social justice and equality, which included universal suffrage. Recognizing that their political strength would come from the ballot box, they were interested in women as voters and possible party members. But including women in the "body politic" had specific implications for the political parties and the male political elites. They had to respond to female mobilization and to decide where women would "fit" in their organizing and structure. To what degree and how would they recruit female members? Would women be integrated fully into political bodies, or would they be given separate but theoretically equal spaces? How should the parties relate to the existing women's groups, particularly the GDD, which were unitary and not necessarily partisan in their membership?

Beyond these structural questions, the parties also had to define what they thought were Italy's most pressing economic and social needs and to develop plans for postwar recovery. Women's issues were central to these preoccupations, and in the formulation of policies and programs, the political parties either incorporated existing attitudes toward women's roles in society or attempted to redefine those roles as part of a vision of Italy transformed. Women were not simply passive pawns in these political maneuvers. They, too, had ideas about recruitment and organization, about the policies and programs that would shape the nation emerging from war. The pages that follow describe the process of political decision-making and the relationships between political actions and reactions.

As of June 1944, Ivanoe Bonomi had headed a "government of national unity," but there were still major conflicts among the political parties, the CLNAI, the king, and the Allies. Among the unresolved issues were whether Italy would be a republic or a monarchy and how that would be decided, the fate of the Fascists and their collaborators, and the degree of influence the partisan organizations in the north would have in setting Italy's future course. In finding solutions to these problems, the parties negotiated alliance pacts, compromised with or struggled against the recognized government and the Allies, and, as necessary corollaries, developed their own mass organizations and defined their political agendas.

## Women and the Socialist and Action Parties

All of the parties recognized the importance of women's support for resistance activities and, in varying degrees, encouraged women to participate in the range of functions previously described and to join political organizations. The result was the creation of women's groups attached to the parties and the publication of newspapers devoted to women's issues.

In Milan and Turin, women associated with the Action Party began meeting in their own groups, which by late 1944 were formally organized in the Women's Movement of "Giustizia e Libertá" (MFGL). The stated goals of MFGL were to aid political victims and the families of partisans, to contribute in all ways to the war of liberation, to encourage and develop women's social and political sense, and to begin to discuss the most important women's issues to be addressed in the postwar era: political equality, rights in the workplace, and public support for mothers and children.[2] At the same time, the organizers of the MFGL in their founding manifesto made it clear that they had no intention of "masculinizing" women or imitating men and that they would not "negate or destroy in the name of some undifferentiated psychological and social equality, the typical female virtues of devotion and sacrifice."[3]

Longtime activist Ada Gobetti was a primary mover for the MFGL, as she brought together a group of women, many of them professionals, who founded the movement. In January 1944, Ada Della Torre, a professor serving as a *staffetta-partigiana* who was "inclined to work with women," approached Gobetti, and by February they had developed a basic pamphlet to recruit women.[3] The MFGL was open to sympathizers as well as women Pd'A members, and some of its most active participants were Communists or Socialists. In August 1944, in Turin, Gobetti met with Frida Malan, another professor who was working with the regional partisan command of the party, and began to discuss founding a newspaper for the MFGL. According to Gobetti, "After long discussion, it was decided that the title would be 'La nuova realtá' (The New Reality). The new reality is exactly what everyone, men and women, hopes to create for the future."[4]

The first edition of *La nuova realtá* in Turin appeared on February 27, 1945; separate editions appeared sporadically in other Italian cities, and, in Rome in the spring of 1945, women of the Pd'A also published *Uguaglianza!* (Equality!).[5] The small but militantly anti-Fascist Italian Republican Party, which often worked in tandem with the Pd'A, revived its women's organizations during the Resistance. By May 1945 it was publishing *L'ora della donna* (The Woman's Hour), which generally supported women's public participation in a democratic republic as well as entry into the workplace with certain necessary protections.[6]

The Socialist Party (now the Italian Socialist Party of Proletarian Unity, PSIUP), which historically had separate women's sections, created a structure of women's organizations in the summer of 1944. In 1943, Giuliana Nenni, the daughter of Socialist leader Pietro Nenni, returned to Italy from exile in France and with other experienced political women helped build a Socialist women's network in central and southern Italy. Beginning in July 1944, the Socialist Party paper, *Avanti!* (Forward!), included a fortnightly supplement entitled "La donna socialista," and by April 1945, with the establishment of the Socialist Women's Center in Rome, another publication appeared, *Lettera alla donna* (A Letter to Women). In the north, even though conflict was more intense and lasted longer, similar developments occurred. Aurelia Zama, a Socialist housewife in Bologna, helped organize one of the first Socialist women's groups, which had 55 members by 1944. These groups published various editions of *La compagna*, the first of which was a typewritten copy appearing on November 30, 1944.[7] As Zama put it, their writings were "above all a message of solidarity which we sent to the *compagne* in the city and the province who needed to feel themselves united in the struggle....In general they were simple women...,unknown combatants who in the majority had moved out of the shadow of their homes."[8] In August 1945, Lina Merlin left Milan and moved to Rome to assume leadership of the party's national women's commission, which by late 1945 brought together the northern and southern women's organizations.

The Socialist Party leadership in these years discussed whether women should be organized separately and what issues would be of greatest concern to women. In reality, as demonstrated, the party had women's sections, but this was assumed to be provisional, and more formal or definitive policy would call only for separate offices or commissions to promote the study of women's problems. Resolution of debate on the Socialists' theory and practice relating to women was often overshadowed or influenced by conflicts and an eventual split within the party. Additionally, the positions of both the Socialists and the Pd'A frequently depended on what the Communists did and said, just as parties on the Right were tied to Christian Democratic actions and principles.[9] The PCI and the DC served as focal points around which political issues were formulated. Thus, questions of organizing women and the inclusion of women's issues in party platforms are most clearly articulated and illustrated in the activities of the Italian Communist Party and of the Christian Democrats during the course of the Resistance and in the immediate postwar period.

## The PCI Approach to Women and the "Woman Question"

The Italian Communist Party was effective in mobilizing and structuring support for the Resistance. At the same time, this activity and the emerging vision of a new Italy were accompanied by a redefinition of the party itself. The "new" party, as described by leader Palmiro Togliatti in 1944, would be a mass movement that appealed to social groups other than the traditional working class. The party's commitment to the electoral process and to progressive democracy meant that it would participate in government and establish alliances with other political groups. A focus on pragmatic political strategies that would increase party power replaced revolutionary rhetoric and plans for sweeping reforms. These changes represented major shifts in the party's course and also were in contrast to many of the ideals and goals of the Communist partisans fighting in the northern Resistance.[10]

The new directions had particular implications for women as well, especially since women were obviously targets for recruitment to mass organizations and women's votes could be important to electoral success. Through resistance activities, large numbers of hitherto unorganized and apolitical women were engaged in public politics. The party encouraged this participation but at the same time recognized the need to educate women and to recruit them to the party itself. In these efforts, the Communist (and Christian Democratic) leadership sought a balance between preserving cooperation and unity with other parties in resistance efforts and paying attention to specific party needs. This approach was particularly evident when it came to relating to the GDD, which the PCI insisted were not Communist groups but non-partisan organizations dedicated to Italy's victory and regeneration.

The party faced another contradiction when it had to formulate policies to appeal to women. A theoretical history committed to revolutionary emancipation for women had to be re-examined because of the need to appeal to a predominately Catholic, and assumed conservative, electorate and because the alliance strategy required working with parties of the center and even those of the moderate Right. In both cases, theory or ideology was driven by practice, and ideals bowed to reality.

## Recruiting Women Members

In the early months of the Resistance, the Communist Party clearly recognized in the mass mobilization for the war "an ever growing activism of large social strata not yet politically qualified and not enrolled in and controlled by political parties." In turn, party leaders predicted that "the party that gains the greatest prestige among the youth and women will be the party of the future."[11] Heeding its own warnings, the party went about organizing previously ignored segments of the population with the result that the face of the "new" party emerging from the war would clearly reflect the nature of the groups mobilized during the Resistance.

Joining a political party was not the automatic outcome of participation in the Resistance, as figures from the sample indicate. Of the 936 women in the sample, only 239 or 25.5 percent had a party affiliation by the end of the war. It can be argued that women were more inclined or had more opportunity to join a party during the war years because of those who were party members, 31.4 percent had joined a party prior to 1943, while 65.3 percent had joined by 1945. The PCI had some success in recruiting women among the partisans, as 141 of the 239, or 59 percent, were on its rolls; of the 141, 34.8 percent had been members before 1943, and 65.2 percent by 1945. In broader terms, women were increasingly incorporated into the party's mass base, as by late 1945 there were between 250,000 and 280,000 female party members (approximately 14-15 percent of the total membership), and by 1946, of an estimated total membership of 1,676,013, 401,202 were women.[12]

The party not only sought more women members but also hoped to appeal to wider or different sectors of the female population. Success in this regard is less marked. Since the party had formerly focused on a working-class constituency, its traditional centers of strength had been in the more industrialized and urbanized northwest and in some sectors of central Italy, while numbers in the northeast and south were smaller. Recruitment drives during the Resistance apparently did not alter significantly the geographical distribution of membership, as most PCI women in the sample, regardless of the date they joined the party, tended to come from the same regions—the Piedmont, Lombardy, Emilia Romagna, Tuscany, and Lazio. There was, however, a change in the occupational base of the members. In the sample, of pre-1943 party members with known occupations, 89.7 percent were industrial or commercial workers, students, teachers, or other professionals. Among those who joined by 1945, the proportional share of these groups fell to 73.5 percent of those with known occupations, and there were noticeable increases among agricultural workers. From the Resistance experience, the party learned "that non-working women, those shut away in the private sphere of home and family, had provided a base of support—albeit passive—to the Fascist mass organizations" and determined that this group "would never again be written off...."[13] This new awareness had practical results, as of the 400,000 women in the party in 1946, 134,306 were listed as housewives.

While in the prewar era family ties often drew women into the party, during the Resistance these connections are less obvious as the sole explanation for party membership. Of pre-1943 party women, 63.3 percent had a spouse or other family member who was also actively anti-Fascist; this figure dropped to 48.9 percent for the group who joined by 1945. Disruption of family structures and patterns of daily life resulting from the war and occupation allowed or even forced individuals to fend for themselves and provided opportunities for them to make their own decisions about political activity. Whereas in the past the party might have used networks of working-class families for their recruiting activity, the "new," mass party had to recruit individuals or to approach families that had no political history. Analysis of the data confirms these changes and points to lessened importance of family connections as the motive behind party membership. As the party broadened its base, family ties proved to be a double-edged sword both for women and for the party in its organizing efforts. On the one hand, commitment to family and close ties to family members might encourage women to take defensive actions, but these same forces could also prevent women from joining a political party. Fathers and husbands might be reluctant to have their daughters and wives in mixed organizations or at public meetings, and women themselves would find it difficult to live up to both party and family expectations.

The fact that a woman's name appeared on party membership rolls did not always represent a genuinely conscious commitment to the party during the course of the Resistance. Cecilia Pron, who was nineteen when the Resistance began, admitted that she and many others "lacked preparation and political knowledge; therefore our adhesion to the party was above all emotional." Prior to 1943, her only knowledge about communism came from the propaganda put out by the Fascists, and the first Communist she knew was a young factory worker whom she helped during the Resistance. One day in 1944 after a bombing, when Pron was helping him move arms and other materials, she found a packet of PCI membership cards. When she asked her companion what they were, he gave her a card. "Thus in two minutes I gained my first membership." Maria Michetti, who had been involved in anti-Fascist activities in Rome as early as 1941 and had often worked with PCI members, recalls her surprise when, after the liberation of Rome in June 1944, the party asked her to assume a role in the local federation, informing her that she had been a party member since February 1943.[14]

Enrolling women into the party was a major goal, but reaching women and convincing them of the advantages of membership were not easy tasks. Nadia Spano, who organized women in the area of Rome after it was liberated, noted that since "it was difficult for them to go to the party, the party went to them."[15] She and her colleagues quickly learned to go into the courtyards of blocks of multi-story buildings and, with a loudspeaker, to talk to the women who listened from their windows while "pots boiled on the stoves." Joyce Lussu's experiences in organizing for the Communists and Socialists are also telling accounts of the difficulties faced in recruiting women. She remembers that often she would arrive at a gathering and there would be no women present. She would ask the men in attendance where their wives were and why they had not come to hear her.

> A chorus of justifications responded to my question: the women were
> minding small children, or preparing the noonday meal, they had gone to
> mass, or they weren't interested in politics, didn't like to go out of the
> house or were not used to being in mixed company...."Oh yes?" I respond-
> ed. "They stay at home because they are honest women! And I who go with
> you to the piazzas and the taverns, what am I? Your position is a criticism
> that I do not accept, for me as a woman."[16]

Sometimes, after Lussu threatened to leave, the men would go home and bring their spouses to the meetings but apparently never with great enthusiasm.

## *Organizing and Educating Women*

To realize its electoral goals, the party had to enroll and politically educate women while taking into account, if not overcoming, traditional attitudes about appropriate gender behaviors. An article entitled "The PCI and Work Among Women," which appeared in the party *Bulletin* in August 1944, confronted these problems and set forth a solution. Though decidedly in favor of recruiting women, the party also had to take into account the "historical characteristics of Italy, the almost absolute economic dependence of Italian women on the family, and the Catholic tradition."[17] Recent experience in areas liberated from the Germans indicated that women were uneasy about joining Communist cells and that men were unwilling to have their wives and daughters join mixed groups. Because of this, the party recommended the creation of separate women's cells. In these groups women could study their own problems and move toward solutions; women would be freer to speak out and act in leadership roles; and with separate organizations women could meet at times that were most convenient to them. Political education for women was a primary goal of the groups. In ensuing months the PCI recognized that old prejudices lived on in the party, and it often reproached male comrades for their "indifferent or suspicious" attitudes toward working with women.[18]

In addition to adopting the policy of separate organizing of women's cells, the party also assumed that the logical people to do the organizing were the experienced political women. For the party, these decisions seemed the most realistic way to educate and raise the consciousness of hitherto apolitical women, but some established women leaders challenged the policies and expressed the humiliation they felt at being put in separate groups; women in the north who were giving their all to the party and to the Resistance were especially resentful about the decision and stated their objections in *La nostra lotta* (Our Struggle) in November 1944. "As Communists, we feel ourselves members of the party with rights and duties equal to those of the men, and we do not therefore find it just to differentiate among us, creating inside the party 'women's cells.'"[19] Individual women resisted the creation of separate cells, and some refused to work with such groups. Marcella Ferrara, a party member since the beginning of the Resistance and an active participant in a Rome GAP, made it clear that working with women alone was a mistake. "Men and women comrades should work together....Enclosing oneself in a ghetto, as I always define the women's committees, was something that cut oneself off from the outside."[20]

Other women, even those who actually helped organize and worked with the separate cells, were at best ambivalent about the policy. Nadia Spano, to whom Togliatti had given the precise responsibility of organizing women, records her reactions to the situation. "It seemed strange: the communist party, those of the vanguard, creating female cells! And I have to tell the truth, at the start it hit me. I was embarrassed, perplexed: what did these cells of only women mean? Didn't it mean falling again into the usual ghetto, contradicting the progressive direction of the party? And then, talking at length, Togliatti convinced us."[21] Joyce Lussu, who knew very well how hard it was to bring women into the party and who worked with women's sections, actually believed that "subordinate women's organizations should not be created and that all political women should involve themselves directly in the parties or unions to oblige them to make the 'woman question' a general question....[Separate sections] reproduced in political institutions domestic aspects of the family and the 'separation of the sexes.' In this way, the women's section was the devoted wife and the Party was the authoritarian husband who kept the power."[22] For the male leaders in the party, organizing women separately was practical, given the nature of the society in which they were working. It was harder for the "elite" political women to accept the strategy because the reality that dictated the need for such a policy was the very reality that they hoped to change. As Giulietta Ascoli explains:

> The reluctance to devote themselves to women's issues was understand-
> able in those years. For the communists and socialists who came from
> prison, from exile, from internment, from the clandestine struggle and who
> felt themselves first communists or socialists and then women; for the
> younger women who had been members for a short time and who wanted to
> leave the ghetto of second class conditions and to participate with full rights
> in the politics of their respective parties, doing women's politics...did not
> always seem gratifying; there was the sense of being confined in a sec-
> ondary role....To understand that women's politics, the "woman question"
> were not secondary problems, would be the result of a long struggle.[23]

The existence of separate cells remained an issue in the PCI long after the war was over, but it was not the only site where theoretical commitments to equality confronted practical politics determined by gender differences.

## Gender and Party Goals

Tied as it was to Marxist theory, in abstract and ideological terms the party was committed to women's emancipation and the incorporation of women into the public life of the nation. This "emancipationist thesis," as described by sociologist Lesley Caldwell, assumes "women's emancipation is similar or parallel to that of men. For both, access to waged work is central....In addition to waged work, the emancipationist tradition has stressed political activity and social relations outside the home."[24] Equal participation in politics, equal treatment before the law, and self-definition and fulfillment in work rewarded with equal pay were the cornerstones of the PCI approach to the "woman question." No one can deny the positive effects party support for these issues would have for women. At the same time, emancipation defined solely in terms of equality with men had some significant flaws: first, it often meant women had to deny their differences and were limited in their own analyses of the social signficance of sex or gender; secondly, since the party's goal of equality was in the public sphere, it did not confront private issues or envision major transformation in the private sphere. Finally, regardless of stated theory and dogma, in practice the party often assigned different roles to men and women, did not create parity of leadership for men and women, saw men's and women's "interests" as different, and, as a result, often appealed to women differently.

The limitations in theory and conflicts between ideology and practice were even more pronounced when the needs and characteristics of the "new" party came into play. Attempting to build electoral support and to participate in government as allies of other parties, the Communists could not ignore public opinion and thus had to temper their rhetoric and moderate their policies. If these things were not enough to establish at the very least ambiguity in responding to women and to the "woman question," the party also had to take into account the immediate demands of rebuilding a war-torn Italy and establishing a stable, democratic government. Whether party actions and programs were driven by ideology or by pragmatic political, economic, and social considerations, it is important to remember as well that the party was made up of men and women with varied personal backgrounds and attitudes, differing levels of consciousness, and individual reactions to proposed changes.

In the fight against fascism and the establishment of a more just, democratic society, the roles and interests of men and women often were *assumed* to be identical. Women and men were comrades in arms in the struggle for liberation. This would hold true especially for the vanguard of Communist women in positions of some authority and with connections to male leaders. Laura Ingrao, who participated in the Roman resistance and campaigned for the PCI after the war, explained that being a woman had nothing to do with her entry into politics. "I was drawn to Communism as an Italian, a democrat, anti-Fascist, in the search for justice, in the attempt to continue a discourse interrupted by Fascism....In that, there was the idea of freedom for men and also for women. But it wasn't specific. Nothing that was a promise to women as women."[25]

Some women went even further, denying that gender affected their position or activity in the party. During the Resistance, Lina Fibbi, who had joined the Young Communist League in exile in France in 1935, was attached to the General Command of the Garibaldi Brigades and thereafter served in various party and labor union offices. When asked if she thought there were difficulties for women in the party, her response was that she did not find any obstacles and that "the limits, if there are any, are mine." Her remarks are especially interesting since she also worked organizing women and in the last year of the war was pregnant (her daughter was born in June 1945).

Other women felt themselves men's equals, saw their work as important, and would have preferred to ignore gender but found that to be impossible in the party. Luciana Viviani participated in the Roman resistance and in 1944, after Rome was liberated, married a comrade, and then both returned to their birthplace, Naples, where they engaged in party work. Viviani remembers that in those first years "I lived, and with me all my generation, schizophrenically, being a Communist and being a woman, because in reality, as a Communist I had not overcome my role as a woman in the society...because in that time people said, 'She does politics and yet it is clear that she is a good wife, a good mother.' "[26]

The party was quite clear in insisting that all citizens, male and female, had certain basic rights that should be guaranteed by the law. The right to vote was of paramount importance to the emerging democratic state and was a right first granted to women in 1945. Additionally, the party, in public written and verbal statements, supported women's right to work, equal pay for equal work, equal access to education, and equal rights to participate in political organizations and to run for political office. In the immediate postwar years, party positions on these issues were reflected in a new, national constitution that was eventually promulgated in January 1948. The first article of the constitution declared Italy to be a democratic republic "founded on work," while Article 3 guaranteed equal rights to all citizens regardless of "sex, race, religion, political opinion or personal and social conditions." Among the guaranteed rights was the right to work (Article 4) and, most importantly, that "the working woman has the same rights, and, for the same labor, the same pay as working men" (Article 37). The right to vote, access to education, the right to run for political office and to associate in political parties were spelled out clearly in other provisions.[27] Emancipation through work, equal opportunity in the material world, and equality before the law had been Communist principles for several decades and, with the support of other political parties, were adopted as fundamental laws of postwar Italy.

This clear support for the principles of equal rights and equal opportunity was balanced by equally firm policies and actions that emphasized differences between men and women, thereby reinforcing socially traditional "separate spheres" and limiting women's opportunity to exercise defined rights. Whether in its recruitment efforts, its appointment of leaders, or its development of policies on family matters and the church, the party failed to live up to its stated goal of gender equity.

In assessing women's interests and motivations for activism, the party (not without some justification) assumed women were fighting against those things that "threatened their lives and their families; they fight for bread and milk for their children."[28] The woman the party was trying to reach was married, devoted to her family, altruistic, and probably not very interested in politics. In a party report of February 1945, Togliatti reaffirmed support for female suffrage but warned that "in certain regions women could vote against our interests [and in favor of the DC]. We should interest always broader masses of women and make sure they vote approximately like the [their] men. But in certain localities this will be unsatisfactory for us given that because of the war there are families that do not have a male head."[29] Slightly later in 1945, Togliatti continued to argue for women's right to vote and to participate in political life but also assured his readers that in assuming these functions women would not "lose their femininity, their attributes as women, wives and mothers. We do not want to destroy the family; we want to regenerate it, to make family sentiment live again filled with a new spirit."[30] Though supporting full public citizenship for women, the PCI also reinforced traditional female stereotypes and women's "private" roles. On a practical level, women were often assigned to committees or brought into policy discussions that dealt with family matters such as maternity and infant care, health issues, support for orphans and refugees, and food and housing.

The "new" Italian woman citizen could be a party member and a worker, but she was fundamentally a wife and a mother, and the responsibilities associated with those latter roles took precedence. The constitutional guarantee of the right to work was accompanied by the statement (which the party accepted) that for the working woman "the conditions of labor must permit the fulfillment of her essential family function and assure to mother and child a special adequate protection."[31] In practice, this provision failed to confront segregation in the labor force and separate wage scales for women; instead it reaffirmed women's role as primary caretakers of children and encouraged protective labor legislation that, as is often the case, heightened labor segregation.

Defense of the family and childhood were cardinal principles of PCI policy and served to validate "separate spheres." Though calling for greater equality in marriage, and assistance for single mothers and widows, husbands legally remained as heads of families, and the party avoided issues of divorce and birth control. As Togliatti asserted in his speech to the first Conference of Communist Women in June 1945, "We need a renovated family,...that is a center of simple human solidarity. It is because of this that we are opposed to setting up any problem which tends to disrupt or weaken family unity....In the end, to resolve the problems of children we need to defend the family."[32]

Later, as the Constituent Assembly prepared the constitution for a new republic, there was little debate on the family and marital law. Article 29 of the constitution recognized "the rights of the family as a natural association founded on matrimony. Marriage is organized on the moral and legal equality of the partners, within the limits established by the law to guarantee marital unity."[33] The last phrase is particularly important, as it meant that specific legal provisions regarding marital rights and conjugal equality would not be dealt with in the constitution. This either left intact previous civil laws that gave authority to fathers and husbands or allowed the judiciary or future legislative bodies to reform the law.[34] The PCI did not argue with these basic provisions and structures because, as Judith Hellman points out, the Communists sought "to outdo the Catholics in their commitment to the family as the central unit of Italian society....The family was regarded as the natural cell of society and…was posed as the key element in the reconstruction of post-war Italian society."[35]

These views, combined with the realities of electoral politics, led the party to deny vehemently that they were immoral destroyers of traditional values, specifically those tied to family and church. In the 1930s, as the party had sought to build an anti-Fascist movement, it distinguished between "Catholic institutions" and "religious sentiments." The former were criticized for their support of the regime, while the latter were described as "tied to the defense of peace and freedom" and therefore inherently antifascist.[36]

Extolling of Christian values continued during the Resistance, and eventually women's spirituality and religious ties were also seen more positively. In fact, in 1945 Togliatti asserted that he did not believe women's religious sentiments were "the cause of their backwardness, [nor did he] believe that such spirituality should be an obstacle in women's struggle for emancipation and democracy."[37] The party insisted that anticlericalism was really a "bourgeois" view and that most attacks against the Church had occurred before the PCI was even organized. In adopting the goals of freedom of conscience and cooperation between Communists and Catholics, the PCI argued, "It is false that the Communists are enemies of personal property and the family" and proclaimed in March 1945 that their Catholic friends should have nothing to fear from the Communists.[38] When the constitution was eventually adopted, the PCI voted for the provision that reaffirmed the favored position of the Catholic church.

## Gender Prejudices Live On

The "new" party that sought broad electoral support among both men and women avoided issues that were controversial or at least untested politically. Committed to bringing peasant women and middle-class housewives as well as female industrial workers into the party, PCI leaders felt it important to temper their approaches. Party directives that guided organizers and recruiters always pointed to the need to recognize differences in women's experiences and interests even if this meant moderating language and party goals so as not to frighten away potential members. As late as August 1947, the party directorate, disturbed by what appeared to be decreases in female membership in some areas, found it necessary to caution the editors of *Noi Donne* (by then the publication of a new organization, the Union of Italian Women, UDI) that it was imperative that all the women's publications reflect "that decorum, that dignity, that liveliness, while still giving these the maximum popularity do not drive away or offend anyone but instead respond to the mentality and requirements of the masses of women."[39] But concern for what the masses of women might think was not the only factor operating. The party also was sensitive to the interests and needs of the fathers, husbands, and brothers of these women, and it was certainly true that within existing party organizations there were many Communist men who firmly believed that women's place was in the home.

Party leaders were well aware of these attitudes. During the Resistance they recognized that "in all levels of our organization the residue of prejudice, bias, and suspicion toward women has not been completely eliminated" and in the postwar era warned that "there no longer should be comrades who consider work [with women] with scepticism and irony."[40] But such pronouncements did not necessarily change behaviors.

Anna Bechis, a worker from Turin who was a *staffetta* with a Garibaldi Brigade and a GDD organizer, pointed out when referring to political leaders' commitment to women's emancipation, "Not only have they not helped, but they have hindered it....[Despite] the constant talk of female emancipation,...in reality women have been relegated to the most modest and self-sacrificing work."[41]

Nelia Benissone Costa, who helped to organize GAP and SAP in Turin and recruited for both the GDD and the PCI, expressed similar frustrations. Male leaders "did not give us the help that they should have. I always denounced this, [telling them] you don't give importance to women....The work of political education of women is work of usefulness to our general political goals." In particular, Costa urged her male comrades to bring their wives and daughters to section meetings. When they asked if she were joking, she was adamant: "No, no, I'm not joking. Why don't you bring them? Are you afraid that your socks won't be mended tomorrow? That your soup won't be well-prepared tomorrow?"[42] Within the party, women and their issues often were segregated from the major political considerations, and this meant that, on the highest levels of party decision-making and among the parties themselves, the "woman question" was not debated.

Despite these deficiencies, the party recruited women in unprecedented numbers and also included some women in positions of leadership. At the December 1945 party congress in Rome, of the 1,626 delegates, 282 were women, and by 1946 9.4% of party leaders were female.[43] These figures are hardly overwhelming, but they do represent significant gains from prewar conditions, and the number of women in party leadership positions was higher immediately after the war than in the succeeding decades. It is also clear that "the PCI employed its rhetoric and public actions to provide a political agenda that identified women as an important segment of Italian society...[and an] electorally crucial political category."[44] However, when the party supported female emancipation, it did so largely in political and legal terms while reaffirming traditional family functions and never directly confronting the contradictions between an acceptance of women's private roles and the newly proclaimed public freedoms.

The discrepancies between theory and practice with regard to women were not unique to the PCI. Most Communist parties before and after the Second World War faced similar dilemmas, and as Sharon Wolchik, a specialist on Eastern European women, explains, the concrete measures adopted "appear to have been determined by consideration of other goals rather than by the ideological commitment to women's equality, [as strategies of economic recovery] would have been difficult if not impossible to implement had political leaders and planners not been able to count on women both to increase the labor force and continue to provide the valuable services they contribute by their unpaid work at home."[45] Facing a nation in economic ruins, with meager public resources for social assistance, neither PCI leaders nor their colleagues in other parties could afford to tamper with gender divisions of labor that fulfilled economic needs and provided some stability to counter the upheavals brought by fascism and the war. This point is evident when Christian Democratic structures and policies are considered and compared to those of the PCI.

# Christian Democratic Politics and Gender

As a newly formed organization, the Christian Democratic Party (DC) had to clarify and promote its ideology, recruit members, and establish relations with other political groups. Like the Communists, Christian Democrats had to decide how to appeal to women, what role women would play in the party, and how to strike a balance between partisan interests and needs for unity in the Resistance efforts. Additionally, it was necessary for the DC to define its relationship to the Catholic church. A 1944 DC paper entitled "Ideas on Christian Democracy" stated quite clearly that "the DC is not, as some would say, the party of Catholics or the party of the Church....Catholicism is not a party; the Church is universal. The DC is the party of those Catholics—practicing or non-practicing—who see and feel the necessity of reorienting social life in new forms."[46] While the party sought to distance itself from Catholic conservatism, and adopted goals of social, economic, and political reform and renovation, it could not ignore the existence of the numerous apostolic groups organized under the umbrella of Catholic Action.

## The Christian Democrats and Catholic Organizations

As noted previously, during the Fascist years Catholic women's lay organizations had continued to function. On the eve of the Resistance the Union of Catholic Action Women (UDACI) had nearly half a million members, while the Young Women of Catholic Action (GF) and the women's branch of the University Federation of Italian Catholics (FUCI) attracted younger women.[47] In general, the memberships of the women's groups surpassed those of the men; for example, by 1946 the GF listed 885,000 members compared to 367,000 in the young men's union. During the years of resistance, these organizations had become decidedly more anti-Fascist and could be the vehicles through which women participated in resistance activities and public life. Alda Micelli, who had joined the GF in 1928 and headed a Catholic girls school in Milan in the 1930s, remembers that "before the war there was no civil or political outlet, only the religious one....During the war the structure of Catholic Action expanded little by little as the regions were liberated. Then we quickly joined CIF [the Center of Italian Women organized in 1945] and campaigned for the vote."[48] Although the relationship of AC to the DC remained ambiguous and informal, duplication and networks of members, as well as pronouncements of similar political positions, demonstrate the importance of the lay groups to the success of the DC.

Given the fact that UDACI was not supposed to be a political organization, the Christian Democratic leaders established women's groups specifically affiliated with the party (Movimento Femminile DC, MFDC) and then a more broad-based women's organization (Centro Italiano Femminile, CIF), both of which were overtly political with public agendas. In the spring of 1944, already active Catholic women, many of them spouses of DC leaders, organized the first sections of the Movimento Femminile DC (MFDC) in Milan, Genoa, and Reggio Emilia, and by late summer a national network of these groups was established. When the Central Division of the party met in Naples in August, it included Angela Maria Cingolani Guidi, a former member of the Popular Party and the Young Women of Catholic Action, who had been doing clandestine work for the party. In March 1945 the party formally assigned Cingolani Guidi to organize the women's groups and recognized her as the group's national delegate.[49]

Like their Communist counterparts, the Christian Democratic leaders recognized the lack of political experience and ideological awareness among their potential constituents. Both the creation of the women's sections and the publication of a variety of newspapers were intended to help educate women and involve them in national political life through what might be termed the role of the "moral mother." When the separate organizations were initially introduced, they were assumed to be provisional. Cingolani Guidi defined them as transitional and indicated they would be unnecessary when women gained political maturity and men better understood women's political value. Later, in 1946, when the first national party congress was held, there was discussion about the separate sections, and, even though several women leaders objected, they became formal institutions in the party.[50] Christian Democrats and Communists thus established similar goals and faced similar problems in organizing women and, at least superficially, came up with the same structures for their women members.

## Women's Causes in the Party

As a "modern," progressive political party, the Christian Democrats developed a program for women's rights and supported various women's causes. In so doing, their policies stated quite directly what the Communists had implied: that the private and public worlds were separate, that women had, in essense, two roles, and that men and women were both equal and different. Writing in the magazine of the MFDC, Guido Gonella, a longtime anti-Fascist, a leader of FUCI, and representative of the more conservative elements in the DC, made it clear that in political society men's and women's status and human rights were identical, but "in the orbit of family life, which requires a hierarchy, the status of the woman is a status of subordination."[51] Separating the natural equality of citizenship from differences based on activity or function, the DC insisted that "every activity, no matter how humble, has equal moral dignity. A woman because of her mission as a wife and mother, as the educator and the helpmate of man, should enjoy equality of political rights, parity in working conditions."[52]

With this as its basic ideology, the DC could call on women to assume a wide range of responsibilities in the building of a "new" nation. For example, in a 1944 Christmas message, DC leader Alcide De Gasperi affirmed support for female suffrage as an expression of women's role "in any social and political renovation, and at the same time the safeguard of the institution of the family.…We urgently need the spirituality of women and the impulse of their ideal sentiments....The party is a large family. You can act as mothers, wives, and sisters. In the struggle you will be our ideal guide."[53] The DC consistently emphasized the need for women to insert their "private values" into the public world, and these appeals were reinforced by leaders of the Catholic church. At the end of the war, Pius XII called on the women of Catholic Action to enter politics, because in coming out of their homes and family spheres they would be able to better defend these, and simultaneously when addressing the young women of the GF he underscored that it was "incumbent on all Catholic young people to participate in political life."[54]

In 1946, as the Christian Democrats formulated the positions for which they would argue in the Constituent Assembly, they included proposals on women's issues. As might be expected, they opposed divorce and birth control on the grounds of defense of the sanctity of the family, as well as natural and divine law. But they also opposed privileges based upon sex, race, party, class, or religion and insisted that women should enjoy equality in public rights and equal treatment in the world of work.[55] When it came to practical measures and constitutional guarantees of women's equality, there was considerable consensus between the DC and the PCI. On the other hand, the Christian Democrats were more direct in their assertions of the importance of women's traditional roles than were the Communists. Whereas the PCI had trouble finding a theoretical "place" for women's private, reproductive responsibilities, the DC, without apology or equivocation, elevated the roles of wife and mother and then appealed to women on that basis.

## Recruitment and Leadership Issues

Like the PCI, the DC successfully recruited women. By 1946 party leader De Gasperi announced that of the 1 million party members, 250,000 were women.[56] While the PCI clearly used Resistance organizations as recruiting grounds for women, it is probable the DC drew more of its membership from Catholic lay organizations; thus the correlation between new recruits and Resistance activists is much less obvious for the DC. Returning to the sample, of 239 women with known party affiliations, only 24 were associated with either the Popular Party or the Christian Democrats. Unlike the PCI women, the occupation most often listed for Christian Democrats was teacher or other professional (13), while agricultural and industrial workers are noticeably absent. As with the Communists, family connection was more important among women who were active before 1943 (70 percent) than those who joined the party by 1945 (21 percent). DC party membership data for the postwar period consistently lists three-quarters of female members as housewives; thus, it would appear that the DC women connected to Resistance work might not be typical of overall women in the party. The high proportion of housewife members has been explained by Lidia Menapace, who notes that wives, mothers, daughters, and sisters of men members were often simply put on party lists to provide a block of secure votes.[57] This would mean, as well, that being listed as a party member would not necessarily reflect a particularly conscious political commitment.

The Christian Democrats also included women among party leaders and did run women for national political office but never in the proportions that reflected their membership base. In 1945-46 two women served in the party National Council, Angela Maria Cingolani Guidi and Maria Jervolino de Unterrichter, both of whom were spouses of important party leaders. Of the 208 Christian Democrats elected to the Constituent Assembly in 1946, 9 were women, and of general DC leadership in that year, 4.4 percent was female.[58]

There is no question that the political parties that led the Resistance provided new avenues for women's activism, saw the electoral potential in the female population, and were committed to extending political and some legal equality to women. Equally clear was a general consensus on the importance of traditional gender roles in the reconstruction of the nation, the separation of women and women's issues from other party concerns, and the absence of women in the parties' decision-making bodies. There was, indeed, a "new" political woman in Italy, but the parties created her in their own image and on the basis of what *they* thought women wanted.

## Autonomous Women's Organizations and the Parties

Closely connected to party recruitment efforts and development of policies and programs on the "woman question" were the parties' responses to and impact on groups like the GDD and UDACI. Both of these groups existed as unitary and apparently non-partisan women's organizations, which were in some ways beyond party control. There were advantages to women in autonomy and separation, as these associations could appeal to women from diverse backgrounds, serve as valuable training grounds by educating women politically, and possibly pressure the political institutions to deal with women's issues. However, the actual degree of autonomy was always at issue since many GDD organizers were associated with "Left" politics and UDACI's religious character linked it to "Christian" political organizations.

Both the PCI and DC recognized that the autonomy of the GDD and UDACI could make them effective channels for reaching women with no political experience; at the same time, since electoral success was the goal, the groups could not be too independent. In effect, the major parties would compete for influence among the separate women's groups and eventually created two national, mass-based women's organizations, the Center of Italian Women (CIF) and the Union of Italian Women (UDI), which, though supposedly autonomous, were increasingly linked to the major parties.

From women's perspectives, the new organizations helped to institutionalize women's activism and to ensure that earlier spontaneity became regular activity for women. On the other hand, they also divided women along ideological lines not necessarily of their own making and contributed further to a "ghettoization" of women's politics. The significance of the separate organizations to women and to the political parties, and the pros and cons of autonomy, were evident early on in the Resistance as the leadership of the CLNs recognized the existence of the GDD and debated what status the groups would have in broader Resistance structures.

## The GDD

As indicated in the previous chapter, the GDD grew out of spontaneous mobilization of women during the Resistance; equally true was the fact that it was often Communist or Socialist women who actually organized the groups, though the rank and file were not necessarily Communist and party affiliation was not a prerequisite for GDD membership. For example, three GDD zones in Emilia Romagna reported the following at the end of 1944: In one zone there were 55 members, 19 of them in the PCI; in another, 55 members with 11 in the PCI; and in the third, 20 members with 8 in the PCI. Reports from Ravenna in 1945 showed that in one area there were 60 Republicans, 43 Communists, and 8 independents, while another district listed 368 GDD members, of whom 201 were political independents. An unnamed Rome sector in February 1945 reported 112 members, of whom 68 were PCI.[59] In the sample of the 136 women who worked with the GDD, 81 (59 percent) had a party affiliation, while 71 (52 percent) were either Communists or Socialists. Given the nature of the sources for the sample, these figures probably inflate PCI influence because an organizing report from the PCI in northern Italy early in 1945 concluded that only about 10 percent of women belonging to GDD were Communist. It warned that "if we do not rapidly reinforce the Communist fractions, we run the grave risk of leaving that mass organization in development at its own mercy without a guide or a spinal column to support it."[60] For the PCI, the apolitical or varied character of the GDD was of considerable concern.

Throughout the Resistance, the PCI balanced, often uneasily, between support for GDD autonomy and recruitment of women to the party. Party press and executive memos to local sections and zones in 1944-45 recognized deficiencies in recruiting women, asked for reports on GDD and women in each sector, and specified how women should be incorporated into party activities.[61] These same directives were often accompanied by the admonition that "to support the work and exercise a constant control [over such groups as the GDD] does not mean that these organizations should be blended or confused with the party. Each of these organizations should act as a separate circle...with its own headquarters and methods of organizing."[62] While the PCI welcomed the growth of the GDD, the large numbers of women mobilizing and moving into the public sphere caused apprehension that the groups were too independent. For its part, the DC was suspicious of Communist influence in the GDD and what it saw as the groups' lack of autonomy. These opposing views crystallized when the CLNs debated giving formal recognition to the GDD.

As already noted, by the summer of 1944, the CLN in Milan, because of its established strength, had become the directing center (CLNAI) in northern Italy and had been recognized as such by the Rome government of liberated Italy. The CLNAI was to coordinate civilian and military resistance and included representatives of the major parties as well as mass organizations supporting the Resistance. Therefore, it was logical that in a June 18, 1944 letter, the GDD National Committee in Milan requested financial support and representation on the CLNAI. Negotiations on this question among the GDD, the CLNAI, and the various parties continued until October 16, when the Milan body formally recognized the GDD as an organization belonging to the Committees of National Liberation.[63] This decision was backed by support from the PCI, Pd'A, and PSIUP.

On September 15, the Liberal Party had stated its opposition to such representation on the basis that the GDD was a "pre-existing organization monopolized by a single party with newspapers of a clearly Marxist tone." The Christian Democrats also opposed recognizing the GDD as the only women's organization and insisted that women's groups should not be political but instead dedicated "to the simple military struggle and the Catholic faith."[64] GDD leaders continued to insist that their groups represented all women regardless of political affiliation, but debates on recognition of and support for the organization continued into 1945, and, in some cases, local CLNs would not accept a GDD representative.[65] On February 11, 1945, the DC took a stronger stand when the party executive committee for northern Italy, acting on orders from the DC National Council, declared that since the GDD program and publications "are inspired by principles and methods not corresponding to our thought," henceforth DC women would not be members of the GDD.[66]

Regardless of attempts to maintain party cooperation and the rhetoric of unity, the reality was that party lines were being drawn both ideologically and structurally. Another source of tension stemmed from the fact that developing party hierarchies were centered in Rome, a situation often objected to by northern units and groups that had their own base of power, a tradition of autonomy, and, in some cases, a different view of Italy's future. These problems are evident in the process of creating the two "new" national women's organizations, the Center of Italian Women (CIF) and the Union of Italian Women (UDI), which occurred simultaneously with the debates over the status of the GDD.

## UDI and CIF

The impulse for the organization of UDI came from PCI leaders in liberated Italy in the summer of 1944. Palmiro Togliatti encouraged visible and experienced women from the PCI to begin to build a national women's organization that could pull together all the existing women's groups and continue to mobilize women after the war of liberation was won. In Rome, on September 15, an organizing committee for UDI was established. The committee included Rita Montagnana and Egle Gualdi (PCI), Bastiana Musu (Pd'A), Giuliana Nenni and Maria Romita (PSIUP), and Marisa Rodano Cinciari and Luigia Cobau for the Catholic Communists.[67] Organizational and theoretical goals were clearly stated. There were to be local circles, provincial committees, and a national executive; all officers were to be elected democratically, and previously constituted women's groups could affiliate with UDI by simply sending their membership lists to the national office. Recognizing the existence and important contributions of the Resistance organizations, UDI directors insisted that these had been "a first step, but it is necessary to do more in the interests of the nation. There is need to unite these groups in a large organization of all Italian women,…in which all ideologies and principles which are not fascist, nor against the people will be respected."[68]

One of UDI's first activities was the creation of the Committee for Suffrage, which was a broad coalition that included members from the women's organizations of the DC and Republican Party, as well as other CLN groups and labor and educational associations.[69] Pressuring the Rome CLN to support suffrage, the Committee argued that Italy could not begin on its new, democratic course while excluding women from a role in politics. Since the CLN parties were for the most part sympathetic and the women's groups unanimous on the issue, the fight for the vote was fairly quickly won.

Pro-suffrage cooperation was quickly replaced by divisions among the women's groups and the parties themselves. In Rome, shortly after the founding of UDI, various Catholic officials met with Maria Rimoldi, representing the women's organizations of AC. In response to UDI's appeals, Rimoldi indicated her interest in forming a similar group, but of "Christian inspiration."[70] The goals of the proposed organization would be to enable women to assume more responsibility in the civic life of a democratic state. In 1945, Amalia di Valmarana, who had participated in the Resistance, was a leader of the DC women's movement, and then served as president of CIF, articulated the purposes and ideals of the new group. She first pointed out that "the times ahead are not such that a woman can limit her interests only to family and professional life, or spend all her energy on religious and charitable activity.…[She now must be ready] to contribute to the reconstruction of her country," and that would include discussion and defense of women's rights, although these were defined in relation to a maternal role and defense of the family, which was seen as the cornerstone of a healthy, Christian society.[71] Issues such as child and health care, education, and improved working conditions for women were supported but only in a familial context.

CIF was organized so that individuals could join but was also a federation that gathered together associations and institutions of Christian inspiration arranged hierarchically from communal to provincial to national councils and commissions. During 1945, CIF groups were founded in all sectors of Italy, usually as the result of bringing together previously existing organizations, especially women's branches of the AC, but also women already involved in the Movimento Femminile DC (MFDC).

In the meantime, UDI was extending its structure as well. In central and southern Italy new groups were founded, often in areas where there had been little partisan activity and there were no women's political associations. For example, between October 1944 and the end of the year, UDI committees were established in Catania (Sicily), Viterbo and Frosinone (Lazio), Perugia (Umbria), and in Ancona and Pesaro (the Marches), where there were 500 members in twenty-two circles. In areas further to the north, occasionally new UDI groups were organized, but more common would be a process of simply absorbing the existing GDD, and sometimes, as in Siena (Tuscany), UDI circles and GDD co-existed for a time. As areas were liberated from Nazi-Fascist control, UDI organizations appeared. In April 1945, *Noi Donne* reported that five UDI circles had "sprung up" in Bologna, a city "liberated only yesterday."[72] In some cases a local GDD might vote to affiliate with UDI, but the formal merger of the two associations was carried out by their leaders and occurred after the northern areas were liberated. On May 20, leaders of UDI and the GDD National Committee met in Milan to agree on fusion of the two groups and subsequently began planning for a national congress to be held October 22-23 in Florence, at which time a unified program would be developed.[73]

At this point, both UDI and CIF claimed to be mass organizations open to all women regardless of political affiliation. In fact, UDI even adopted a motion stating that members of CIF and any other Catholic association could join them. CIF, on its part, insisted that it was not an arm of the DC, that its origins were in Catholic Action, and that it was open to all Christian women. The reality was that with more formal national organizing, at least in a vertical fashion, and through their leadership, the two organizations became more explicitly tied to the existing parties, either of the Left or of the center.

After February 1945, when the DC formally pulled out of the GDD, it increasingly turned to CIF as a mechanism for organizing women and aided in the funding of the group. Ecclesiastical directives also advised DC and Catholic women not to join UDI, while in August of 1945 the executive committee of the Liberal Party announced its formal withdrawal from UDI. Women in these parties apparently accepted the schism as inevitable but not necessarily desirable. DC leader Maria Federici later noted that especially in the north, in fighting both against the Fascists and for their own rights, women activists had found common terrain; however, "the unity among the women could not be maintained for long, because of the influence that certain parties began to exercise on the women's groups." Social Democrat Aurora Guarini, whose party also broke with UDI, stated, "We left UDI unwillingly....We had to do it to follow the party line."[74]

Meanwhile, to confront the charges of partisan bias, the PCI kept insisting that UDI remain an autonomous organization. A 1945 party memo announced, "We must abandon definitively any sectarian attitude, any tendency to dominate, any attempt at propaganda by the party within UDI....It would be a grave error to reduce UDI to a competition among the parties."[75] UDI leaders voiced similar sentiments and at a June 1945 meeting agreed with Marisa Rodano that "UDI must be a mass organization and, as such, should not be tied to any party." Regardless of words or intent, structural divisions among the women's groups occurred and were symbolized by the fact that, whereas in the summer of 1945 the CLN for Lombardy included a representative of the GDD, by October there were two women on the committee, one representing UDI, the other CIF.[76]

It is clear that whatever unity existed during the war of liberation was increasingly disrupted, at least in a formal way, by the end of the conflict. The women's organizations were thus affected by broader political forces whether they liked it or not. The reality of this impact is better understood by looking at the political affiliations of GDD members, how the creation of UDI and CIF affected women, and women's own responses to ideological divisions and party directives.

Examining the membership figures and political affiliations of GDD groups reveals several important factors. First of all, women who were part of the GDD were more likely to be party members than were other women who participated in Resistance activities. As one woman pointed out, when you joined the GDD "they did not tell you *which* party to join, but that you should join one."[77] This is borne out by sample data.

Of the total of 936 women, only 24.5 percent had a party affiliation, while of 136 GDD members, more than half were also party members; and, of those, 63 percent joined a party after 1943. Equally true is the fact that large numbers of GDD women had no identifiable political connection. Socialist Pina Palumbo, who was active in the Milan GDD, remarked that "there were not, at the beginning, distinctions of political faith, and women party members were so close to those without a party that it would be hard to determine how many and who were the socialists."[78] This lack of political identity was evident in 1945 when GDD groups were absorbed into UDI. For example, in April, Forli (Emilia Romagna) reported 5,115 members, 1,000 of whom were without party affiliation, while two circles in Ravenna reported, respectively, 368 members, 201 of them political independents, and 171 members, with 68 independents. Even as late as October 1945, UDI's provincial committee in Modena included 3 independents out of 10 members.[79] Certainly, joining the GDD served as an impetus for party affiliation, but, as in the total population, neither GDD membership nor Resistance activity brought automatic political affiliation.

The second important finding that emerges from membership records is that among women with party affiliations there was a considerable mix. Besides the 3 independents, the Modena committee mentioned above also included 2 Socialist members, 3 PCI, 1 Pd'A, and 1 DC member, and the Ravenna circle of 171 had

60 Republican members. Given the origins of the GDD, it is understandable that Socialist and Communist women were more highly represented in the groups, but it is also interesting to note that even when DC policy and ecclesiastical messages advised Catholic women not to join the GDD or, later, UDI, the reality was often different. Prominent DC woman Lina Cecchini served on the GDD directorate in Reggio Emilia after September 1944, while in Turin, the GDD representative on the local CLN remained a DC woman until the war ended, and in many other areas women from AC as well as the DC continued to participate in their local groups. Formal enunciations of ideological differences were more characteristic of national organizations, while on a practical, local level, interparty unity continued.[80] It should be noted as well that party identification and ideology that marked women leaders were not necessarily duplicated among the rank and file, and when GDD sections were absorbed into UDI and Catholic Action associations federated with CIF, the masses of women were not involved in these decisions and did not see the affiliations as necessarily tying them to a particular party.[81]

While rank-and-file women may not have been aware that their participation in the GDD, and later UDI or CIF, connected them to a party, women leaders with greater political understanding were not necessarily pleased with the situation. Ada Gobetti, who had helped to found the women's movement in the Pd'A and was part of the GDD directorate in Milan, recalled her thoughts in September 1944 when the GDD sought recognition from the CLNAI. "There is no question that it was the Communists who created the GDD; it is on the communist women that propaganda work is grounded. It is undeniable that the tie between the GDD and the Communist Party is watched-over and continuous." Although Gobetti asked why the GDD, and not other of the women's groups, should have an official position in the Resistance structure, she eventually supported the decision. As she pointed out, "What else could I do?…Protest, be obstinate, create a split?"[82]

Even Communist women were uncomfortable with their party's influence on the women's organizations. Irma Franceschino, a GDD leader in UDI who had also worked for the PCI, said that "from the start I deplored the excessive weight of the parties inside [UDI] and above all of the PCI." As a result, she worked increasingly for UDI and less for the party. Another important PCI leader, Gisella Floreanini, finds the word "excessive" to be inappropriate but also admits that the party saw UDI as its instrument, while UDI wanted autonomy. Throughout the next several decades, various UDI women would resist having their organization function as a "transmission belt" for the party, while simultaneously tensions continued to exist between the Milan chapter, the home of the first autonomous GDD, and the hierarchical structure of UDI centered in Rome. Women in CIF had similar problems in trying to remain autonomous and keeping their local bases in the face of an increasingly centralized approach on the national level.[83]

# Conclusion

In summary, Italian politics was transformed in the fight against the Fascists and during the course of the Second World War. The "new" parties that emerged were dedicated to participatory democracy and constitutional, parliamentary government, but they faced massive problems related to recovery and reconstruction. As these parties developed structure, organization, and programs, they had a direct impact on Italian women and their social and political associations.

In the first place, in seeking electoral success, the parties were committed to female suffrage and recruitment of women members. Because of the need both to appeal to women and to regain stability and rebuild the nation, women's concerns were given public recognition on an unprecedented scale. Women's work and wages, education, social assistance programs, and child and maternity welfare were all considered of national importance. Responding to previously existing women's groups, the parties created their own women's sections and ultimately helped sponsor the growth and institutionalization of the mass-based women's organizations—UDI and CIF. For the first time, women were given a place in the structure of Italian political life, but as we have seen, there were boundaries to the political arena that women had trouble crossing and the new public roles accorded women were often contradictory.

Though the parties recruited women, many who were mobilized during the Resistance remained outside formal party structures. Women who were most active and politically conscious still came from the same occupational groups (industrial workers, teachers and other professionals, and students), but the disruption of family cohesion resulting from the war created new concerns for "housewives" and forced political parties to reexamine their recruitment strategies. Within the parties, women were underrepresented in decision-making bodies. While the creation of separate women's sections could provide women with political education and training, it also served to segregate women and marginalize their concerns. All the parties, in varying degrees, continued to see women primarily as wives and mothers and did little to challenge traditional divisions of labor and gender roles. Women were brought into discussions of national policy only when proposed projects were assumed to interest women as mothers and housewives, such as those involving transportation, schools, medical care, food distribution, and aid to orphans.

Finally, UDI and CIF clearly were organizations important to and supported by Italian women, but their development served various political "agendas," and the degree to which the existence of such mass movements represented an overwhelming surge of women's political consciousness must be examined. This leads to the final set of questions, which the next chapter will address: What were women's expectations and practical or strategic goals? How were these tied to the motives that had propelled women to act, and how were these affected by mobilization during the Resistance? Was there an emerging feminist consciousness, and if so, to what degree and in what ways did it challenge dominant political structures and attempt to alter Italian social and gender relations? To answer these questions, we must return to the women themselves, to their words, lives, organizations, and plans for the future.

# ■ 5 ■

# Feminist Consciousness and Politics in the Resistance: "A Sense of One's Self"

The previous chapters have discussed the factors that led women to take part in the Resistance, the importance of their activity to the success of partisan efforts, and the connections between women's mobilization and the political structures that evolved during the course of the war. The final and perhaps most important topic to be considered is the meaning of Resistance activities to women themselves. As women mobilized, how many women and what aspects of their lives were truly affected? Did participation in the Resistance help to alter women's perceptions of themselves, their capabilities, and their place in Italian society?

Women joined the Resistance for a variety of reasons, responding to the disruption and crises in their lives. It is therefore important to understand what they saw as the most important problems for women and how these were to be resolved. If their hopes and expectations led to female dreams and visions for the future, how successfully were these translated into reality? When the war ended in 1945, Italians could jubilantly claim victory, but just as historians since then have questioned whether "the Resistance had indeed won all its battles," so, too, we must ask what it was that women had won.[1] Answers to these questions appear as we consider the responses and opinions of individual women and examine the structures, operations, and programs of the women's organizations.

## The Evolution of the GDD and UDI

Because the GDD and later UDI were women's organizations concerned with women's issues, their development and activities provide important information concerning what women wanted and what they achieved. Among the specific topics to be addressed are: Which women and how many were actually touched by these networks? How did these organizations define women's problems and needs? And what immediate or long-term goals did they establish?

## The Membership of the GDD

In the spring of 1945 when the GDD prepared to merge with UDI, the initial GDD founding group in Milan had expanded to an organization claiming 70,000 members with sections throughout the northern area. When the GDD sent its membership figures to UDI in April 1945, it listed the following:

| Piedmont | 4,528 members | (1,653 in Turin) |
|---|---|---|
| Lombardy | 4,758 | (3,398 in Milan) |
| Emilia Romagna | 11,402 | (4,000 in Bologna) |
| Liguria | 1,340 | (1,000 in Genoa) |
| Veneto | 2,000 | |

In addition to regular members, provincial groups also listed associates (collegati), who participated in all activities but did not pay the usual dues of four or five lire per month. Lombardy claimed to have 9,823 associates, while there were 6,000 in Emilia Romagna.[2] Though these numbers are impressive, more important are the ways in which the groups were organized and what membership actually meant.

As we have seen, in all areas by late fall 1943, women, either individually or in small groups, were engaged in various partisan activities. Building upon this existing base, a politically experienced woman (often a PCI member) normally would contact the most well known local activists and begin to build an organization that had recognized leaders, an established membership, and defined programs and goals. Originally the groups were urban-centered, consisting of five or six women whose common characteristic was previously demonstrated activism rather than particular political identification. In Bologna, organizing began in the fall of 1943 when Vittoria Guadagnini returned from exile and made contact with committed women. The original group included Vittorina Tarozzi, an activist factory worker; Jordis Grazia, a PSIUP member who was working on the party newspaper; and Rosalia Roveda, a teacher of philosophy and history who had been a volunteer nurse with the Red Cross since 1940 and became directly involved in Catholic anti-fascism by helping to organize a group of young Christian women. By February 1944, a formal organization was in place.

The process in Turin was much the same, as PCI women Maria Negarville and Teresa Testa, both back from exile in the fall of 1943, made contacts with Ada Gobetti and women from the Socialist and Liberal parties. The organization in Reggio Emilia was the result of the efforts of Velia Vallini, a young agricultural worker who had been involved in strikes in 1942, and Laura Polizzi of the

PCI. By September 1944, they had added to their directing group Lina Cecchini of the DC and Malvina Magri, a worker and PSI member. The group in Genoa had a similar history. It was organized in January 1944 largely by Lina Fibbi, also returned from exile, and Elletra Prampolini of the PCI but quickly expanded to include representatives from other parties. People such as Guadagnini, Fibbi, and Polizzi would frequently work in one area, then move on to other organizing, and thus show up in more than one GDD structure. Once regional and provincial structures were created, these women often directed them.

In each of these cases, leadership of the GDD came from politically affiliated women, in particular those who were members of the PCI. In regions where the PCI was less influential (e.g., Padua or Venezia), GDD organizing was apparently also less effective. Nevertheless, once groups were formed and mass membership developed, the base included women from all parties as well as those without political identification.

In a series of interviews, 47 Resistance women were asked whether "differences in social conditions, political organization, and religion created difficulties in the common struggle with other women." Forty-four of them said no, and even Laura Polizzi, who answered affirmatively, indicated that while initially there were problems with Catholic groups, these were overcome by "discussing and deciding on their initiatives and the things that needed to be done."[3] This lack of political differences and the sense of unity among the women is borne out in the responses of 65 women interviewed for a study on the Resistance in Brescia. Only 6 of the respondents had a party affiliation; 2 mentioned they had previously worked with women, but a subgroup of 20 partisans indicated they felt greater solidarity with other women than with their leaders or male partisans.

Adele Bei, who worked with the Rome GDD, noted that she had little connection with DC women, though she did work with women of the Christian Left. On the other hand, "the mass which we directed and organized was made up of Catholic women, women of the people, in the large majority independents who opposed the war and fascism."[4] Diana Franceschi of the Bologna GDD makes much the same point: "Catholic women of the city districts and factories participated in large numbers in the struggle and the demonstrations because then there were no ideological barriers." Stella Vecchio from the Milan organization agreed that political differences played a small part in their activities since, for most, it was the first time they had entered political life. This point was stressed by the GDD National Committee in Milan when they wrote to UDI describing their membership as "masses of women who are just now awakened to political life. These women still do not know how to distinguish between the program of the Communists and that of the Socialists, between the Liberal and Christian Democrat, and that of the Pd'A, but they feel some things unite them to all their sisters whatever the party to which they belong."[5] If political affiliations later divided the women, it appears they were imposed from without, rather than being the result of major internal differences. Women joined the GDD because of common female experiences and goals, not because of precise political ideologies.

Just as the GDD membership crossed political lines, so was it also cross class, usually reflecting the demographic characteristics of a particular region. The initial membership of the Milan group consisted of women who were factory workers, clerks, professionals, and students. By April 1945, the central sector in Milan included 11 clerical workers, 6 professionals, 5 students, 4 artists or artisans, and 1 housewife.[6] GDD organizing tended to focus on occupational groups or locality, usually distinguishing between country and city cells and, in the latter, between those of the workplace and those of the neighborhood *(di strada)*. In Milan, in November 1944, there were 47 groups in the workplace, 32 *di strada;* and by March 1945, 126 workplace and 58 neighborhood groups existed.[7] The situation in Ravenna was a little different. Its organizing report listed 32 city groups, including 2 of factory workers; 8 of students, teachers, clerks, and intellectuals; 5 of housewives; 9 of agricultural workers; and 8 mixed groups; and there were 13 groups in the surrounding countryside. The fact that there were only two factory sections was somewhat unusual, but the report explained that women workers felt their "agitation was easier and less dangerous if directed almost exclusively to immediate economic needs without introducing new national and patriotic motives," and that most of their work was influenced and directed by the PCI.[8]

As GDD membership expanded, urban groups tended to be more numerous; for example, in Liguria, most cells were composed of students, intellectuals, and workers, except in La Spezia, where they were able to recruit peasant women. Conditions in the countryside made organizing both different and difficult. Luciano Bergonzini notes in his study of the Bologna resistance that in rural areas there could be little secrecy or security based on anonymity, as everyone knew everyone else. Thus every successful action required the consent, support, or protection of an extensive, but often invisible, network of people.[9] Resistance organization in the countryside was crucial to the struggle, for farmers and agricultural workers could provide needed supplies and simultaneously deny those resources to the Fascists. GDD leaders were aware of their urban bias and came to understand that issues and actions that mobilized city women might have little impact in the countryside. This fact was made clear to Gemma Bergonzoni as she directed the GDD efforts and tried to organize the female rice-field workers in the area of Medicina (Emilia Romagna). In March 1944, she organized a demonstration of 450 women who protested the fact that their husbands were being drafted and asked for distribution of basic food supplies, and, a little later, a major strike of 2,000 field workers included demands for bicycle tires as without them the women would have to walk several kilometers to work since there was no other transportation. The following year bicycles were again an issue when the local Fascist authority decided to commandeer 500 bicycles for the Germans. This produced another large demonstration, after which the women got to keep and use their bicycles. Through this series of quite specific actions, organization and solidarity among the women developed, and Bergonzoni attributes this to the fact that issues of immediate concern were the basis for their activity. "We said that for demonstrations to occur...we had to have with us not just the organizers, but the majority of women. [We protested] only when a problem was one we all felt."[10]

GDD leaders did make efforts to build their base in the countryside and to appeal to the interests of rural women. In March 1945, the national leadership stressed the need to strengthen ties between urban and rural women, "eliminating the residue of divisions disseminated by fascist propaganda." If the GDD was "to become the organization of all Italian women, it should concern itself with their particular needs, their conditions of life and help them to gain the necessary improvements."[11]

Regardless of these efforts, the average GDD member probably was not an agricultural worker or rural resident. A profile of the 136 GDD women in the sample illustrates this point and indicates other common features of the female membership. Among them there were 17 agricultural workers and 6 housewives, while there were 45 industrial workers, 17 women involved in commercial activity, 13 students, 11 teachers or professors, and 12 in other professions. Fifteen had no known occupation. Most of the women came from the Piedmont, Liguria, Lombardy, and Emilia Romagna and were between the ages of twenty and forty, which was typical of the majority of participants in the Resistance.

In some respects women of the GDD did differ from the overall population considered. Of those in the total sample whose date of joining the Resistance is known, only 19.2 percent were active before September 1943; among GDD women, 59.6 percent had a record of earlier activism. As might be expected, while only 25 percent of all women involved had a party affiliation, for the GDD the figure is 59.6 percent. Additionally, as indicated earlier, for most women in the general sample, there is no known family connection; the opposite is true for GDD women, where 54 percent had a family member, spouse, or companion who was an anti-Fascist or partisan.

Interpreting these figures requires some caution because of the nature of the sources. The GDD women in the sample were probably women in some leadership capacity and therefore not entirely representative of overall membership, while typical rank-and-file women are more likely to be included in the total sample. Even so, the data would support comments made earlier about the organizing process, which usually involved visibly active women with some established political connections, as well as the importance of experienced women in helping to shape and direct the rank-and-file women's responses to fascism and the war experience.

## Activities and Goals of the GDD

Once GDD were organized, their activities were fairly diverse. One of their functions was to raise money to distribute among the partisan units. In November 1944, the Milan GDD provincial committee reported that its sectors had raised more than 400,000 lire, most of which went to the CLN Lombardy, but sums were also given to Socialist and Pd'A Brigades.[12] The GDD also collected food and clothing for the families of partisans and were, of course, the instrumental force in staging demonstrations and strikes as well as the means by which women were recruited to serve brigades and other units as *staffette* and *partigiane*. But the agenda of the GDD went beyond this assistance role by defining and developing solutions for women's specific problems.

The GDD saw their work as a process beginning with recruitment of women to aid in resistance activities; from there women would become more public and political, setting goals and assuming new responsibilities in liberated Italy. In some senses, they saw this process in rather simple or inevitable terms. If women joined the Resistance, and helped to defeat fascism and end the war, they would de facto have a place in the direction of Italian society. As the problems they faced were attributed to fascism and the war, the answers lay in national liberation and progressive democracy. Analysis of gender prejudice did not really go beyond its manifestations in the Fascist regime. This certainly left many women unprepared for the difficulties they would face in the new Republican Italy. Marisa Rodano, in reflecting on her experience and the meaning of the Resistance to Italian women, maintained that their activism was not just a temporary phenomenon and that they did connect their own emancipation to the national struggle but that, on the other hand, such activity could not be seen as the beginning of an inevitable march to equality.[13]

One of the major functions of the GDD was political education, or consciousness-raising as we call it now. For this purpose, GDD units, particularly in urban areas, created "study centers" for the purpose of examining women's present and future problems. Increasing women's awareness of their political potential, involving women in this aspect of public life, and convincing them that they had special needs and general rights were difficult ventures. One woman organizer in the south recounts that she and her colleagues usually focused on immediate material issues rather than ideology or general women's status because "the *compagne* did not always understand."[14] Giuseppina Garemi describes the early organization of the GDD in Pisa: "We were a group of women who met to discuss whatever was going on and above all to be ready to help if tomorrow something happened. Politically we were little prepared, because we came from twenty years of fascism, and then, I have to say it, our respective parties didn't pay much attention to an autonomous political organization of women."[15]

Gabriella Rossi, who worked with the Youth Front in Emilia Romagna, remembered that in the spring of 1944 when she attended a meeting to organize the GDD, the goal of women's emancipation was discussed: "It was a word that, when uttered for the first time,...was a shock."[16] Rossi also asserts that it was fairly easy to recruit women to transport arms, medicine, and supplies, "but no one wanted to accept a political role." Gina Borellini confirms this by indicating that in the GDD it was often "the first time that the real significance of liberty, democracy and emancipation was spoken about. It was much easier to accept the task of collecting medicine, supplies, to carry orders and transport arms."[17] Assisting the partisans was a natural role; moving to act in their own interests required a break from traditional attitudes and activities. Clementina Succio, a factory worker from Turin whose political career had begun in the twenties and included exile and acting as a PCI courier before 1943, stated that the men saw women as inferior beings, but "we also had a sense of inferiority."[18] Reluctance to identify themselves as political actors was certainly an obstacle to be overcome, but, additionally, there were numerous women in highly visible positions of leadership who failed to see the importance of gender issues and to connect their work with women's emancipation.

When Ada Gobetti, who had a long history of public activism, was first approached about forming the GDD in Turin, she stated: "I confess that after the enthusiasm for suffrage of my long-past adolescence, I had not occupied myself with women's issues....Was there really a 'woman question'? Perhaps not seeing the problem is my own deficiency."[19] For some women, there was a clear separation between their activity and identity as a woman and other political functions they might assume. As one woman put it, "I felt myself first a Communist and then a woman," while another said, "I did both things, the 'party' and 'women'." In a similar vein, when Luisa Bertini, who had been a member of the Popular Party, was asked what needed to be changed in the society, she stated: "The freedom to say what you think; but not as a woman, as a citizen, because that is how I identified and identify."[20]

Diana Sabbi, who came from a Socialist and longtime activist family and was decorated for her military actions in the 62nd Garibaldi Brigade in Bologna, indicated what the struggle meant to her. Working with her partisan comrades from all classes "for me, was the discovery of a new world; it was the end of that hateful discrimination which fascism had tried to institute between the categories of urban and rural workers, the middle classes and the intellectuals." Cross-class unity, not gender equality, was what concerned her most.[21] Such broad political ideals were fairly common. The GDD women of Pisa, preparing to affiliate with UDI in 1945, explained: "UDI, then, is not a charitable institution, nor a forum for feminist exercises, nor an exaltation of female abilities; it represents the fraternal union of all the women of Italy in the struggle against prejudice and selfishness."[22]

Some women refused to work with the GDD. For those who hoped to be "real partisans" or to "act like men," gender-segregated groups often associated with traditional "women's work" were considered unacceptable. Mariolina Beltrami was an eighteen-year-old student when she joined the PCI Youth Front in 1944. She apparently rejected the GDD, preferring a male model of activism, and went on to command an SAP unit in Reggio Emilia.[23] It is of interest to note here that among the 33 women in the sample who had military rank and command positions, 19 were aged 20-29, 7 were students, and, while 20 had a party affiliation, only 7 worked with the GDD and 2 others with party women's sections. Thus these women were not typical of the broader group. Neither was this most non-traditional behavior—military leadership—necessarily connected to the gender-based activities and goals of women in the Resistance.

## Education and Identity

Convincing women that they should become active politically and that there was a 'woman question' they needed to address was not a simple matter, and the GDD had to develop a variety of strategies to achieve these goals. In their discussion groups and numerous publications, the GDD consistently made the connection between their resistance work and the new role women would play in liberated Italy. Typical of this approach is the statement from *Noi Donne* (Bologna) in May 1944: "In fighting for the independence of Italy we are also fighting for our freedom as women and as workers."[24]

A wide variety of newspapers, pamphlets, and broadsides were used to reach, recruit, and educate the masses of Italian women. In most cases, the GDD center in Milan prepared the material and sent it to local groups, which would add items of local interest and then publish the material in whatever way they could (many early editions were simply mimeographed). The most important GDD publication was *Noi Donne,* the origin of which was a clandestine and anti-Fascist paper printed in Paris in the mid-thirties. *Noi Donne* appeared in Emilia Romagna in May 1944 and was followed quickly by similar provincial publications in the Piedmont, Lombardy, Liguria, and Tuscany, as well as by more limited regional appearances in Novara (Lombardy) and Friuli (Tre-Venezia). An open, "legal" version of *Noi Donne* also began in Naples in July 1944 under the direction of Nadia Spano and Laura Bracco. With the liberation of Rome and the founding of UDI, this edition moved to Rome.

GDD groups also published their own independent papers that focused on local events and people. A multi-party paper, *Il pensiero femminile* (Women's Opinion), first released in Milan on International Women's Day, 1945, was intended as an organ for theoretical discussion rather than news reporting. Party women were also printing their own news sheets, and the close connections between those and the GDD are evident in the fact that they often reported similar news items and carried the GDD message. Because of the technical difficulties in printing, *Noi Donne* in Milan began with only 500 copies, but within a few months it had increased to 6,000 and generally ran between that figure and 10,000.[25]

The subject matter of the various publications reveals which issues were considered to be of importance, as well as the development of responses to women's conditions in Italy. The focus of most material in 1944 was the recruitment of women to the national struggle. Women were encouraged to aid the partisans, to join resistance organizations (whether women's or not), and to demonstrate against German and Fascist control. Many of the women's actions already recounted in previous chapters were described in the press. Detailed accounts of the women who were arrested and tortured, who evaded capture by the Fascists, or who were awarded medals for valor furnished headline items and provided models of vigorous action and patriotism. Exhortations to resist encouraged "unfeminine" behavior, as, for example, the broadsides from both Bologna and Modena that called on mothers and wives "to respond to violence, with violence."[26] Rewards for women's resistance activity were also clearly stated: Women would be equal citizens, would have the right to vote, and, in a democratic order and in the "new" society, Italian women would play an important role.

The publications stated unequivocally and repeatedly that equality and emancipation were women's goals and made frequent references to women emerging from the slavery of their previous existence. In November 1944, *Noi Donne* in Liguria specifically referred to "the struggle for liberty and women's emancipation."[27] *La voce delle donne* in Bologna in December 1944 affirmed that women were showing by their actions that they were "not second to anyone, but that our work has earned the esteem of our men and all the world, that we have properly redeemed our rights and conquered the place that belongs to us in the future society of popular democracy."[28] Other articles referred to the "prejudice and superstition which favor the slavery of women in the family and society," to women's united struggle to cease being "the passive and undervalued victims of a reactionary society," and to the fact that "women's traditional exclusion from the political life of the nation is due, not to incapacity, but to a narrow-minded and overwhelming conception of the construction of society in force even now."[29] Awareness of women's subject status was clearly articulated in these publications during the years of the Resistance; the writers viewed this subjection as grounded in reactionary Fascist society and promised that, with liberation, justice would be done.

## Feminist Ideology in the Women's Organizations

Denunciation of past injustices, reaction to a "second class" status, and demands for change were common themes for Italian women of the Resistance. But deciding what should be changed and moving from rhetorical statements to practical proposals were much more difficult. In August 1944, an article in *Noi Donne* asked, "What Do We Want?" and answered:

The women of Italy want to remain mothers, wives and exemplary women, but at the same time we who are half of the population, want to understand political life, to be able to express our opinions on the great problems of the country. We ask our government…to accord us those civil, human and social rights we demand.[30]

## Women As Political Protagonists

Women sought equality with men and rejected discriminatory treatment. At the same time, they recognized gender differences, especially those based on roles in the home and family, and in claiming their rights were not prepared to reject all aspects of women's "double burden." As a result, the programs and goals that were proposed rested on three basic assumptions: first, that as workers and citizens, women would be equal to men; secondly, that as wives and mothers, women needed material support to ease the "double burden"; and thirdly, that the work of wives and mothers should be recognized as benefitting all of society, not just the individual family members. Given the fact that it was often the separate and unique aspects of women's experience that had led them into the Resistance in the first place, and that women continued to be segregated during the Resistance, this was an entirely appropriate response. Equal citizenship in the public world was combined with an enthusiastic affirmation of separate spheres and defined gender roles. In fact, gender difference was seen as a source of strength rather than of conflict or antagonism. Possible contradictions between equality in the public sphere and rights and duties in the private were not resolved.

In more concrete terms, politics, work, education, and careers were the areas where women's and men's opportunities and status would be the same, and, consequently, legal and institutional barriers were to be eliminated. Gaining the right to vote was, of course, a major, first step, and women's organizations encouraged women to become political beings, to use the ballot box, to run for office, and to participate in decision-making at all levels of Italian society. This was an area where women did achieve some success.

By the end of the war, some women began to see politics as the vehicle for social transformation and realization of their own aspirations; for many, this was a new phenomenon. Coming from a world in which it was assumed women had no place or interest in politics, and a society that had isolated women from political concerns, the experience of working in an organization like the GDD, where specific goals and plans for the future were discussed, added new dimensions to women's lives. Gisella Floreanini describes this new perspective as that of "becoming political women, of considering politics the instrument to carry forward our battle" and above all of developing a "sense of one's self…,of being a person," while Giuliana Beltrami affirms that in their activities some "began to act in the first person, to disobey....They wanted, for once, to live like men."[31] Diana Franceschi, a *staffeta* and part of the provincial directorate of the Bologna GDD, indicated that "the fact of being part of the GDD, where I participated in the decisions, in the direction of what initiatives we should take, gave me the chance to acquire an autonomy and a personality of my own, finally."[32] According to Laura Polizzi, other women with whom she worked in the GDD had similar feelings: "For some it was the first time they participated in discussions of a political sort and they were very interested."[33]

Many women, remembering their experience in the Resistance, refer to the formation of a "civil and political consciousness" and an emerging identity as "political protagonists," creating what PCI leader Rina Picolato has referred to as a "new" woman.[34] Catholic activist Clara Obici, who was president of CIF in Ravenna, agrees, noting that, during the war, a conscious grasp of women's rights and duties in the new society began. The first steps into political life were often made cautiously and tentatively, but not lightly. Clelia Minelli, a PCI member from Modena, recalls exercising the vote for the first time: "It was an incredible emotion, my hands, legs and arms shook....The vote for women was the first, great conquest that would put women on the same level as the men."[35]

Both the GDD and UDI encouraged women to run for political office and pressured parties to include women in their candidate lists; they also were willing to voice their disappointment when this did not happen. Success in this arena can be measured precisely by looking at women elected to office and their backgrounds. Between 1945 and 1948, as Italy moved to create a popularly elected, democratic government, women were involved in each step of the process. Thirteen women served in the Consultative Assembly (Consulta Nazionale) from September 1945 to May 1946 (of a total of 440 members), and 21 were members of the 655-person Constituent Assembly from June 1946 to April 1948. When Italians voted in favor of a republic in 1948, women were 53 percent of the voters, and, finally, when the first legislature was elected in May 1948, women held positions in the national government for the first time. Thirty-nine women were elected to the Chamber of Deputies (of 568), and 2 to the Senate (of 233).[36] Though one must recognize the importance of this historical moment to women's political development, it is obvious that in none of the elected bodies were women a dominant force.

As one might expect, most of Italy's postwar political leaders were individuals who had experience in the anti-Fascist and Resistance movements. This background is significant for women as well as for men. More than 50 percent of the women elected to Parliament had a history of partisan activity, and both of the senators and 26 of the deputies were elected from the areas of major resistance activity (i.e., Rome and north of it). A more detailed profile of the women in the sample who were elected to city, regional, and national governments, or to national party or labor group offices, reveals several significant facts. Sixty-three women held such positions, in itself not a very impressive number. Generally they were between 20 and 40 years of age; of the 50 with known occupations, 37 were factory workers, students, or teachers/professors or other professionals. Forty-nine percent of the group had a family member, spouse, or companion connected with anti-Fascist or partisan activity, a correlation much higher than that of the overall female population participating in the Resistance.

As one might expect, and in contrast to the general sample, almost all of the elected women were party members (61), though only 25 had joined a party before 1943, indicating some "new" women did enter political life. PCI or PSIUP membership dominated among the elected women (45 of the 63), just as it did in the general sample, but, unlike the broader group, 66 percent (42 women) were members of UDI, CIF, their party's women section, or some combination of these. This latter point reinforces the conclusions that membership in the women's organizations stimulated political consciousness and that these groups provided important encouragement and support for women candidates.

A final factor distinguishing the women elected to office from the overall female partisan population was their function in the Resistance. Whereas, among the total group, the most common activity was work in a GAP or SAP, only 7.9 percent of the women who went on to hold office had such a background; instead, they tended to be concentrated in the work of organizing, leading demonstrations, and contributing to and distributing propaganda. Thus, for women, simply engaging in and supporting resistance activity did not inevitably lead them into postwar political leadership. More important was the specific nature of their resistance work, and most significant was whether or not they were recruited into one of the political parties.

Overcoming the attitudes and obstacles that kept women from joining a political party or running for office would require more than an act of rebellion or heroism in the Resistance. As other histories have shown, women's activities in wartime can easily be explained and perceived as being only "for the duration." The GDD, then UDI and CIF, wanted women to become forceful political beings, but if measured in sheer numbers, the success of their efforts was limited. In part, this can be explained by the attitudes of the parties to women's activism but also to the inability of the women's organizations to exert independent political influence, to overcome certain stereotypes related to women's role, and to persuade women that non-traditional behavior was both desirable and acceptable. To measure successes and failures in the latter areas, we must return to the agenda and programs of the women's groups. Did the organizations adopt policies that might have challenged those of their parties and the male elite, and did they provide sufficient definition and support for female activism, as well as specific strategies and goals with which women might identify and pursue to the point of overcoming traditional gender structures?

## Women As Workers

In addition to equality in the political sphere, the GDD and UDI also insisted on women's rights in the world of work. Equal pay for equal work, improvement in wages and benefits, as well as increased representation of women in workplace organizations were repeated demands during the Resistance. Fascist discrimination against working women was strongly denounced, and the specific economic hardships suffered by women under the regime were frequently discussed. After 1943, at different levels of government there were attempts to respond to economic pressures, especially male unemployment, by restricting the work available to women, and the women's organizations criticized and resisted these efforts, insisting on women's right to work. For example, the prefect of Palermo had established a "Defeminization Commission" for this purpose, but largely due to the pressure of UDI, which denounced this new discrimination, the body was abolished in September 1945.[37]

Both the GDD and UDI recognized the necessity of incorporating women into official labor unions in order to defend their rights and address their own problems, and here the organizations had some success. As early as December 1944, UDI had organized a special commission to work for this purpose and had begun to pressure local Chambers of Labor and organizations such as the General Confederation of Labor (CGIL) to include women in decision-making bodies. In April 1945, UDI participated in a general worker's conference held in Naples that resulted in the inclusion of women in the National Committee of the CGIL and the creation of a women's council that would work with both the General Confederation and local chambers.[38] These sorts of actions were accompanied by frequent calls for educational reform and training to enable women to pursue careers and professions of their choice.

Arguments for women's rights in the workplace often began with the simple recognition that women *were* working and probably would continue to do so. The fact that *some* women would have to be self-supporting was explained by the numbers of men lost in the war and the overall economic problems facing the nation. Given this reality, women should be treated equally. From the words and tone of speeches and newspaper articles, one could conclude that the women's groups sought to reassure their membership and society at large that in their concern for equality in the workplace they were not trying to take men's jobs or denying women's primary responsibilities in the private sphere.[39] The acceptance of women as workers was balanced by the recognition that women were also mothers, and thus the women's organizations consistently emphasized the need to provide special support in the form of child care, food subsidies for children, and maternity benefits. With this assistance, women would be able to advance in the world of work, contribute to the welfare of their families, and properly raise a new generation of children, all of which were necessary if Italy was to recover and progress.

Economic and workplace rights for women were often linked to stability of family life. Christian Democrat and Catholic Action women called on the state to help restore the economic security of the "traditional" family (usually meaning one headed by a male). But they also acknowledged the rights of female heads of households and supported equal pay for equal work because these were seen as necessary adaptations to reality. They recognized that mobilization for war had "irrationally" expanded the world of work for women and insisted that whatever work women did should not "harm their psycho-physical characteristics and their virtues, ordained principally to managing the home."[40] Programs for family assistance were important for all the women's groups, as were moves to have women designated as "heads of household," thereby meeting the criteria for public aid.[41] These issues and others were discussed during the summer of 1945 as the GDD and UDI prepared for a national women's conference to be held in Florence in October and were included in the major resolutions addressed at that meeting. Among UDI's demands related to working women were equal pay for equal work, equal professional and employment opportunities, adequate assistance for working mothers, and support for the children of workers in the form of food, adequate housing, and medical care. Going beyond these fairly standard issues, UDI also expressed concern for housewives who had no compensation, no protection, and no limit on the hours they worked.[42]

When the Constituent Assembly began to meet in June 1946, UDI proposed similar provisions for inclusion in the legal structure of a democratic Italy. As we have seen, these specific provisions were not always supported in practice by the major parties, though all, in theory, advocated equal treatment in the world of work. In a sense, the women's groups did go beyond the traditional parties in their assertions of women's economic needs and their recognition that all women were not necessarily supported by men. However, while they might call for a "new and healthy environment" where women could develop their abilities and begin to participate in the public world, this would occur without abandoning "those occupations which are particularly feminine."[43]

## Women's "Nature" and the Link Between Private and Public Spheres

During the Resistance, women were keenly aware of connections between the public and private spheres and had clear ideas about "natural" male and female differences. These attitudes, in turn, directly affected their understanding of the meaning of equality and emancipation for women. Common attitudes held that women were especially suited to certain functions in the "private" sphere, that their virtues and values in the public world emanated from that separate sphere, and particularly from their roles as mothers. In this view, motherhood was a physical and moral activity important to the nation as well as to the individual family. Women leaders and their organizations sought to elevate this sphere and to build public and political recognition of its importance and social utility. They argued that women could handle the "double burden" of private and public responsibilities if they received institutional support, and although they challenged segregation in the workplace, they did not question a fundamental division of labor in the home. If men exhibited prejudices or sexist behaviors, these were often seen as individual failings or the results of unexamined customary attitudes. Patriarchal institutions were usually viewed as the product of fascism rather than as a part of more fundamental social structures. Custom and tradition, reinforced by fascism, were the culprits, and these would be transformed with the birth of a "new" and progressive Italy.

## Women's Role in Reconstruction

During the Resistance, notions of separate spheres and particular feminine attributes often were used to move women to act and to support various programs. In January 1945, *Noi Donne* in Liguria pointed out that "we women have, as women, common interests, never antagonistic to those of men, but specifically diverse; we have particular virtues and particular defects." The same article argued that traditional female virtues and sensibilities were motives for participating in the Resistance and would also contribute in the future, liberated Italy. Bologna's *La voce delle donne* (Woman's Voice) welcomed women's entry into political life but insisted that it "should not be considered as exhibitionism or a masculine pose; we will know how to reconcile our profound femininity with our political activity; in fact, it is this which will permit us to defend and maintain the attributes of our sex."[44] Because of their particular character and experience, women were especially qualified to deal with certain aspects of reconstruction; after all, who, better than women, understood the problems and requirements of daily life? Often quite explicit links were made between women's experiences and responsibilities in the home and the role they should play in public life.

The first issue of *Noi Donne* published in Naples, in July 1944, began with an article entitled "Our Duty." After noting that for twenty years fascism had disrupted their families and forced women to become heads of household, the editors announced that their journal would offer to all women "the possibility to discuss the problems which, because we are women, are of particular interest, [and that] we want to reconstruct the family and for that reason we are directly interested in all the problems of national life."[45]

Both the GDD and UDI recommended that committees and government organizations be created to deal with fundamental issues of day-to-day survival and proposed a prominent place for women in such social welfare bodies. Rina Picolato, who was appointed to the Consulta Nazionale (Consultative Assembly) in 1945, when asked what her contribution would be, responded, "solving and discussing basically all the very complex problems of existence, [especially] that very severe one of feeding [the population]."[46]

For some time, individual women had been scrambling to feed and care for their families, and a primary function of the GDD always had been to provide assistance in the form of collecting and distributing food and money, not only to the partisans but also to other individuals or families in need. With the cessation of hostilities, UDI took on many of these responsibilities, showing particular concern for orphans, refugees, and unemployed women. Given the decline in production, food shortages, material destruction, and financial crisis characteristic of Italy at the time,[47] it made sense for women to focus on these issues.

In its program for the new constitution, UDI included a variety of related recommendations. In addition to work for all men and women, it called for "a dignified tenor of life for workers, a healthy home for every family, adequate support for maternity, the protection of the physical and moral health of children, the right to assistance for the aged, infirm and invalid, and the distribution of primary goods on the basis of need."[48] These proposals, which came under the heading "The Defense of the Family," echoed more general views of the time, as the major political parties also saw healthy family life as a prerequisite for a healthy society and democratic government. The traditional family that everyone seemed to be talking about was itself most likely a myth and, at best, an ideal, given the changes in family life in the 1920s and 1930s and the disruption of personal relationships during the war and Resistance. Nevertheless there was little serious or systematic critique of that institution, however it was defined.

## *Motherhood, Marriage, and Family Life*

The meanings, requirements, and responsibilities of motherhood and maternity were critical to all of the discussions or pronouncements about family and gender roles. Various publications made it clear that motherhood was woman's mission, not her destiny, and as such it should be a joyous, positive, even worry-free experience, valued and supported by the society as a whole. Though attempting to emphasize the public and collective rather than the private and individual responsibilities of mothers, many of these messages reflected traditional views of women's place and often echoed the rhetoric of Mussolini and his regime. In September 1944, *Compagna* in both Lombardy and the Piedmont described a Socialist future in which "the young woman would return to school in the air of freedom, beauty and health; the wife to her husband and home; the mother to her children because with socialism the man alone could adequately support his family." The following March the same journals referred to women's "exclusive social function: maternity." A broadside of the women's movement of Justice and Liberty (MFGL) presented its hopes in similar terms. "We want a society in which our children can grow up physically and morally healthy: women have not only the duty, they have above all the right to be mothers. We must struggle that this right be respected and protected."[49]

Given the difficulty and even anguish associated with the experience of motherhood in the previous years, these sentiments were highly appropriate and struck a responsive chord. The problems associated with this line of appeal are also clear. First, it was questionable whether there would be resources for public support of maternity and how much of a state priority the "new" motherhood would be. Second, it is doubtful that public opinion would accept the idea of "social motherhood" in the place of traditional views of motherhood as a "private" matter. Finally, such statements tended to reinforce traditional views of women's nature and place. Female self-sacrifice, altruism, support, and assistance were acceptable behaviors, and women as wives, mothers, cooks, nurses, and consolers were familiar figures. While a vanguard of women may have begun to think of themselves in different terms, the vast majority probably did not and were not encouraged to do so through these sorts of appeals and proposals.

In addition to maternity and child care, the women's organizations also discussed housework, and though they did not question this as women's work, they did at least begin to think of it in more political terms. A February 1945 article in the Socialist *L'nuova realtá* (The New Reality) entitled "The Problem of Housewives" began by asking what place the "woman in the home" would have in the future of the nation since, in reality at least, 50 percent of Italian women were, and for some time would be, exclusively housewives. The author stated that existing responses to the question were unsatisfactory. Some simply denied women the right to leave the home to create an economically and socially independent position for themselves because of their "natures." In response, the author suggested they remember it was 1944, not 1744. On the other extreme, some argued that housework should be mechanized and child care done by specialists provided by the state, thereby according it dignity and worth commensurate to work in the public sphere. Here the author admitted that such schemes, though interesting, were also idealistic and utopian, as they would be costly and neither the state nor the society was in a position to effect such a transformation. In the meantime, housewives would have to continue to work in "the limits of their own families," but they could at least organize and gain a sense of their own worth and the value of political participation. Through the press and influence on social institutions, individual experience and sentiment could be translated into action affecting issues of greatest concern to them: "infant and maternity protection, provisioning in general, housing and restoring the physical and psychological health of the race."[50]

*Il pensiero femminile,* in its attempts to raise theoretical or philosophical issues, also included discussion of women's work in the "private" sphere. One article insisted that housework should be considered socially productive, and to that end it needed to be organized and rationalized. According to the author, this could be accomplished by creating collective work groups with divided functions and by utilizing more advanced technology, which would free "the mother to fulfill her higher functions."[51] In all of these proposals for transforming housework, tasks in the home and maintenance of the family were seen as exclusively female occupations, and nowhere were male responsibilities evaluated or a more equitable division of labor considered. Certainly there was a "double burden," but heroic and vigorous womanhood was equal to the task.

Occasionally the women's groups did venture into the arenas of marital reform and sexual equality, but such forays were fairly isolated and rarely supported by established political forces. An article in *Compagna* that stressed women's maternal function and marriage and family as the "secure guarantee" for the physical and moral health of individuals and the nation also accepted "divorce because we want the same morality for both sexes [as well as marital reform so that] both partners have equal rights of decision in all the circumstances of family life."[52] In general, however, divorce was not a central or visible issue among the women's groups and certainly not something the major political parties were willing to support. The Christian Democrats were most adamant in their opposition because in their view divorce encouraged "lack of fulfillment of family responsibilities and an attempt by civil law to corrupt natural and divine law."[53]

Even those who might have been sympathetic to divorce felt it would contradict too many Italian social and cultural traditions, no doubt spelling political suicide. On this and other "touchy" women's issues, women leaders determined what they considered to be the mentality and interests of most Italian women and decided to follow a middle course. Ada Gobetti remembers her response when she was first asked to help in organizing the GDD and to read an early GDD manifesto:

> It didn't quite talk about women's rights;...instead it attempted to
> explain to simple women the significance of the war and how, as women,
> they could collaborate....It tried to speak the language that could best
> appeal to feminine qualities; that, while affirming a theoretical equality
> [among women and between men and women], sought to recognize the
> existence of basic differences that create diverse sensibilities, interests and
> impulses.[54]

In May of 1945, a group of women from UDI met with the Christian Democratic Minister of Justice, Umberto Tupini, to discuss women's legal status and to recommend possible reforms, particularly in the marriage and family codes. The women argued for changes in those marital laws that presently gave fathers and husbands almost absolute authority over wives and children and dictated harsher penalties for women in cases of adultery. They pointed out that much of existing law was antequated, that the war had increased the responsibilities and duties of women, and that in gaining the vote women had entered into public life. "For all of these reasons it is imperative and at the same time just that women have greater autonomy and authority in the family.... [After all], who could argue that women were not concerned about their children?…And yet, legally mothers have no power or authority over their children."

Minister Tupini affirmed his belief in the indissolubility of marriage and the legal necessity of designating a "head of family." However, he also agreed that the idea of a patriarchal despot should be eliminated and instead family authority "should be exercised jointly by both spouses" and family property held in common. Though Tupini would make no specific commitments, the UDI representatives expressed satisfaction that their concerns had been heard and that those responsible for framing a new constitution would consider women's legal status and "give legal recognition to the position women had spontaneously acquired in the society."[55] In the long run, as was already pointed out, these reforms would not be fully reflected in that constitution.

Throughout the Resistance, in public forums and in publications, analyses of family life and personal relations were made, but these were never the focus of women's thought or actions and were phrased so as not to be threatening or too strident. Transforming relations between private and public spheres was always overshadowed by demands for political and economic rights and needs. The goal of equality meant that women would have the same rights and duties as men in politics and the world of work, if necessary; women would have more opportunities, but they would continue to shoulder the responsibilities of the private sphere, and little would change in the lives of men. Gender differences in political rights, wages, or criminal punishments could be challenged because they were unjust but would be reinforced in other arenas because they were "natural" and fundamental to an ordered and stable society. Some women complained that the men of the Resistance assumed women would return to the home, "where they belong," once the fighting was over, but women themselves mirrored this viewpoint as well. Just at the conclusion of the war, on May 15, 1945, the *Noi Donne* edition in Rome ran the headline, "Leaving Our Rifles, We Will Rebuild Our Families."[56]

## Conclusion

By way of summary, an overall consideration of the content of the women's publications in these years provides a general impression of the messages being delivered to Italian women and what were perceived as women's interests and desired female behaviors. By far the largest percentage of articles in all the journals reported on women's contribution to the Resistance struggle—their support of the partisans and their heroic military actions and demonstrations. Next in importance were pieces that dealt with economic issues, women's work, and political participation. In contrast, there were few theoretical, feminist discussions or analyses of the sex/gender system. Instead, traditional female virtues were reinforced in the emphasis on supportive and nurturing functions, and, in fact, after May 1945 more and more of the material reported on assistance activities (for children, the war wounded, and the homeless) and less on women in non-traditional and militant roles.

Those issues most often discussed in women's publications also varied by region. For example, the Roman issues of *Noi Donne* from 1944 through the summer of 1945 had regular features and special articles on child care, homemaking, fashion, and film. Normally, these occupied between two and three pages in a sixteen-page publication and included recipes for using rations creatively and instructions on how to make laundry white or how women could "make over" their clothing so that "all of our dresses can be elegant." One issue even reported on a conference devoted to the theme "The Social Value of Fashion."[57] Such articles were less prominent in editions published in the north, where fighting continued for a longer period.

No doubt, in a world torn apart by war, there was a sense of assurance or "normalcy" in discussions of everyday activities associated with food and clothing. Contradictory themes often appeared simultaneously, as forecasts of the emergence of a "new" woman were accompanied by articles extolling traditional female attributes and functions. In a somewhat schizophrenic manner, calls for women to assist and support were blended together with insistence on independence and autonomy. Communist Rita Montagnana's article, "Our Contribution to National Rebirth," appearing in September 1945 in *Noi Donne,* listed all that UDI had done in assistance and support but also adamantly insisted that they were not limited to these activities. UDI had "its own defined program,…[and had carried on] widespread campaigns for the rights of women workers and to guide women to become actively involved in the social and political life of the nation."[58]

Claims to what might be termed a "double" life, and recognition of women's special virtues along with their universal human rights, were problematic because little was done to explain *how* these oppositions could co-exist and what they would mean for women's experience. Feminist demands and potential remained limited or unexplored, and as Margherita Repetto and others who have studied this period in the evolution of Italian feminism conclude, "The lack of a theoretical reorganization of the 'woman question' was not casual and neither of little moment were the consequences that derived from this."[59]

In general, women's organizations during the Resistance sought consensus rather than confrontation and tried to promote issues and attitudes that could appeal to most women. Fascism had divided Italy; therefore, unity among men and women, and among all women, was stressed, even though this was not always the reality, as political differences showed up among women leaders and in the eventual creation of two supposedly unitary women's organizations. Even so, at the local level there was a sense of solidarity and common goals. Women were organized on a large scale and were guaranteed the right to participate in politics, and some of their issues were inserted into national political discourse. As a result of their activities in the Resistance, some women *did* gain a "sense of themselves."

Olga Prati cites the testimony of a peasant woman as evidence of the "new horizons which opened to women's eyes. 'Women are tired of being behind, like the cart behind the horse. I understood that to make a difference I had to make a political choice.' "[60] Anita Lenza, a member of Catholic Action and CIF in Bologna, echoed these sentiments in her remembrance that there was "a general wish for renewal and change of the climate in which Italian women had been kept." What they actually would be able to do and how far and in what direction this new consciousness might take them are different matters.

Giovanna Petti Balbi, who interviewed numerous rural women for her study on the Resistance in Liguria, concludes that "for some, the experience of the Resistance remains an episode, an interlude in their lives."[61] More generally, throughout Italy there were also many women who saw the Resistance as the beginning of a new era. What remains to be considered is the degree of continuity or change in women's lives in the immediate postwar era.

No one can argue with the fact that the Second World War, and especially the period of the Resistance, had profound impact on the lives of most Italians, and certainly on the women who were connected to partisan activity. There were probably many women like Elsa Oliva, who remembers that it was in a Nazi interrogation that she was first called a rebel. "Well good, I told myself. I will always be a rebel; it is a word that I like."[62] If Oliva, and others, effectively resisted Nazi and Fascist oppression, did this rebellion have other results? Were there long-term, tangible, and even emotional results of this rebellion? The final chapter attempts to measure changes in "the relations between women and men, in their relative positions in society, and…in the social meanings of masculinity and femininity."[63] In turn, this assessment leads to more general conclusions about the connections between gender, war, and revolution.

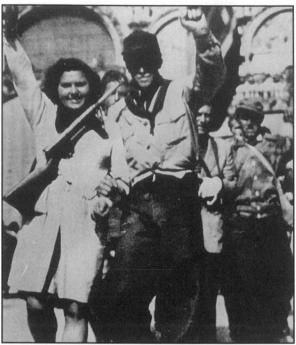

Partisans in Venezia
celebrate liberation.
Beltrami collection.

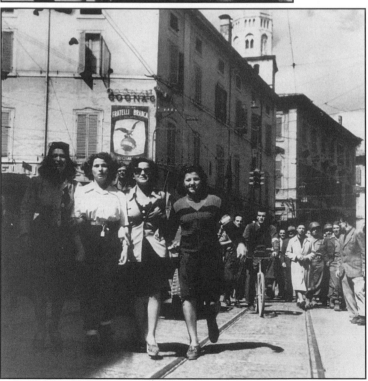

A fascist "collaborator" is captured and escorted by three *staffete,* Modena,
24 April 1945. Courtesy Still Photo Collection, National Archive.

# ■ 6 ■

# War and Resistance
# As Forces for Change:
# "Renewal and Tradition"

By the summer of 1945, Italian women could congratulate themselves on having helped to defeat fascism and to end the war. They could take pride in and even marvel at the unprecedented number of women who had engaged in political and military activities historically considered beyond the range of usual female experience. And they could look forward to exercising their newly won civic rights and responsibilities. But beyond the immediate elation and relief accompanying these "victories," what had Italian women won? What had changed in their lives? What factors remained the same?

Since the conclusion of World War II, women veterans of that conflict as well as scholars studying Italian women in the postwar era have drawn conclusions about the effects of the war and Resistance and described women's experience in the years following 1945. But they do not necessarily agree in their assessments. As noted at the beginning of this study, ex-partisan, Communist activist, and elected deputy Gina Borellini saw the Resistance as "the decisive moment in the process of female emancipation," while Nilde Jotti, also a former partisan and one of Italy's most prominent political women, asserted in 1964 that during the Resistance there was "the first grasp of collective consciousness by impressive new masses of women about their position and their responsibilities in the life of the nation."[1] In even stronger language, Aida Tiso, in her work on the Communist Party and the "woman question," argues that "the end of the war signaled the beginning of a new epoch for the country, an epoch in which traditional injustices, among these the problems of women, would be eliminated." Less enthusiastically, Daniela Colombo maintains that "since the end of World War II, one of the most important social changes in Italy has undoubtedly been the increasingly widespread trend among women toward individual autonomy and social impact."

In contrast, scholar Laura Conti says of women's participation in the Resistance: "It was not a fact of political maturity, a manifestation of political consciousness, but only a passionate explosion, a sadly angry adhesion to the choice of their men...to move and act and fight for others and not for themselves in history." Less critically, Maria Vittoria Ballestrero notes that in addition to female heroism, the Resistance also exalted "traditional female virtues—self-denial and the spirit of sacrifice....[Women were] glorified in words, but undervalued in fact." And finally, the conclusions of partisan and political activist Marisa Rodano bear repeating. She maintains that, although the Resistance provoked a sort of consciousness-raising among women, it was not necessarily the beginning of an inevitable march to emancipation.[2]

So how can we make sense of Resistance experience and reconcile these diverse judgments? Historian Franca Pieroni Bortolotti, who was active in the Communist Youth Front in Florence in 1944-45, believed that the activities, organizations, and people of the Resistance reflected the intertwining of "renewal and tradition."[3] Such a perspective has value, as it allows one to see both continuity and change, to consider different levels of social experience and time, and, above all, to recognize the diversity of women who fought in the Resistance. With these things in mind, it is possible to begin to determine the meanings and results of the Resistance. To do so involves a blending of descriptions of material conditions with those of personal opinions, attitudes, and images and the simultaneous use of participants' self-identities and feelings with the scholar's definitions and judgments based on hindsight.

## Postwar Economic and Social Conditions

At the outset, it is important to recognize that at the close of hostilities no one in Italy could afford to sit back and rest on their laurels. The Fascist regime was gone, but since it had built on basic structures in Italian society and integrated many traditional values, much of fascism still remained. Outright fighting was over, but now came the task of struggling to recover and rebuild in the face of massive destruction and disruption. Industrial and agricultural production was below prewar levels; dams, roads, bridges, and railroads had been blown up; and even as late as 1948 there were between 1.5 and 2.5 million people unemployed. All goods were scarce, and inflation was running wild; the price of bread rose from 12.34 to 96 lire per kilogram between 1944 and 1951; and the costs of milk and pasta increased by over 500 percent in the same time period. As scholar Donald Sassoon has concluded: "What one could have bought for 100 lire in 1938 would have required 858 lire in 1944, 2060 in 1945, 2884 in 1946 and 5159 in 1947."[4] Thus, most Italians experienced a worsening of material conditions as a result of the war.

## Table 6.1 – Price Index (Base 1913=1)

| Year | Wholesale Price Index | Consumer Price Index (Based on families of workers and employees in firms) |
|---|---|---|
| 1901-10 | .840 | .927 |
| 1911-20 | 2.434 | 1.714 |
| 1921-30 | 5.372 | 4.451 |
| 1931-40 | 4.134 | 3.996 |
| 1941-45 | 33.259 | 36.373 |
| 1946-50 | 228.030 | 191.320 |

Source: ISTAT, *Sommario di statistiche storiche dell'Italia (1861-1965)* (Rome, 1968), Table 87, p. 13.

## Table 6.2 – Male/Female Sex Ratios

| Year | Men/1000 Women |
|---|---|
| 1901 | 990 |
| 1911 | 967 |
| 1921 | 973 |
| 1931 | 957 |
| 1936 | 964 |
| 1951 | 949 |

Source: *Un secolo di statistiche italiane nord e sud, 1861-1961* (Rome: Svimez, 1961), Table 35, p. 26.

Beyond these concrete economic difficulties, what other measurable factors can be used to consider what impact the war and Resistance might have had? If we move forward in time into the period of reconstruction, and to 1951 when the next census was taken, in terms of employment, in that year, 20.2 percent of Italian women were working, constituting 25.19 percent of all those employed; these figures are only about two percentage points above the figures for 1931. The nature of women's work had not changed much either, as women were still concentrated in the service sector, and only in the area of public administration had the female component increased over the 1921 level.[5]

Other demographic characteristics for the postwar period are also revealing.[6] Women continued to outnumber men in postwar Italy, while life expectancies for both sexes rose significantly by 1960. Marriage rates fluctuated considerably, rising rapidly immediately at the close of the war, dropping to a postwar low in 1951, and then increasing gradually to exceed the rates of the

Fascist era. It is also of note that in 1951 a considerable proportion of females (20.8 percent) between the ages of eighteen and fifty-nine were either unmarried or widowed, and while divorce remained illegal, separation and annulment could be granted by the courts. Requests for such action were still relatively few for the total population, but they almost doubled between 1941 and 1947 and continued to grow in the next two decades. Given these factors and the overall economic conditions, it is not surprising that the birth rate continued to fall. In 1951, it was 18.48 per 1000, the lowest level since Italy became an independent and unified state, and even with an increase thereafter, reaching a postwar peak in the 1960s, the birth rate did not duplicate the prewar levels. Regional differences remained characteristic of Italy, where birth and marriage rates were lower and requests for marital separations higher in the northern and central zones than in the south.

## Table 6.3 – Requests for Marital Separation (Cases Decided)

| Year | Personal Separation | | Annulments | |
|------|---------|---------|---------|---------|
| | Request | Granted | Request | Granted |
| 1911-20 | 2499 | 1006 (40%) | 39 | 26 (67%) |
| 1921-30 | 5012 | 1375 (28%) | 75 | 53 (71%) |
| 1931-40 | 6093 | 1583 (26%) | 56 | 41 (73%) |
| 1946-50 | 11047 | 6288 (56%) | 91 | 73 (80%) |
| 1951-60 | 8434 | 4882 (58%) | 78 | 59 (76%) |

Source: ISTAT, *Sommario di statistiche storiche dell'Italia, 1861-1965* (Rome, 1968), Table 39, p. 52.

Economic crises, problems of survival, and the shift in some family responsibilities that had shaped the lives of Italian women in the interwar years were not eliminated with the cessation of hostilities. Many women still had to support themselves and their families, but opportunities for work remained limited. Consequently, one could argue that many chose to postpone childbearing until brighter economic prospects appeared on the horizon.

Desires for upward mobility through professional training and university education, which had been frustrated during the thirties, were not suddenly fulfilled in the forties or fifties. In 1951, 15.2 percent of women were illiterate (compared to 10.5% of men); this represents an appreciable improvement over the pre-Fascist era, in which 24 percent of males over the age of six and 30 percent of the females of the same ages could not read. However, regional differences remained striking, as in the early 1950s in the south, where at least 30 percent of the women could not write their names on their marriage certificates. It is also true that the percentage of female students in the universities grew from 9.3 percent in 1920-21 to 25.4 percent in 1948-49, but since that latter figure reflects only 42,000 women, this change did not have widespread impact. Women did receive training as teachers and constituted between 75 and 100 percent of kindergarten and elementary school faculty, but as late as 1961 only 1.6 percent of university professors were women. In 1951, while women were 51 percent of the total population, they constituted only 27% of professionals.[7] Assessment of these factors leads one to agree with Joanne Barkan that "even a decade and a half after liberation, the basic situation of women in Italy had not changed a great deal."[8]

## Table 6.4 – Women in Universities

| Year | Total Enrolled | Women % of Total | % of Women Eligible to Enroll (Estimate) |
|------|---------------|------------------|------------------------------------------|
| 1920-21 | 53,239 | 9.3% | 1.48% |
| 1930-31 | 46,262 | 13.3% | 1.13% |
| 1938-39 | 77,429 | 19.5% | 1.76% |
| 1945-46 | 189,665 | 25.0% | 4.26% |
| 1948-49 | 168,001 | 25.4% | 3.68% |

Source: ISTAT, *Annuario Statistico dell'Istruzione Italiane, 1948-49,* Table 171, p. 225.

## The Meaning of Equal Rights

It was in politics and the law that the greatest changes occurred during the course of the Resistance and immediately following. As indicated in Chapter 4, the new constitution contained provisions designed to ensure equality among all citizens; an equal rights clause, the extension of suffrage, and at least a limited concept of women's right to work were all part of the law of the land. The principle of equality that was adopted, however, was directed to the public sphere, as in private matters older power relations prevailed. The privileged position of the Catholic church was maintained, as the new constitution included an updated version of the Concordat arrived at by the church and the Fascist regime. A harmonious and stable family and socially acceptable, "natural" gender roles in many instances had the force of law.

The Christian family, which was a cornerstone of the new democratic state, "legitimized traditional roles of husband and wife and their duties to each other and their children."[9] Efforts to ensure equality of opportunity and treatment in the workplace were always affected by desires to provide special treatment for women so as not to disturb their familial and maternal functions. Family decisions regarding children, use of property and resources, and even place of residence were made by men, as a patriarchal hierarchy was reaffirmed in law. Laws on birth control and abortion, divorce, and even punishment for adultery remained unchanged and reflected older standards of private behavior and morality. Thus, in the public sphere, where a certain degree of equality was guaranteed, women had few realistic options, while in the private sphere they remained second-class citizens. Since the public and private spheres are connected, the contradictions in women's lives remained, and the possible transformations that the Resistance seemed to promise failed to occur.

## Women in the Political Parties

Participation in political parties, election to government offices, and the appearance of mass-based women's organizations represent some of the most significant changes for women when compared to the prewar situation. Most impressive were the parties' successful efforts to recruit women, which are reflected in membership figures. Through the mid-fifties women constituted between 25 and 26 percent of PCI membership, while, for the DC, figures fluctuated from about 25 percent in 1946 to a high of over 36 percent in 1954.[10] This was a far cry from the pre-Fascist era when women were a very small minority in all the political parties. Most parties continued to organize women separately in the postwar years, either in separate cells or through female branches, and maintained women's commissions or congresses to keep in touch with women and respond to their problems.

These successes were not unqualified, as organizational segregation served to isolate women and in neither the PCI nor the DC were membership figures reflected proportionately in leadership positions. Through the mid-fifties, PCI women were between 8 and 10 percent of the party directorate, while their showing in DC leadership was even lower, usually around 3 percent. As other studies of the parties in this period have concluded, "Politics was a man's business," and "throughout the 1950s and 1960s, the PCI addressed few issues of specific importance to women and offered minimal policy initiatives on women's behalf. Neither active recruitment of women into the party leadership nor promotion of the few female notables within the party occurred."[11]

The figures for women elected to the national government reflect a similar pattern: initial impressive gains but then a fairly rapid drop in both numbers and percentages so that by 1958 each party had only 10 women deputies, representing 7 percent of the PCI contingent and about 4 percent of that of the DC.[12] Mass-based electoral politics, the momentum of the Resistance, and the promise of rewarding those who had given so much to the effort briefly helped to propel women into public office, and for the women who had been pushing for civil equality for several decades this was a victory that represented at the least a shift in Italy's political culture. But power relations were not altered, and moderate sympathy for women and their issues did not expand into energetic efforts to change the faces of the parties and their programs. Women were still removed from equal activity and influence in the "universe of political discourse."

## Permanent Women's Organizations

The creation of mass-based women's organizations, UDI and CIF, was certainly one of the most important results of the Resistance. For the first time, significant numbers of women from all social groups were brought together in formal structures for the purpose of developing national solutions to their own problems. Through UDI, and to a slightly lesser degree CIF, women had the opportunity to discuss their own experiences, to gain political knowledge and skills, and collectively to have some impact on national policy-making. In the 1950s both UDI and CIF could count over 1 million members and supporters in affiliated organizations, but even with this mass base, their ability to change concretely the basic patterns of women's lives remained limited.

The problems and limitations that had characterized UDI as it developed before 1945 continued in the postwar years. In the first place, no matter how often UDI insisted it was an autonomous organization open to all women, the reality was that it became increasingly tied to the parties of the Left and was viewed by those parties, particularly the PCI, and by the general population, as their "transmission belt." Such a perception is understandable, given UDI's origins in the GDD, which were often founded and led by women from the Left and supported by that political tradition. Though it had grown out of spontaneous, grassroots activism, UDI became increasingly hierarchical in the immediate postwar period, particularly under the leadership of President M. Maddalena Rossi, who ruled "with an iron hand [and] held to her view that participation in UDI should be primarily an apprenticeship for party politics."[13] The close connections between the parties and the women's organizations are symbolized by the fact that the presidents of these organizations were also important party members. Both Rossi and CIF president Maria Federici had worked for their respective parties during the Resistance, represented them in the Constituent Assembly, and then were elected to the first national government.

The issue of autonomy did not die out completely, and eventually, by the late fifties, it emerged as a major point of controversy within the organizations. During the Resistance, women's organizations had envisioned emancipation in the worlds of work and politics while accepting women's private roles and responsibilities, and gender questions that were either divisive or controversial were side-stepped or ignored. This stance continued in the postwar years, and, in fact, UDI became more and more conservative. At least until the mid-fifties, the agendas of both CIF and UDI appeared driven by PCI and DC interests rather than being focused on women's issues.[14]

## The Responses of "Political" Women

As a result of the Resistance, Italian women had the opportunity to enter the sphere of public politics and to become protagonists in unprecedented ways.[15]

However, the women who could and did take advantage of these opportunities were still few in number; of the women in the sample, only 63 (7 percent of the total) were identified as holding party, labor union, or government office after 1945. Most women leaders had been politically conscious and active before 1943. Karen Beckwith describes "a pattern typical of many female deputies on the left":

> (1) initial political involvement through women's organizations or women's sections of a political party, followed by (2) a period of partisan activity under Fascism...,followed by (3) activism in founding UDI, and culminating in (4) a seat in Parliament.[16]

If one considers Christian Democratic women such as Maria Federici, Angela Cingolani Guidi, Maria Jervolino, and Tina Anselmi, the same pattern holds true. In fact, in many ways these women had more in common with their male comrades than they did with the majority of women. A study of Italian deputies in the postwar decades found that "those on the left joined a political party by age twenty-one and were influenced by 'their reaction to fascism, the resistance and the promise of a bright future.' "[17] These factors would hold true for both men and women.

At the same time, being "like men" created particular problems for the political women like Luciana Viviani, partisan and deputy after 1948, who spoke of living "schizophrenically," behaving like a good Communist but being judged on whether she was a good wife and mother. Others felt similar contradictions. Anita Pasquali, from a partisan family in Verona, joined the PCI at the end of the war at the age of 15 and later worked for UDI and in the municipal government in Rome. She comments that working to organize women and struggling for equality developed consciousness and solidarity among the women but brought with it

> complete sublimation of all of our reality as women. We, and the Party, lacked any analysis of the connection between private and public....Our private lives had to adapt rigorously to the male model....I felt a revolt inside me...but tried to keep calm thinking [that when the Socialist revolution came] women's conditions would be changed and our private lives also would be liberated.[18]

Finally, Giuliana Dall Pozzo, another longtime PCI activist and director of *Noi Donne* for many years, concludes, "I am from a generation in which theory sacrificed private life, and all my life has been a difficult balance between my life as a woman and my obligations. I have to say that among communist women there was a myth of competency, of placing any personal issues in the background." Many women chose not to live a "split" life, and like Laura Ingrao, whose husband Pietro Ingrao was an important PCI leader, did not pursue public office after the war because "apart from having five children, which requires a certain amount of work, I have always taught, and it would have been a little too much to be a deputy as well. [Having two politicians in the house] would be a bit strange. He is a deputy, she a senator; she is a senator, he a deputy. That is not something that appeals to me."[19]

In postwar Italy, as scholar Yasmine Ergas has pointed out, civil equality co-existed with social inequality. For women, this created contradictions and tensions between their importance as wives and mothers and their value in politics and the workplace. Ergas argues that in a strange way, "equality erases identity," and women could choose between integrating into the public world, which meant assimilation, or continuing to operate in a private world, which, though marginal, also provided a clear female identity.[20]

During the Resistance, activist women experienced unprecedented autonomy and influence and saw a bright future in political and legal terms. Simultaneously, their lives, like those of most Italian women, continued to be constrained by a traditional sex/gender system that defined the worlds of work, marriage, home, and family. The "elite" of visible, active women were touched by these forces and thus, in some sense, were typical of all women. It is interesting to consider the maiden speeches of Communist Rina Picolato and DC member Angela Cingolani in the 1945 Consultative Assembly. Their texts differed little, and while insisting that they did not want to be treated as "the weaker and gentle sex, objects of formal gallantry," they also stressed that women's interests were in "home, family, childhood, physical and moral education, and instruction of young people."[21] What made them different from their less active sisters was how they chose to represent and further those interests. They certainly would not have agreed with the results of a 1951 poll by the DOXA Institute that asked Italian women whether they should have precise political opinions and join a party. Fifty-two percent of the respondents thought it better if women had no interest in politics.[22]

Women leaders, even as they might understand such attitudes and be aware of the contradictions in their own lives, could also express frustration with the status quo and annoyance at the values and expectations of "rank-and-file" women. In 1953, Ada Gobetti provided a caustic judgment of the goals and values modern women were encouraged to adopt. "[What are their ideals?] To catch a man who offers them substantial gifts, who has a secure position, and a car, possibly not Italian....Then they need to make him marry them...and to reach that noble goal any means are good: deceit, falsehoods and lies."[23] At the same moment, Communist educator, intellectual, and union leader Dina Jovine regretted all the emphasis in the women's press on female virtue: "The fundamental characteristic of that virtue is passivity: the obedient daughter, sister, wife and even the mother who, confronting the problems of educating her children, is incapable of initiative."

Italian society during the years of the war and Resistance was destabilized enough to open doors to some women, but when the conflict was over, return to a patriarchal order occurred quite quickly. Though a few "uncommon" women made it through the doors of politics, they continued to have to do battle with the social boundaries common to their gender, and their consciousness, ambivalent or contradictory as it sometimes was, was insufficient to bring about a revolution.

The messages women had been hearing for decades continued to be forcefully articulated, especially in women's magazines such as *Grazia,* which, in 1950, featured articles that encouraged husbands "to dedicate some of your time to 'form' [women politically]," or reported on women scientists who, though not interested in fashion, were "women like you…who don't sacrifice their own femininity." In 1951, *Gioia* argued that "the women who stay at home are the happiest. Only unhappy women look for a job outside the home in order to try to find distraction."[24] And woe to the woman who separated from her husband or even tried to find care for her children outside her home. As one woman remembers, she was thought to be "incapable of adapting to a normal role and as such a failure, she was finished."[25] In the postwar era, few women, "common or uncommon," had found the emotional and ideological weapons, or the material resources, to confront and successfully challenge this powerful credo.

# Conclusion

As women acted publicly and collectively, their goals were most often practical ones, determined by immediate material needs and problems rather than by analysis of fundamental factors leading to women's subordination and by development of openly alternative forms of social relations. Because fascism had been the common enemy, and unity had been required to defeat the regime and to end the war, women's problems received little attention, and potentially divisive sex-related issues were never brought to the fore. Though for a brief time, many of women's domestic functions that sustained human life took on political meaning, the functions themselves and basic divisions of labor were not transformed by rhetoric that labelled them "patriotic." It seems clear that successful political and military rebellions often do not permanently alter basic material conditions; nor do they automatically produce fundamental social change. The most oppressive of regimes, in this case fascism, provoked violent and radical reactions and resistance, but focus on the struggle itself allowed little time to discuss and unmask basic causes for gender inequality. Certainly, tsarist tyrannies, military despotism, and Fascist dictatorships must be blamed for oppression and exploitation, but because active opposition is so dangerous and intense, it is difficult to see beyond the regime to long-term social forces that create inequities. As Leslie Rabine has argued, "No single, central struggle against a totalized adversary could by itself overturn the old order and cause a dialectical transformation into a new one."[26]

The Italian case also makes it clear that the impact and effectiveness of female networks and communities, women's mobilization, and the development of feminist consciousness are shaped by men's interests and priorities and general structures of political power. The radical potential that had characterized certain factions of the Resistance was dissipated as parties of the Left modified revolutionary goals in favor of moderate and pragmatic political agendas and a focus on electoral victory and parliamentary cooperation. Though female activism forced leaders to include women in their broader political strategies, Italian women had little chance to disrupt political and social hegemony, and their autonomy and self-determination were increasingly limited by others' agendas, as the histories of UDI and CIF illustrate.

Political revolutions and resistance may offer women the opportunity to act collectively, to acquire skills and an awareness of basic human rights, and concepts of social justice. During wartime, individual women may well gain a sense of their own competence and of their ability to perform like men, as the personal accounts provided in this volume illustrate. At least in the eyes of some of the participants, war did produce a momentary egalitarianism, a sort of androgyny. It may be true, as a World War I rhyme put it, that "Girls are doing things / They've never done before....All the world is topsy / turvy / Since the War began."[27] But battlefield experiences, of whatever kind, do not translate automatically into political consciousness, permanent political strategies, or tangible changes in women's status in a civilian world. Transformation of gender structures is rarely the focus or result of wars of "liberation."

The example of the Italian Resistance illustrates the fact that women's participation is an important component of revolutionary struggles, but what this means is less clear. In the Italian case, the goal of equality was defined as participation in politics and modeled on men's rights and responsibilities. Simultaneously, gender differences were accentuated, and functions and attributes associated with women were acknowledged and even exalted. Because these characteristics were described as "natural," ahistorical, and even absolute, they inevitably posed major obstacles to change and became the mechanisms to put women in "their place" once again. As we have seen, it was very difficult for women to claim authority and power in either public or private arenas. But there was one place where they were sovereign—in their own memories of their Resistance experience.

Anna Bravo, who conducted interviews with Italian women survivors of Nazi concentration camps, found that "the events which brought such a radical break in these people's lives became paradoxically the thread which lends continuity to their memory, and the core around which their sense of self is rebuilt; whatever else they may become, they will always be survivors."[28] Similarly, many Resistance women would always be partisans, or even "rebels," and they would not forget that "in those past days they were able, however partially and briefly, to break their chains."[29] This volume rests on their memories and is testament to the fact that, eventually, the women of the Resistance in Italy began to write their own histories, to set the record straight, and, in this fashion, provided crucial points of reference for future generations who would grapple with the meaning of freedom and seek to devise strategies for human liberation.

# NOTES

## Introduction

1. Giovanna Zangrandi, *I giorni veri*, 1943-45 (Milan: Mondadori Editore, 1963), p. 213. Bruna Betti's testimony, which follows, is from an interview in Massimo Papini (ed.), *La donna e la Resistenza nell'anconetano* (Ancona: Tipografia Artigiana, 1987), pp. 106-7.

2. Zangrandi, *I giorni veri*, p. 183; Cinnani's experience is cited in Claudio Pavone, *Una guerra civile; Saggio storico sulla moralitá nella Resistenza* (Turin: Bollati Boringhieri Editore, 1991), p. 544.

3. Joan Scott, "Introduction" to Margaret R. Higonnet, et al. (eds.), *Behind the Lines: Gender and the Two World Wars* (New Haven: Yale University Press, 1987), pp. 4, 6.

4. Franca Pieroni Bortolotti, *Le donne della Resistenza antifascista e la questione femminile in Emilia Romagna, 1943-1945* (Milan: Vangelista, 1978), p. 64.

5. Gina Borellini, "Discorso d'apertura," Convegno "Donne e Resistenza," 13-15 May 1977 (Unpublished paper in Union of Italian Women [UDI] archives).

6. Temma Kaplan, "Female Consciousness and Collective Actions: The Case of Barcelona, 1910-18," *Signs* 7:3 (Spring 1982), p. 551.

7. Ethel Klein, *Gender Politics: From Consciousness to Mass Politics* (Cambridge, MA: Harvard University Press, 1984), p. 86.

8. Maxine Molyneux, "Mobilization without Emancipation? Women's Interests, the State and Revolution in Nicaragua," *Feminist Studies* 11:2 (Summer 1985), p. 228. An excellent study of politicizing motherhood is Marguerite Guzman Bouvard, *Revolutionizing Motherhood: The Mothers of the Plaza de Mayo* (Wilmington, DE: Scholarly Resources, 1994).

9. Mary Katzenstein points to the need to consider the less visible or orthodox ways in which women pursue their agendas. See "Introduction" to Katzenstein and Carol M. Mueller (eds.), *The Women's Movements of the U.S. and Western Europe* (Philadelphia: Temple University Press, 1987), p. 3. Anna Bravo and Anna Maria Bruzzone, *In guerra senza armi: Storie di donne, 1940-45* (Bari: Laterza, 1995), pp. 15-16, 20 argue that we need to reconsider what "resistance" means, and that military action (usually male) should not be privileged over civil activity (more likely female).

10. Drude Dahlerup, "Overcoming the Barriers: An Approach to How Women's Issues Are Kept from the Political Agenda," in Judith Hicks Stiehm (ed.), *Women's Views of the Political World of Men* (Dobbs Ferry, NY: Transnational Publishers, 1984), p. 33.

11. The relationships between women's organizations and political institutions and state structures are described in detail in Katzenstein and Mueller (eds.), *The Women's Movements*; Janet Saltzman Chafetz and Anthony Dworkin, *Female Revolt: Women's Movements in World and Historical Perspective* (Totowa, NJ: Rowman and Allenheld, 1986); Sylvia Bashevkin (ed.), *Women and Politics in Western Europe* (London: Frank Cass and Co., 1985); Sharon Wolchik and Alfred Meyers (eds.), *Women, State and Party in Eastern Europe* (Durham, NC: Duke University Press, 1985).

12. See, for example, Rosalind Delmar, "What Is Feminism?" in Juliet Mitchell and Ann Oakley (eds.), *What Is Feminism?* (New York: Pantheon, 1986), p. 11.

13. Maxine Molyneux, "Mobilization without Emancipation?," pp. 232-33.

14. Klein, *Gender Politics*, pp. 3, 101. Molyneux, "Mobilization without Emancipation?," p. 231 and Dahlerup, "Overcoming the Barriers," pp. 42-43 also discuss the importance of causal explanations.

15. Anna Maria Bruzzone and Rachele Farina, *La Resistenza taciuta* (Milan: LaPietra, 1976), p. 12.

16. Pavone, *Una guerra civile*, p. 29.

17. Nancy Cott, "Feminist Theory and Feminist Movements: The Past Before Us," in Mitchell and Oakley (eds.), *What Is Feminism?*, p. 59.

18. Ibid., p. 50.

19. Estelle Freedman, "Separatism as Strategy: Female Institution Building and American Feminism, 1870-1930," *Feminist Studies* 5:3 (Fall 1979), pp. 512-29 and Kathryn Kish Sklar, "Hull House in the 1890's: A Community of Women Reformers," *Signs* 10:4 (1985), pp. 658-77 both discuss these issues in an earlier historic context. The fact that contemporary Italian feminists refer to isolation in traditional parties as "ghettoization" is referred to in Karen Beckwith and Jane Slaughter, "The Italian Communist Party: The Position of Women as an Index for Measuring Theoretical and Practical Change" (Unpublished paper, 1980), p. 10.

# Chapter 1

1. Historian Emilio Gentile suggests that "fascism can be placed within the historical framework of the chronological and geographical limits of Europe between the two world wars." "Fascism in Italian Historiography. In Search of an Individual Historical Identity," *Journal of Contemporary History* 21 (1986), pp. 183, 199.

2. George L. Mosse, *Nationalism and Sexuality: Respectability and Abnormal Sexuality in Modern Europe* (New York: Howard Fertig, 1985), pp. 130-31.

3. The following are most helpful for discussions of women's status in Europe in the interwar years. Renate Bridenthal, Atina Grossman, and Marion Kaplan (eds.), *When Biology Became Destiny: Women in Weimar and Nazi Germany* (New York: Monthly Review Press, 1984); Renate Bridenthal, "Something Old, Something New: Women Between Two World Wars," in R. Bridenthal, Claudia Koonz, and Susan Stuard (eds.), *Becoming Visible: Women in European History* (Boston: Houghton Mifflin, 1987), pp. 473-97; Atina Grossman, "The New Woman and the Rationalization of Sexuality in Weimar Germany," in Ann Snitow, et al. (eds.), *Powers of Desire* (New York: Monthly Review Press, 1983), pp. 153-75; L. Coveney, et al. (eds.), *The Sexuality Papers* (London: Hutchinson and Co., 1984); Judith Friedlander et al. (eds.), *Women in Culture and Politics* (Bloomington: Indiana University Press, 1986); Barbara Brookes, "The Illegal Operation: Abortion, 1919-39," and Sheila Jeffreys, "Sex Reform and Feminism in the 1920's," in London Feminist History Group (eds.), *The Sexual Dynamics of History* (London: Pluto Press, 1983); Bonnie Smith, "The New Woman," Chapter 8 in *Changing Lives* (Lexington, MA: D. C. Heath, 1989), pp. 317-63.

4. Bridenthal, Grossman, and Kaplan, "Introduction" to *When Biology Became Destiny*, p. 10.

5. Susan Kent, "Gender Reconstruction After the First World War," in Harold L. Smith (ed.), *British Feminism in the Twentieth Century* (Amherst: University of Massachusetts Press, 1990), p. 71, and B. Smith, *Changing Lives*, p. 435.

6. For France, see B. Smith, *Changing Lives*, pp. 398-99; for Britain, Martin Pugh, "Domesticity and the Decline of Feminism, 1930-50," in H. Smith (ed.), *British Feminism in the Twentieth Century*,

pp. 149, 158. For these patterns across Europe, see Bonnie S. Anderson and Judith P. Zinsser, *A History of Their Own*, Vol. II (New York: Harper and Row, 1989), pp. 207-16.

7. Lesley Caldwell, "Reproducers of the Nation: Women and the Family in Fascist Policy," in David Forgacs (ed.), *Rethinking Fascism: Capitalism, Populism and Culture* (London: Lawrence and Wishart, 1986), pp. 110-11.

8. Mosse, *Nationalism and Sexuality*, pp. 160, 180, and Bridenthal, Grossman, and Kaplan, *When Biology Became Destiny*, p. xii.

9. Stein Larsen, et al., *Who Were the Fascists?*, quoted by Stanley Payne in "The Concept of Fascism," New York *Review of Books* (3 March 1983), p. 14, and Mosse, *Nationalism and Sexuality*, p. 176.

10. See Barbara Jancar-Webster, *Women and Revolution in Yugoslavia, 1941-45* (Denver: Arden Press, 1990).

11. Alexander De Grand, *Italian Fascism: Its Origins and Development* (University of Nebraska, 1982), p. 63. This is probably the most lucid summary of fascism in Italy and is recommended reading as general background for the period.

12. Ibid., pp. 32-33.

13. Alexander De Grand, "March on Rome," in Frank J. Coppa (ed.), *Dictionary of Modern Italian History* (Westport, CT: Greenwood Press, 1985), p. 256.

14. Victoria De Grazia, *How Fascism Ruled Women* (Berkeley: University of California Press, 1992), pp. 2, 8-9.

15. De Grand, *Italian Fascism*, p. 78.

16. Victoria De Grazia, *The Culture of Consent: Mass Organization of Leisure in Fascist Italy* convincingly illustrates this process (Cambridge University Press, 1981).

17. The best work on the early Fascist women is that by Denise Detragiache, "Il fascismo femminile da San Sepolcro all'affare Matteotti (1919-1924)," *Storia contemporanea* (April 1983), pp. 211-51; for an excellent discussion of the literature on women's involvement in the movement and of Fascist organizations and women, see Maria Fraddosio, "Le donne e il fascismo: Ricerche e problemi di interpretazione," *Storia contemporanea* (February 1986), pp. 95-135.

18. Annamaria Galoppini, *Il lungo viaggio verso la parità: I diritti civili e politici delle donne dall'Unità ad oggi* (Bologna: Zanichelli, 1980), pp. 89-90.

19. For discussion of the Fasci Femminili see Victoria De Grazia, "Fasci Femminili," in Philip V. Cannistraro (ed.), *Historical Dictionary of Fascist Italy* (Westport, CT: Greenwood Press, 1982), pp. 202-4; Claudia Koonz, "The Fascist Solution to the Woman Question in Italy and Germany," in Bridenthal, et al. (eds.), *Becoming Visible*, pp. 504-8; and Maria Antonietta Macciocchi, *La donna "nera"* (Milan: Feltrinelli, 1976), pp. 88-94.

20. Franca Pieroni Bortolotti, "Femminismo e socialismo dal 1900 al primo dopoguerra," *Critica Storica* 8 (31 January 1969), p. 51; Judith Adler Hellman, "The Italian Communists, the Women's Question, and the Challenge of Feminism," *Studies in Political Economy* 13 (1983), pp. 58-59.

21. Teresa Noce, *Rivoluzionaria professionale* (Milan: La Pietra, 1974), p. 43.

22. Mosse, *Nationalism and Sexuality*, p. 185. Hellman, "The Italian Communists, the Women's Question, and the Challenge of Feminism," pp. 60-61, describes discussions of and controversies surrounding the "woman question" in the PCI in these years.

23. Cited in Nadia Spano and Fiamma Camarlinghi, *La questione femminile nella politica del PCI, 1921-1963* (Rome: Editore Donne e Politica, 1972), pp. 21, 38.

24. For general discussion of the Socialist and Communist parties in these years, see Franca Pieroni Bortolotti, *Socialismo e questione femminile in Italia, 1892-1922* (Milan: Mazzotta, 1974); Claire LaVigna, "The Marxist Ambivalence Toward Women: Between Socialism and Feminism in the Italian Socialist Party," in Marilyn Boxer and Jean Quataert (eds.), *Socialist Women* (New York: Elsevier, 1978); Partito Comunista d'Italia. Secondo Congresso Nazionale, Roma, 20-24 Marzo 1922. Relazione del Comitato Centrale, in *Il primo anno di vita del Partito Comunista d'Italia. Strumenti di lavoro. Archivi del movimento operaio*, No. 9 (June 1966), mimeograph, Milan; Camilla Ravera, "Come nacque nel PCI una politica per l'emancipazione femminile," *Donne e politica* 2 (February 1971), pp. 5-11; and Spano and Camarlinghi, *La questione femminile*.

25. Francesco Maria Cecchini (ed.), *Il femminismo cristiano: La questione femminile nella prima democrazia cristiana, 1898-1912* (Rome: Riuniti, 1979), pp. 128-30.

26. For the early organizations, see Francesco Traniello and Giorgio Campanini (eds.), *Dizionario storico del movimento cattolico in Italia, 1860-1980,* 2 Vols. (Turin: Marietti, 1981); Paola Gaiotti de Biase, *Le origini del movimento cattolico femminile* (Brescia: Morcelliana, 1963); and for Coari's "Programma minima femminista, 1907," see Cecchini, *Il femminismo cristiano*, pp. 188-96.

27. Traniello and Campanini, *Dizionario storico,* II, pp. 188-96.

28. Elisa A. Carrillo, "Christian Democracy," in Edward Tannenbaum and Emiliana Noether (eds.), *Modern Italy: A Topical History Since 1861* (New York: NYU Press, 1974), p. 81. Marina Ceratto, *Il "Chi é" delle donne Italiane, 1945-81* (Milan: Mondadori, 1982), pp. 145, 320 and Marina Addis Saba, "Rappresentanza e non-questione femminile alla Consulta Nazionale," *Storia e problemi contemporanei* 2:4 (July-December 1989), p. 23 discuss Cingolani Guidi.

29. "Il lavoro tra le donne," *Bollettino del PCI* (January 1931), pp. 8, 9.

30. Noce, *Rivoluzionaria professionale*, p. 46.

31. Gualdi quoted in Ilva Vaccari, *La donna nel ventennio fascista, 1919-43* (Milan: Vangelista, 1978), pp. 196-97.

32. Estella [Teresa Noce], "Il Congresso mondiale delle donne contra la guerra e il fascismo," *Lo stato operaio* 8:8 (August 1934), p. 603.

33. From an article in *Compagna; Giornale delle donne lavoratrice* (1936), reprinted in *Il prezzo della libertá* (Rome: Associazione Nazionale Perseguitati Politici Italiani, 1958), p. 169. Among Noce's articles are "La religione non deve impedire l'unione di tutti gli sfruttati" (PCdI pamphlet, Paris 1932) and "In prima fila le lavoratrici per il pane ed il lavoro!" (PCdI pamphlet, Paris 1931).

34. Traniello and Campanini, *Dizionario storico,* II, pp. 359-61, and Charles Delzell, "Catholics in the Italian Armed Resistance," *The Italian Quarterly* (Winter 1983), pp. 59-60.

35. *Enciclopedia dell'antifascismo e della Resistenza,* Vol. 1 (Milan: La Pietra, 1968), p. 557, and *Noi Donne,* No. 1 (31 September 1945), p. 2. The history of this movement is well documented in Carlo Felice Casula, "Il movimento dei cattolici comunisti e la Resistenza a Roma," *Il Movimento di Liberazione in Italia* (October 1973), pp. 37-68.

36. De Grand, *Italian Fascism,* p. 76; S. Portaccio, "La donna nella stampa popolare cattolica: *Famiglia Cristiana,* 1931-45," *Italia Contemporanea* 143 (June 1981), pp. 65-67 argues that Catholic anti-feminism did not need Fascist anti-woman theory and that the church used Fascist political and cultural conditions to pursue its own agenda and goals. Though information on the women's groups is limited, see Ilva Vaccari, *La donna nel ventennio fascista,* (1919-1943) (Milan: Vangelista, 1978), pp. 114-15; De Grazia, *How Fascism Ruled Women,* pp. 243-46, and Gianfranco Poggi (ed.), *L'organizzazione partitica del PCI e del DC* (Bologna: Il Mulino, 1968), p. 417.

37. Cecilia Dau Novelli, "'Daremo sei millioni di voti' Il Movimento delle donne cattoliche nei primi anni della Repubblica," *Memoria*, No. 21 (1987), pp. 51-52.

38. Ibid., p. 49 from a 1984 interview with Micelli.

39. Luisa Passerini, "Oral Memory of Fascism," in David Forgacs (ed.), *Rethinking Fascism* (London: Lawrence and Wishart, 1986), p. 195. An excellent discussion of this issue is found in Dianella Gagliana, et al., "Culture popolari negli anni del fascism," *Italia contemporanea* 157 (December 1984), pp. 63-90.

40. Steven White, "Italian Popular Education Between Fascism and Democracy, 1943-1954" (Dissertation, University of Virginia, 1985), p. 48.

41. ISTAT, *Sommaria di statistiche storiche dell'Italia, 1861-1965* (Rome, 1968), Table 4, p. 13 indicates that in 1931 66.5 percent of the male population was listed as active, dropping to 65.6 percent in 1936. In those same years, the female population active remained at about 25 percent, the major drop having occurred after 1921 when the figure was 27.6 percent. For a discussion of state control over labor and attempts to compensate for wage losses through fringe benefits, see De Grand, *Italian Fascism,* pp. 66, 111, and De Grazia, *The Culture of Consent,* pp. 52-53.

42. *Cento anni di vita nazionale attraverso le statistiche delle regione* (Rome: Svimez, 1961), Table 8, pp. 10-13, and De Grand, *Italian Fascism,* p. 67. For a detailed discussion of one area's immigration patterns and their effects, see Comitato per la Celebrazioni del XXX della Resistenza, *La*

*Resistenza nelle campagne modenesi* (Modena: Quaderni dell'Istituto Storico della Resistenza, 1976), pp. 149-56.

43. For the statistics and demographic data that follow, see ISTAT (Istituto Centrale di Statistica), *VI (Sesto) Censimento della populazione del Regno d'Italia al 1 dicember 1921. Relazione generale,* 2 Vols., reprint (Rome: Stabilimento Poligrafico, 1928); ISTAT, *VII Censimento generale della populazione. 21 Aprile 1931 IX. Relazione generale,* Vol. IV, Parte Seconda, and *Indagine sulla fecondità della donna,* Vol. VI (Rome: Istituto Poligrafico della Stato, 1935); *Un secolo di statistiche italiane, Nord e Sud, 1861-1961* (Rome: Svimez, 1951); and *Cento anni di vita nazionale attraverso le statistiche delle regione* (Rome: Svimez, 1961). Although both the 1921 and the 1931 census records are flawed, they can be used for their qualitative remarks and corrected by use of data from later publications.

44. ISTAT, VII *Censimento. Indagine sulla fecondità,* Vol. VI, especially pp. 18-38.

45. Antonio Santini, "Cicli economici e fluttuazioni demografiche: Nuzialitá e natalitá in Italia, 1863-1964," *Quaderni storici* 17 (May/August 1971), p. 569.

46. Macciocchi, *La donna "nera,"* p. 46; article cited by Laura Lilli, "La stampa femminile," in Paolo Murialdi, Nicola Tranfaglia, et al. (eds.), *La stampa italiana del neocapitalismo* (Bari: Laterza, 1976).

47. "Tu é gioiosa per l'Italia Imperiale," *Gioia* (23 May 1937), p. 2.

48. De Grazia, *How Fascism Ruled Women,* p. 77. For a full discussion of the contradictory Fascist "discourses" and theories regarding women, see Robin Pickering-Iazzi (ed.), *Mothers of Invention: Women, Italian Fascism and Culture* (Minneapolis: University of Minnesota Press, 1995).

49. De Grazia, Ibid., p. 168. Chapter 6 of that work fully discusses the complexities of women in the work force.

50. Claudia Koonz, "The Fascist Solution to the Woman Question," pp. 511.

51. Alexander De Grand, "Women Under Italian Fascism," *The Historical Journal* 19:4 (December 1976), p. 962. For discussion of the National Foundation for Maternity and Infancy (ONMI), see Vaccari, *La donna nel ventennio fascista,* pp. 95-99. For discussion of incentives and punishments, see as well Lesley Caldwell, "Reproducers of the Nation," pp. 117-19, 121-33; and Claudia Koonz, "The Fascist Solution to the Woman Question," pp. 510-11.

52. See Santini, "Cicli economici e fluttuazioni demografiche," pp. 555-86, and Koonz, "The Fascist Solution to the Woman Question," p. 512, fn. 19.

53. Emiliana Noether, "Italian Women and Fascism: A Reevaluation," *Italian Quarterly* 23 (Fall 1982), p. 73.

54. ISTAT, *Sommario statistico delle regione d'Italia* (Rome: n.p., 1947), tables on pp. 54, 76, 119, 130, and 65, respectively.

55. Vaccari, *La donna nel ventennio fascista,* p. 130, and Francesca Bettio, *The Sexual Division of Labour* (Oxford University Press, 1988), pp. 117-18. Excellent detail on all the dimensions of women's work experience in these years can be found in Perry Willson, *The Clockwork Factory* (Clarendon-Oxford Press, 1993).

56. De Grand, *Italian Fascism,* p. 111.

57. De Grazia, *The Culture of Consent,* pp. 4, 5, 16, discusses the attempt to balance costs of the regime with benefits for the people, especially through *dopolavoro* (leisure-time) recreational circles.

58. Stefania Bartolini, "Il fascismo femminile e la sua stampa: la 'Rassegna Femminile Italiana' (1925-30)," *Nuova donnawomanfemme* 21 (1982), pp. 153, 166-67. The fate of an elite, intellectual women's organization is discussed by E. Scaramuzza, "Professioni intellettuali e fascismo: L'ambivalenza della Alleanza Muliebre Culturale Italiane," *Italia contemporanea* (September 1983), pp. 111-33. For other aspects of women's politics and social activism, see De Grazia, *How Fascism Ruled Women,* pp. 262-71.

59. Richard J. Wolff, "'Fascitizing' Italian Youth: The Limits of Mussolini's Educational System," *History of Education* 13:4 (1984), p. 288; Nadia Forloni and Floriana Cantarelli, "La donna nella scuola," in Partito Socialista Italiano, *La donna in cinquant'anni di lotte socialiste, 1924-74* (Milan: Circolo De Amicis, November 1974), pp. 72-75; and Tracy Koon, *Believe, Obey, Fight: Political Socialization of Youth in Fascist Italy, 1922-1943* (Chapel Hill: University of North Carolina Press, 1985), pp. 176-77.

60. Koonz, "The Fascist Solution to the Woman Question," p. 507. Fascism's diverse impact on young women is cogently explained in Chapter 6, "Growing Up," pp. 116-65, in De Grazia, *How Fascism Ruled Women.*

61. Vaccari, *La donna nel ventennio fascista*, pp. 164-89 provides details of these protests while additional records of the actions can be found in Roberto Finzi, *La unitá operaia control il fascismo* (Bologna: Consorzio Provinciale Pubblica Lettura, 1974); Luciano Bergonzini, *La Resistenza a Bologna*, 5 Vols. (Bologna: Istituto per la Storia di Bologna, 1967), especially Vol. III; and Paris Tassinari, "Settemila a fianco dei 'ribelli' di Bulow," in *Donne emiliane nella Resistenza* Special Edition, *Quaderni de "La Lotta,"* No. 3 (Bologna: 1964). Perry Willson describes anti-fascism in the factory in *The Clockwork Factory*, pp. 222-25.

62. See Susan Zuccotti, *The Italians and the Holocaust* (New York: Basic Books, 1987), pp. 30-36 for the growth of anti-Semitism, and pp. 36-41 for the racial laws.

63. Raimondo Luraghi, "Dal 25 luglio all'8 settembre," and Vincenza Baldazzi, "L'8 settembre a Roma," both in Franco Antonicelli (ed.), *Trent'anni di storia italiana, 1915-1945: Dall'antifascismo alla Resistenza* (Turin: Einaudi Editore, 1961), pp. 294-95, 318. Good detail on cost of living and wages in the period 1920-1945 can be found in ISTAT, *Sommario di statistiche, 1886-1965,* Table 93, p. 119; and in Claudio Dellavalle, "La classe operaia piemontesi nella guerra di liberazione," in Aldo Agosti and Gian Mario Bravo (eds.), *Storia del movimento operaio del socialismo e delle lotte sociali in Piemonte,* Vol. III (Bari: De Donato, 1979-81), pp. 305-62.

64. Examples from *Annabella* include "Donne Italiane in Linea" (11 June 1940), p. 9, and "Le donne possono vincere la guerra" (25 June 1940), p. 9. The latter became a regular column, but, interestingly enough, by 1944 there is almost no mention of the war in the magazine.

65. Luraghi, "Dal 25 luglio all'8 settembre," pp. 295-96.

66. Mario Lizzero, "Virginia Tonelli 'Luisa' partigiana," *Quaderni della Resistenza* 1 (Comitato Regionale dell'ANPI del Fruili-Venezia Giulia, 1972), p. 75.

67. De Grand, *Italian Fascism*, p. 126.

68. De Grazia, *How Fascism Ruled Women*, p. 275.

# Chapter 2

1. For coverage of these general political developments, see S.J. Woolf (ed.), *The Rebirth of Italy, 1943-50* (London: Longman, 1972); and James Edward Miller, *The United States and Italy, 1940-1950* (Chapel Hill: The University of North Carolina Press, 1986).

2. Alexander De Grand, *The Italian Left in the Twentieth Century* (Bloomington: Indiana University Press, 1989), p. 85.

3. Marisa Diena, *Guerriglia e autogoverno: Brigate Garibaldi nel Piemonte Occidentale, 1943-45* (Parma: Guanda, 1970), pp. 31-32.

4. Benedetto Dalmastro, "L'organizzazione delle bande partigiane," in Franco Antonicelli (ed.), *Trent'anni di storia italiana, 1915-1945: Dall'antifascismo all Resistenza* (Turin: Einaudi Editore, 1961), p. 355. Claudio Pavone, *Una guerra civile* discusses how the bands became institutionalized, and the importance of the leaders in establishing the political character of the units, pp. 124-68, 152-54.

5. The GAP (Gruppi di Azione Patriottica) were small, fairly exclusive and completely clandestine assault and sabotage groups, generally under Communist direction but also affiliated with the Pd'A. The SAP are harder to describe. Defined as Squadre d'Azione Patriottica (Patriotic Action Squads) by most, a January 1945 issue of *L'Attacco: Giornale della Brigata Bolognese (SAP)* refers to them as Squadre d'Ardimento Patriottico (Squads of Patriotic Courage). (I:1 January 1945, reprinted in L. Bergonzini [ed.], *La resistenza a Bologna,* p. 994). The SAP were more widely recruited and served as reserve, auxiliary, and support units for the partisan army and the GAP. See C. Pavone, *Una guerra civile,* pp. 387-88 for descriptions of the GAP and SAP.

6. Giorgio Vaccarino, "La Resistenza armata," in Antonicelli (ed.), *Trent'anni di storia italiana,* pp. 342-43.

7. Testimony in Luciano Bergonzini (ed.), *La Resistenza a Bologna,* Vol. I (Bologna: Istituto per

la Storia di Bologna, 1967), pp. 475-78.

8. Mario Lizzero, *Virginia Tonelli: 'Luisa' partigiana* (Venezia Giulia: Comitato Regionale dell'ANPI del Friuli-Venezia Giulia, 1972), p. 48.

9. For information on Fibbi, see *Enciclopedia dell'antifascismo e della Resistenza,* Vol II (Milan: La Pietra, 1971), p. 340; for Gobetti, see Ibid., p. 592 and Ada Gobetti, *Diario partigiano* (Novara: Einaudi Editore, 1956), pp. 9-11.

10. For details on the prison experience, see John Cammett, "Communist Women and the Fascist Experience," in Jane Slaughter and Robert Kern (eds.), *European Women on the Left* (Westport, CT: Greenwood Press, 1981), pp. 163-79; for an excellent discussion of the political and private lives of anti-Fascist women, see Giovanni De Luna, *Donne in oggetto: L'antifascismo nella societá italiana, 1992-1939* (Turin: Bollati Boringhieri, 1995). Lucia Scarpone's testimony appears in Bianca Giudetti Serra, *Compagne,* Vol. II (Turin: Einaudi, 1977), pp. 345-50. For biographical material on Merlin, see *Enciclopedia dell'antifascismo e della resistenza,* Vol. III, p. 673 and Lina Merlin, *La mia vita* (Florence: Giunti, 1989), pp. 36, 60. Merlin's memoir was first published after she retired from public life in 1963; thus a certain idealization of previous behavior is possible. Committed anti-Fascists might well have had to deal with the Fascist bureaucracy in less romantic ways, simply to survive. Just as for the more general population, the line between consensus and opposition was blurred at times. John Cammett describes how women who were political prisoners negotiated with the nuns who ran the prisons in which they were incarcerated; he also makes clear that pragmatic decisions about survival often haunted the women the rest of their lives. Cammett, pp. 170-71.

11. Paola Gaiotti de Biase, *Questione femminile e femminismo nella storia della Repubblica* (Brescia: Morcelliana, 1979), p. 29. For biographical sketches of the women whose names follow, see Marina Ceratto, *Il "Chi é?" delle donne italiane, 1945-1982* (Milan: Mondadori Editore, 1982).

12. Comitato Femminile Antifascista per il XXX della Resistenza e della Liberazione in Toscana, *Donne e Resistenza in Toscana* (Florence: n.p., 1978), p. 49.

13. For the evolution of FUCI activism, see Carla Tagliarino and Enrica Andoardi, *Cattolici e "Azzurri"* (Novara: Istituto Storico della Resistenza in Provincia di Novara, 1973), p. 45; Antonio Cucchiari (ed.), *I cattolici dal fascismo alla Resistena* (Rome: Coines Edizioni, 1977); and Vittorio Giuntella, "I cattolici nella Resistenza," in Francesca Traniello and Giorgio Camparini, *Dizionario storico del movimento cattolico in Italia, 1860-1980,* Vol. II (Turin: Marietti, 1981), p. 119. For biographical information on Anselmi, Menapace, and Federici, see, respectively, Ceratto, *Il "Chi é?"* pp. 16-17, 195, and 108-9. Dau Novelli, "Daremo sei milioni di voti," *Memoria,* No. 21 (1987) discusses Federici's political development, p. 47.

14. Giovanni Pesce, *And No Quarter: An Italian Partisan in World War II,* transl. by Frederick M. Shaine (Milan: Feltrinelli Editore, and University of Ohio, 1972), p. 42. Pietro Secchia, *Il Partito comunista italiano e la guerra di Liberazione, 1943-1945: Ricordi, documenti inediti e testimonianze* (Milan: Istituto Feltrinelli, 1973) focuses primarily on Spanish Civil War veterans and those previously imprisoned.

15. C. Pavone, *Una guerra civile,* p. 15.

16. Nuto Revelli, *La guerra dei poveri* (Turin: Einaudi, 1979), pp. 127, 147.

17. G. Quazza, "The Politics of the Italian Resistance," in Woolf, *The Rebirth of Italy,* p. 17.

18. Judith Adler Hellman, *Journeys Among Women* (New York: Oxford, 1987), p. 114 points to the inadequacy of focusing only on "legendary women" who "moved well beyond the usual female characteristics."

19. As is often the case in historical analysis of this sort, the sample and data are not "pure" or random. The nature of sources for the topic does influence the material considered; in this specific case, references to women were more frequent in some regions (particularly Emilia Romagna), and among the political parties the PCI and PSI were more likely to detail women's experience and activities. The variables used to develop the general profile were the following: region of activity; occupation; personal or family connections to others engaged in opposition either before or after 1943; date of joining and functions in the Resistance; military rank or command; arrests; work among women specifically; party membership; government or party position; and feminist activity after 1945. Information on at least five of the variables was necessary in order for a subject to be included in the group analyzed.

20. A more limited study of the area of Brescia comes to the same conclusion. Of 65 women analyzed, only 6 had obvious party affiliation. See Rolando Anni, et al., *I gesti e i sentimenti: Le donne nella Resistenza bresciana* (Brescia: Comune di Brescia, 1989), pp. 6-7.

21. P. Willson, *The Clockwork Factory*, p. 240.

22. "Donne della Resistenza," Special Supplement, *Nuovo Risorgimento,* No. 12 (22 March 1953), p. 13; Gianfranco Bianchi and Bruno De Marche (eds.), *Per amore ribelli: Cattolici e Resistenza* (Milan: Universitá Cattolica del Sacro Cuore, 1976).

23. Orlandi Bastia and Dal Pozzo's accounts are in Bergonzini (ed.), *La Resistenza a Bologna,* Vol. III, p. 709, and Vol. V, p. 130, respectively. Borellini is cited in Luisa Sturani (ed.), *Antologia della Resistenza* (Turin: Centro del Libro Popolare, 1951), p. 334; Information on Malvestiti can be found in Movimento Femminile della Democrazia Cristiana di Milano, *Donne cristiane nella Resistenza: Tesimonianze e documentazioni* (Milan: Molinari, 1956), pp. 50-51; and in Charles Delzell, "Catholics in the Italian Armed Resistance," *Italian Quarterly* (Winter 1983), p. 59.

24. A recent detailed analysis of Bologna's partisan families points to the importance of the brother/sister relationship. See Claudia Antonini and Milena Brugnoli, "I partigiani: provenienza, composizione sociale, presenza femminile," Unpublished paper (Seminario, Per una storia della Resistenza Bolognese, Bologna, 20 January 1989), 10 pages. Rossi's experience is in Avvenire Paterlini, *Partigiane e Patriote della provincia di Reggio nell'Emilia* (Reggio Emilia: Edizioni Libreria Rinascita, 1977), pp. 426-27; Covina's testimony in Bergonzini, *La Resistenza a Bologna,* Vol. V, p. 242, Magri in Vol. III, p. 129, and Parenti, Vol. V, p. 903.

25. Bianca Giudetti Serra (ed.), *Compagne: Testimonianze di partecipazione politica femminile,* Vol. II (Turin: Einaudi Editore, 1977), pp. 447-49.

26. Mirella Alloisio et al. (eds.), *Mille volte no: dai no di ieri ai no di oggi* (Rome: Riuniti, 1975), pp. 159-60.

27. "Perche fummo partigiane?," in Associazione nazionale dei partigiani italiani [ANPI], *Popolo in lotta: Per la consegna della medaglia d'oro al valor militare alla Cittá di Cuneo* (ANPI, 8 June 1947).

28. Elsa Oliva, *Ragazza partigiana* (Novara: Istituto per la storia della Resistenza in Provincia di Novara, 1969), p. 33.

29. Giuliana Beltrami, co-author with Mirella Alloisio of *Volontarie della Libertá* (Milan: Mazzotta, 1981), interviewed a wide range of women for her work and kindly gave me access to all her records. This is from an interview conducted May 18, 1977. Anna Maria Bruzzone, who also interviewed women for her study, argues that connections to loved ones did not mean that "choices and decisions were not autonomous." "Women in the Italian Resistance," in Paul Thompson and Natasha Burchardt (eds.), *Our Common History* (London: Pluto Press, 1982), p. 277.

30. De Grazia, *How Fascism Ruled Women*, p. 12.

31. From her speech, Comitato Nazionale del ANPI, Rome, "Antifascismo negli ideale della Resistenza: Forza morale che unisce per rinnovare la societá," 8th Congresso Nazionale dell'ANPI [National Association of Italian Partisans], Atti, Florence, 4-8 November 1976. She expressed a similar view to me in an interview in Milan in October 1981.

32. Bergonzini (ed.), *La Resistenza a Bologna*, Vol. III, p. 341.

33. Rifredi's account is in Paterlini, *Partigiane e patriote,* p. 418.

34. Fae's testimony is in Giudetti Serra (ed.), *Compagne*, Vol. I, p. 192.

35. Interview in Bravo and Bruzzone (eds.), *Guerra senza armi*, p. 186.

36. Interview in Anna Maria Bruzzone and Rachele Farina (eds.), *La Resistenza taciuta* (Milan: La Pietra), p. 34.

37. Gina Borellini, "Note sulle partigiane modenesi," in *Donne Emiliane nella Resistenza,* 3rd. *Quaderno de "La Lotta"* (Special Edition, September 1964), p. 15.

38. Giudetti Serra (ed.), *Compagne*, Vol. II, p. 580.

39. Bandiera is the subject of Renata Viganó, "Una piccola grande donna," in *Partigiane della libertá* (Rome: Sezione centrale stampa e propaganda, PCI, 1973), p. 126; Polizzi's testimony is in Paterlini, *Partigiane e Patriote,* Vol. II, p. 458.

40. In Giudetti Serra (ed.), *Compagne*, Vol. I, p. 288.

41. Koon, *Believe, Obey, Fight*, p. 233.

42. Wolff, "'Fascitizing' Italian Youth," pp. 293, 297.

43. In Guido Gerosa, *Le compagne* (Milan: Rizzoli, 1979), p. 284.

44. Lydia Franceschi and Isotta Gaeta (eds.), *La altra metá della Resistenza* (Milan: Mazzotta, 1978), p. 67; Erica Scroppo, *Donna, privato e politico: storie personali di 21 donne del PCI* (Milan: Mazzotta, 1979), pp. 105, 109. An interesting discussion of generational vs. class revolt is found in Bruno Wanrooij, "The Rise and Fall of Fascism as a Generational Revolt," *Journal of Contemporary History* 22 (July 1987), pp. 401-18.

45. Shelley Saywell, *Women in War* (Ontario, Canada: Penguin Books, 1985), p. 76, in her chapter "Via Rasella" interviewed Capponi and Musu.

46. *Noi Donne*, Nos. 6-7 (31 October-15 November 1945), p. 2.

47. Alloisio, et al. (eds.), *Mille volte no*, p. 199.

48. Steven White, "Italian Popular Education: Between Fascism and Democracy, 1943-1954," dissertation (University of Virginia, 1985), p. 41, and pp. 42-44 for following information.

49. Bianca Montale, "La donna nel campo della scuola e della cultura," in G. Benelli, et al. (eds.), *La donna nella Resistenza in Liguria* (Florence: La Nuova Italia, 1979), p. 155; Guarnaschelli's account, which follows, is in Franceschi and Gaeta, *L'altra metá*, p. 96.

50. See Cagossi's memoir, *Da piccola italiana a partigiana combattente* (Modena: S. T. E. M.-Mucchi, 1976) for this evolution.

51. Malavasi's experience is in Paterlini, *Partigiane e Patriote,* p. 300; Laura Polizzi's account is in same, p. 393. Guazzaloca's testimony is in L. Bergonzini, *La Resistenza a Bologna,* Vol. V, p. 719.

52. Interview with Pron, in Scroppo, *Donna, privato e politico,* p. 119; "Intervento di Maria Beltrami," in Partito Socialista Italiano [PSI], *La donna in cinquant'anni,* p. 127.

53. Paterlini, *Partigiane e Patriote*, Vol. I, p. 19.

54. Alloisio, et al. (eds.), *Mille volte no,* p. 64.

55. Giudetti Serra, *Compagne,* Vol. 1, pp. 3-6; also Gobetti, *Diario partigiano,* p. 373.

56. Sandro Contini Bonacossi and Licia Raggianti Collobi, *Una lotta nel suo corso: Lettere e documenti politici e militari della Resistenza e della Liberazione* (Venice: Neri Pozza Editore, 1954), p. 287; Movimento Femminile della DC, *Donne Cristiane nella Resistenza,* p. 71; Cesarina Bracco, *La staffetta garibaldina* (Borgosesia: Provincia di Vercelli, 1976); and transcript of interview with Bracco by G. Beltrami. Brugnoli's study of the family in Bologna's resistance found that mothers, sisters, and daughters often joined the Resistance simultaneously, "I partigiani: provenienza, composizione sociale," p. 5.

# Chapter 3

1. U.S. Office of Strategic Services, Research and Analysis Branch, No. 2993, "The Contribution of the Italian Partisans to the Allied War Effort" (Washington, March 31, 1945), pp. iii, iv (National Archives Building, General Records of the Department of State, Record Group 226).

2. Ibid., p. 11, and Adjutant General's Office, SHAEF; Mission France, Letter, December 1944 (General Archives Division, Washington National Records Center, Suitland, Records of Allied Operational and Occupation Headquarters, Record Group 331).

3. Giorgio Vaccarino, "La Resistenza armata," in Antonicelli, *Trent'anni di storia* notes that the Allies were hesitant about dealing with or encouraging the partisans, yet were forced to recognize their important military contribution. This is evident in the April 1954 report by the commander of the British Special Forces, which concludes that "the contribution of the partisans to the Allied victory in Italy was thus notable and surpassed, by a great deal, the most optimistic forecast. Without these partisan victories, there would not have been such a rapid Allied victory in Italy." See pp. 349-53.

4. "Due ordini di operazione di Kesselring contro le 'Bande partigiane'," reprinted in *Il Movimento di Liberazione in Italia,* No. 20 (Milan, September 1952), pp. 48-50, and copy of Colonel Anselmo Ballarino's weekly report, April 1945 in Paterlini, *Partigiane e Patriote,* II, p. 681.

5. Luciano Bergonzini, *La Resistenza a Bologna,* Vol. V (Istituto per la Storia di Bologna, 1967), p. 35.

6. Interview in Guido Gerosa (ed.), *Le compagne* (Milan: Rizzoli Editore, 1979), pp. 226, 230.

7. Interview with Bruna Betti in Massimo Papini (ed.), *La donna e la Resistenza nell'anconetano* (Ancona: ANPI Provinciale di Ancona, 1987), p. 107. Betti was only seventeen in 1943, but her father was a member of the local CLN, which she admits influenced her choice of activity.

8. For Liguria, see Giovanna Petti Balbi, "La donna nelle compagne e in montagna," in G. Benelli, et al. (eds.), *La donna nella Resistenza in Liguria* (Florence: La Nuova Italia, 1979), pp. 159-86, especially pp. 177-79. Barbara Jancar-Webster, *Women and Revolution in Yugoslavia* (Denver: Arden Press, 1990), p. 99.

9. Reprint of "Il Partito comunista alle compagne staffette," in *Partigiane della Libertá* (Rome: Sezione centrale stampa e propaganda PCI, 1973), pp. 137-42.

10. Terzini testimony in *Donne e Resistenza in Toscana* (Florence: Comitato Femminile Antifascista per il XXX Della Resistenza e della Liberazione in Toscana, 1978), p. 44; Merlin account is in her autobiography, *La mia vita* (Florence: Giunti, 1989), p. 61.

11. Record and testimony in Avvenire Paterlini, *Partigiane e Patriote della provincia di Reggio nell'Emilia* (Reggio Emilia: Edizione Libreria Rinascita, 1977), pp. 30-32.

12. Interview in Chiara Valentini and Laura Lilli (eds.), *Care Compagne* (Rome: Editori Riuniti, 1979), p. 244.

13. Giorgio Bocca, *Storia dell'Italia partigiana* (Bari: Laterza, 1966), p. 251, and Guerrino Franzini, *Storia della Resistenza reggiana* (Reggio Emilia: ANPI, 1966), p. 839. C. Pavone, *Una guerra civile*, pp. 544-47 covers concerns for "morality" in mixed brigades and fears of women in the units.

14. Giovanna Zangrandi, *I giorni veri, 1943-45* (Milan: Mondadori Editore, 1963), p. 107.

15. For these examples, see, respectively, Movimento Femminile della Democrazia Cristiana, *Donne cristiane nella Resistenza: Testimonianze e documentazione sul contributo femminile alla lotta partigiana in Lombardia* (Milan: Molinari, 1956), pp. 96-97; Mirella Alloisio, et al., *Mille volte no* (Rome: Riuniti, 1975), p. 110; Anna Maria Bruzzone and Rachele Farina, *La resistenza taciuta* (Milan: La Pietra, 1976), p. 118; "Donne spezzine nella Resistenza," in *La Resistenza nello Spezzino e nella Lunigiana: Scritti e testimonianze* (La Spezia: Istituto Storico della Resistenza, 1973), pp. 186-87; and Iste Cagossi, *Da piccola italiana a partigiana combattente* (Modena: S.T.E.M.-Mucchi, 1976), p. 69.

16. "Le medaglie d'oro al valor militare," in *Partigiane della libertá* (Rome: Sezione centrale stampa e propaganda, PCI, 1973), p. 199.

17. *Il pionere* I, Nos. 23-25 (December 1944), p. 2.

18. *La Comune (Settimanale Comunista)* (Bologna), Anno 1, No. 5 (February 1944), reprinted in Bergonzini (ed.), *La resistenza a Bologna*, II, pp. 263-64. By May of that year the same paper indicated women should participate "not just in passive ways, but in *vera e reale* activity." Ibid., p. 293.

19. *La Lotta: Organo della Federazione Comunista di Bologna*, I (May 1944), reprinted in Bergonzini (ed.), *La Resistenza a Bologna*, II, p. 570.

20. Interview with Capponi in Shelley Saywell, *Women in War* (New York: Penguin Books, 1986), p. 87. Capponi's activities are also discussed in Mirella Alloisio and Giuliana Beltrami, *Volontarie della libertá* (Milan: Mazzotta, 1981), p. 65.

21. Renata Vigano, *Donne della Resistenza* (Bologna: S.T.E.B., 1955), p. 43.

22. Musu's testimony is in Saywell, *Women in War*, pp. 80, 81.

23. Bruna Curzi, "Le ragazze dei GAP," in *Partigiane della Libertá*, pp. 112-16. See also Federazione Provinciale Comunista Romana, "Le donne di Roma durante l'occupazione" (Rome: n.p., n.d.), pp. 19-22.

24. Saywell, *Women in War*, p. 88, and "Le medaglie d'oro al valor militare," p. 200.

25. *Noi Donne* II:8 (25 June 1945), p. 2.

26. See Beltrami Files and Notes; Etnasi, *Donne italiane*, p. 81, and Ilio Barontini, "Le staffette," in Antonio Meluschi (ed.), *Epopea partigiana* (Bologna: Editrice S.P.E.R., 1947), p. 19.

27. See Avvenire Paterlini, *Partigiane e Patriote*, Vol. I (unpublished manuscript in UDI files), p. 27. The original manuscript is in two volumes but was published in a single volume in 1977 (see fn. 11). Also see Comitato Promotore del Raduno nel ventennale della Resistenza, *76th Brigata S.A.P*

*"Angelo Zanti"* (Reggio Emilia, 1965), no page numbers. This same publication provides an excellent discussion of the units, how they were organized and how they ultimately functioned.

28. Tristano Codignola, "Lotta per la libertá," pamphlet No. 2, 1945, in Partito d'Azione, Documentazione, 1944-45 (collection of pamphlets in the Hoover Institution Archives, Stanford University).

29. Her testimony is in Paterlini, *Partigiane e Patriote*, pp. 393-99.

30. Interview in Bruzzone and Farina (eds.), *La Resistenza taciuta*, pp. 125, 130, 131.

31. Her account is in *Noi Donne* 20:17 (25 April 1964).

32. Sabbi account is in Bergonzini (ed.), *La Resistenza a Bologna*, III, p. 342.

33. Quoted in Saywell, *Women in War*, pp. 84, 101.

34. Judith Hicks Stiehm, "The Man Question," in Stiehm (ed.), *Women's Views of the Political World of Men*, p. 219.

35. There are a number of sources that detail the actions of the gold medal recipients. This is from *Enciclopedia dell'antifascismo e della Resistenza*, II (Milan: La Pietra, 1971), p. 49.

36. "Le donne nella Resistenza italiana," in *Partigiane della Libertá*, pp. 152-53, and Marco Cesarini Sforza (ed.), *Brigata Matteotti nel ventennale della Resistenza* (Rome: Istituto di Studi Storici sul movimento socialista, 1965), p. 65. Her letter to her brother is quoted by Maria Saracinella at a conference in 1986, the proceedings of which are in Papini (ed.), *La donna e la Resistenza nell'anconetano;* see p. 22. Saracinella cites from two other women's letters that have the same theme of seeking pardon and assuring their families that there is no shame in what they have done.

37. Cited by C. Pavone, *Una guerra civile*, p. 544 and fn. 146, p. 779 from Bruzzone and Farina (eds.), *La Resistenza taciuta*.

38. See Rapporto dei GDD al UDI, Milan, 15 April 1945 (UDI Files, Rome), 15 pp., and report CLNAI-CVL to 29th Divisione Garibaldi-Piemonte, 10 August 1944 in Etnasi, *Donne italiane*, pp. 159-60.

39. Pieroni Bortolotti, "Le donne della Resistenza," p. 208, and her appendix, p. 332, which reprints the letter of recognition by the division commander; see also unpublished paper by same author, "La donna nella Resistenza" (UDI Files, Rome), p. 16.

40. I corpi di assistenza femminile, Handwritten Report, 1944 (Rome: UDI Files, Miscellaneous, "Donne e Resistenza"); Emilio Seroni, "Milioni di lire raccolta e ridistributi," in *Partigiane della libertá*, pp. 159-60.

41. Biographical sketch of Madia is in *Noi Donne* (reprint), No. 9 (15 December 1945), p. 2. Alloisio and Beltrami, *Volontarie della Libertá*, p. 71 refer to her work and that of Antonia Colucci.

42. Vincenza Fornaro (ed.), *Il servizio informazione nella lotta clandestina* (Milan: Editrice Domus, 1946), p. 35.

43. Franco Fucci, *Spie per la libertá: I servizi segreti della Resistenza Italiana* (Milan: Mursi, 1983), pp. 266-73; for Silvia Rota, see pp. 67-71.

44. This sort of activity is described in Letter, October 1944 for Florence sector, "Intelligence Reports," ACC Patriots Branch 10000/125/31 (WNRC Suitland, Maryland).

45. The event in Bologna is described by Manzela Sanna in Lydia Franceschi, Isotta Gaeta et al. (eds.), *La altra metá della Resistenza* (Milan: Mazzotta, 1978), p. 103. Panciroli's account is in Paterlini, *Partigiane e Patriote*, p. 371.

46. From *Bandiera Rossa* (21 September 1944), reprinted in Papini (ed.), *La donna e la Resistenza nell'anconetano*, pp. 129-31.

47. Palmerini's testimony is in Alloisio, et al., *Mille volte no*, pp. 196-97; and for Cesarina Bracco, *La staffetta garibaldina* (Provincia di Vercelli: Borgosesia, 1976), p. 24.

48. Numerous references to this sort of work are found throughout the personal testimonies; see especially accounts in Paterlini, *Partigiane e Patriote*, pp. 166, 337, 533.

49. Joyce Lussu, *Portrait: Cose viste e vissute* (Bologna: Transeuropa, 1988), pp. 78-79.

50. For Fibbi's life, see Gerosa, *Le Compagne*, p. 114 and *Enciclopedia dell'antifascismo e della Resistenza*, II, p. 340; for Meglioli and Brunetti, see Paterlini, *Partigiane e Patriote*, pp. 5-6 and p. 122, respectively.

51. Albertini's account is in Ibid., pp. 40-41.

52. Rumori's testimony is in Papini (ed.), *La donna e la Resistenza nell'anconetano,* p. 119; see Paterlini, *Partigiane e Patriote,* pp. 491 and 188, respectively, for Storchi and Cristina's accounts.

53. On founding of the GDD, see Programma d'azione dei Gruppi di Difesa della Donna, 28 November 1943 (Milan, Istituto Nazionale per la storia del Movimento di Liberazione in Italy, ISML, Fondo CLNAI, Busto 18, fasciolo 7), and Rapporto dei Gruppi di difesa della Donna, Milan, 15 April 1945 (Rome: UDI Files). Sources vary regarding the women who actually attended this first meeting, but on the basis of my research I would agree with the account provided by Giuliana Beltrami, *Volontarie della Libertá,* pp. 30, 131.

54. Ada M. Gobetti, "Perché erano tante nella Resistenza," *Rinascita* 18:3 (March 1961), p. 245.

55. Paterlini, *Partigiane e Patriote* provides information for GDD organizing in Reggio Emilia; see especially p. 445 for Rossi's experience. Scarpone is also interviewed in Bianca Giudetti Serra (ed.), *Compagne,* II (Turin: Einaudi, 1977), pp. 319-54.

56. Information on GDD organizing is spread throughout the accounts in Bergonzini, *La Resistenza a Bologna,* but see especially for Guadagnini, I, 477; for Bersani, V, 433-34, and for Bergonzoni, V, 693-94. The author's comments on the GDD are in V, p. 38.

57. "Donne spezzine nella Resistenza," p. 187; "Diece patriote raccontano," in *Donne emiliane nella Resistenza* (Special Edition) *Quaderni de "La Lotta,"* No. 3 (Bologna, 1964), pp. 53-58.

58. Interview by G. Beltrami, 6 May 1978.

59. Rapporto dei Gruppi di difesa della donna, Milan, 15 April 1945, and Forze dei GDD per settore e per zona (ISML, Fondo CLNAI, b. 18/f.7).

60. Martini, who was forty years old in 1943, was a seamstress who worked out of her own home. She had joined the PCI in 1921 and began her Resistance activity distributing party literature. Her testimony is in Bruzzone and Farina (eds.), *La Resistenza taciuta,* p. 180.

61. There are numerous accounts of the Arduino murders and the subsequent protests. For example, Teresa Cirio, who was present during the events, describes them in her testimony in Bruzzone and Farina (eds.), *La Resistenza taciuta,* p. 87. An account, including a reprint of a newspaper story, appears in Commissione Femminile dell'A.N.P.I, *Donne piemontesi nella lotta di liberazione* (Turin: Impronta, n.d.), pp. 24-26.

62. Zangrandi, *I giorni veri,* p. 213. For the two accounts that follow, see Bergonzini, *La Resistenza a Bologna,* V, p. 572 for Generali, and Paterlini, *Partigiane e Patriote,* p. 498 for Tagliavini.

63. Renata Viganó, *Donne della Resistenza,* pp. 54, 57.

64. Most accounts focus on urban protest; however, good description of resistance by agricultural workers and efforts to recruit them to more active roles is available in Comitato per la celebrazioni del XXX della Resistenza, *La Resistenza nelle campagne modenesi* (Modena: Quaderni dell'Istituto Storico della Resistenza, 1976), pp. 171-76. For the effects of the popular protests, see U.S. Office of Strategic Services, "The Contribution of the Italian Partisans to the Allied War Effort," p. 10.

65. These activities and their importance were acknowledged by letters from the commands of the Garibaldi and Fiamma Verdi Brigades of Reggio Emilia to the GDD of that area in "Un mese di lotta armata in Emilia Romagna, Dicembre 1944" (Ministerio dell'Italia Occupata, Documenti, No. 3, Rome, 1945 in the HIA).

66. Comitato di Liberazione Nazionale, Regionale Piemontesi, Giunta Consultiva Regionale, "Relazione sulla liberazione della cittá di Torino" (April 1945), and Luigi Arbizzani, "Contributo per una storia del movimento femminile nella Resistenza bolognese," in *Donne emiliane nella Resistenza,* p. 36.

67. *La nuova realtá,* I (1 February 1945), p. 3. See also Rapporto dei GDD, 15 April 1945.

68. Zangrandi, *I giorni veri,* p. 183.

# Chapter 4

1. Joan W. Scott, *Gender and the Politics of History* (New York, NY: Columbia University Press, 1988), p. 27.

2. Manifesto di costituzione dei "Gruppi Femminile Giustizia e Libertá" (n.p., n.d., on microfilm at the Feltrinelli Institute, Milan), 2 pp. For these early organizing efforts, see also Movimento Femminile "Giustizia e Libertá," "Organi del Movimento" (ISML, Fondo CLNAI, b. 18/f. 7); Sandro Contini Bonacossi and Licia Ragghianti Collobi (eds.), *Una lotta nel suo corso: Lettere e documenti politici e militari della Resistenza e della Liberazione* (Venice: Neri Pozza, 1954), and *Italia Libera: Organo del Partito d'Azione* II:17 (30 November 1944), 4:4.

3. Ada Gobetti, *Diario partigiano*, pp. 77, 81.

4. Ibid., p. 169.

5. Systematic description of these publications, like all of those of the Resistance, is difficult. Sites of publication shifted, names were sometimes altered, and use of volume and issue numbers is not consistent. The most helpful effort to locate and organize the publications of the Resistance is Laura Conti (ed.), *La resistenza in Italia* (Milan: Feltrinelli Institute, 1961).

6. Renata Ballardini, "La pubblicistica del movimento femminile repubblicano dalla clandestinitá alla Costituente," in Pieroni Bortolotti (ed.), *Le donne della Resistenza antifascista*, pp. 221-24.

7. Bergonzini (ed.), *La Resistenza a Bologna, II*, pp. 73-74; Alloisio and Ajo, *La donna nel socialismo italiano*, pp. 85, 87-88. There were various editions of *La compagna;* the Feltrinelli Institute has copies of the Piedmont and Lombardy editions from 1944 to 1945, while at the National Institute of the Liberation Movement in Milan (ISML) there are copies of the same editions plus a few from Emilia Romagna. Titles also vary, as, for example, *La compagna: Giornale delle donne socialiste italiane (Piedmont)* and *Compagna: Giornale dei Gruppi Femminile aderenti al Partito Socialista di Unitá Proletaria* (Emilia Romagna).

8. Cited in Bergonzini (ed.), *La Resistenza a Bologna*, II, p. 74.

9. For discussion of inter- and intra-party relations, see Alexander De Grand, *The Italian Left in the Twentieth Century* (Bloomington: Indiana University Press, 1989), pp. 94-99; and S. J. Woolf (ed.), *The Rebirth of Italy*, pp. 59-69.

10. Aldo Garosci, "The Italian Communist Party," Part III, in Mario Einaudi, Jean Marie Domenach, and Aldo Garosci (eds.), *Communism in Western Europe* (Ithaca: Cornell University Press, 1951), pp. 154-219.

11. Partito Comunista d'Italia, La Conferenza dei Triumvirati Insurrenzionali del Partito Comunista. Serrare le file e vincere ogni difficoltá (Istituto Feltrinelli Fondo Resistenza [hereafter IFFR], Vol. II, b.16/f. 92, 20 pp.), pp. 5-6, and Partito Comunista d'Italia. Ai comitati federale. Ai compagni chiamati a coprire cariche pubbliche. 18 December 1944 (IFFR, Vol. II, b.4/f.21, 18 pp.), p. 9.

12. Partito Comunista Italiano, *La politica dei comunisti dal quinto al sesto congresso: Risoluzione e documenti raccolti* (Rome: A cura dell'ufficio di segretaria del PCI, probably 1948), p. 207; Silvana Casmirri, "L'Unione Donne Italiani, 1944-1948," *Quaderni della F.I.A.P,* Nuova Serie, N. 7 (April 1978), p. 86, fn. 4; *Poggi, L'organizzazione partitica*, pp. 328, 356, 372. Membership figures during the war are questionable, as even Togliatti admitted in a 1945 report that listed 40,191 women in the party in February 1944. (Cited in Poggi, p. 33, fn. 32.)

13. Judith Adler Hellman, "The Italian Communists, the Women's Question, and the Challenge of Feminism," *Studies in Political Economy* 13 (1983), p. 62.

14. Interview with Pron in Scroppo, *Donna, privato e politico,* pp. 119-20; author's interview with Maria Michetti, Rome, 30 September 1981. Gisella Floreanini of the PCI supports this, indicating that most women joined the party at the end of the Resistance (Interview, Milan, 14 October 1981).

15. Spano comments in Gerosa (ed.), *Le compagne*, p. 121.

16. Lussu, *Portrait*, p. 87.

17. *Bollettino di Partito* I:1 (August 1944), pp. 20-22. The policy of separate cells was reaffirmed after the end of the war. See Partito Comunista Italiano, *La politica dei comunisti dal quinto al sesto congresso*, p. 208.

18. Partito Comunista d'Italia. Rapporto organizzativo, p. 7, and "Lettera di direttive del PCI," in *Partigiane della Libertá*, p. 98. *La nostra lotta* II:7-8 (April 1944) (Milan: Feltrinelli Reprint, 1966) had pointed out the deficiencies in their efforts to organize women, p. 18. In 1946 they were still concerned about inadequacies in the incorporation of women into party activities, and in 1947 a special

committee responsible for increasing female membership affirmed the policy of separate cells but also admitted that the women's cells did not "live the full life of the party" like the men's. Partito Comunista Italiano, *La politica dei comunisti dal quinto al sesto congresso*, pp. 85-89, 207-8.

19. "Le comuniste in linee," *La nostra lotta* (25 November 1944), p. 30. This question is discussed in interviews in "Partecipazione delle donne e organizzazione del PCI," *Donne e politica,* Nos. 5-6 (1971), pp. 37-38, and by Rita Montagnana, "Le donne italiane nella lotta per la libertá," *Voce della donna* (Rome: Societa Editrice *L'Unitá*, 1945, pamphlet by same title), pp. 6-12, and in Nadia Spano's comments in Erica Scroppo (ed.), *Donna, privato e politico* (Milan: Mazzotta, 1979), p. 78.

20. Ferrara interview in Scroppo (ed.), *Donna, privato e politico, p.* 94. One of the most famous and oft-quoted women who resisted separate cells was Teresa Noce, who stated her position in *Rivoluzionaria professionale*, p. 339.

21. Spano in Gerosa (ed.), *Le compagne,* p. 119. Spano also is interviewed in Scroppo (ed.), *Donna, privato e politico*, and there she explains more fully why it was important for women to have their own organizations, p. 78.

22. Lussu's comments are in her own *Portrait*, p. 88, and in Franceschi and Gaeta (eds.), *L'altra metá,* p. 113.

23. Giulietta Ascoli, "L'UDI tra emancipazione e liberazione, (1943-1964)," *Problemi del Socialismo* 17 (1976), p. 122. Judith Hellman discusses these issues in *Journeys Among Women*, p. 35.

24. Lesley Caldwell, "Italian Feminism: Some Considerations," in Zygmunt G. Baranski and Shirley Vinall (eds.), *Women and Italy: Essays on Gender, Culture and History* (New York: St. Martin's Press, 1991), p. 99.

25. Ingrao interview in Gerosa, *Le compagne*, p. 169; Fibbi interview in same, p. 114.

26. Viviani interview in Gerosa (ed.), *Le compagne*, p. 292.

27. For these constitutional provisions, see Giovanni Conserva's edition, *Costituzione della Repubblica Italiana* (Rome: Bonacci Editore, 1974).

28. *La nostra lotta* (4 June 1944), p. 2.

29. "Rapporto del Compagno Togliatti tenuto il 5 Febbraio 1945 ai Congressisti Toscani," reprinted in Pietro Secchi (ed.), *Il Partito comunista italiano e la guerra di Liberazione: Ricordi, documenti inediti e testimonianze* (Milan: Feltrinelli, 1973), p. 857.

30. "Per la partecipazione delle donne alla vita nazionale," *Noi Donne* 1:3 (September 1945) (Rome: Reprint, Editrice Cooperativa Libera Stampa, 1978), p. 12.

31. Translation by Joanne Barkan, *Visions of Emancipation* (New York: Praeger, 1984), p. 32. See, as well, Assemblea Costituente. Commissione per la costituzione. Projetto di costituzione della repubblica italiana. Testo approvato della commissione (Rome: Tipografia della camera dei deputati, 1947), p. 9.

32. Palmiro Togliatti, "L'emancipazione della donna: Un problema centrale del rinnovamento dello Stato italiano e della societá italiana," in *L'emancipazione femminile* (Rome: Editori Riuniti, 1973), p. 39.

33. Conserva (ed.), *Costituzione della Repubblica,* p. 59; an earlier version had been more explicit in recognizing "the importance of the family to the moral stability and prosperity of the nation" and guaranteeing "the indissolubility of marriage and the unity of the family" (Assemblea Costituente. Commissione per la costituzione, p. 7).

34. For example, the constitution left in place the 1929 Lateran Accords between Mussolini and the Catholic church as well as legislation from the 1920s that excluded women from certain public offices and activities, particularly jury service and the judiciary. [Piero Calamandrei, "La Costituzione e le leggi per attuarla," in A. Battaglia, et al., *Dieci anni doppo* (Bari: Laterza, 1955), pp. 252, 259, and 263, and Annamaria Galoppini, *Il lungo viaggio versa la parità: I diritti civili e politici delle donne dall'Unitá ad oggi* (Bologna: Zanichelli, 1980), pp. 179-80.]

35. Hellman, "The Italian Communists, the Women's Question, and the Challenge of Feminism," pp. 66-67.

36. Pier Giorgio Zunino, *La questione cattolica nella sinistra italiana* (Bologna: Il Mulino, 1975), pp. 381, 472. For Noce's earlier writings, see fns. 32 and 33, chapter 1; for her later objections, see *Rivoluzionaria professionale*, p. 372.

37. Togliatti, "L'emancipazione della donna," p. 35. Laura Ingrao remembers a discussion with Togliatti in which he insisted that when women went to mass they did so not for a priest but for themselves, and thus these were "moments of liberation." Cited in Gerosa (ed.), *Le compagne*, p. 185.

38. Partito Comunista Italiano. Dichiarazione del Partito Comunista sui rapporti fra i communiste e cattolici, August 1944 (IFFR, Vol. II, b.14/f.76, 3 pp.), p. 1; article on "Family and Religion," in *Tempi Nuovi: Periodico del Gruppo Intellettuali 'Antonio Labriola'* 1:2 (March 1945), reprinted in Bergonzini (ed.), *La Resistenza a Bologna*, II, p. 779.

39. "Risoluzione della Direzione del PCI sul movimento femminile, Agosto 1947," in PCI, *La politica dei comunisti dal quinto al sesto congresso*, pp. 292, 295-96.

40. "Lettera di direttive del PCI per il lavoro tra le donne" (no date, but probably late 1944 or early 1945) in *Partigiane della Libertá*, p. 98; "Le Donne e il Partito," *Quaderno dell'Attivista*, No. 1 (New Series) (September 1946), p. 20. These attitudes are discussed by Silvana Casmirri, *L'Unione Donne Italiane, 1944-48* (Nuova Serie, N. 7, *Quaderni della F.I.A.P.*, April 1978); Carla Ravaioli, *La questione femminile*, p. 151, and A. Tiso, *I comunisti e questione femminile*, p. 64.

41. In Giudetta Serra (ed.), *Compagne*, II, p. 511.

42. In Bruzzone and Farina (eds.), *La Resistenza taciuta*, p. 56.

43. *Il comunismo italiano nella seconda guerra mondiale: Relazione e documenti presentati dalla direzione del partito al V Congresso del Partito Comunista Italiano* (Rome: Riuniti, 1963), p. xxviii. Of the total delegates, 1,044 had been active in the Resistance and 738 were "new" party members, joining after July 1943; Poggi, *L'orgnizzazione partitica del PCI e della DC*, p. 511.

44. Karen Beckwith, "Feminism and Leftist Politics in Italy: The Case of UDI-PCI Relations," in Bashevkin, *Women and Politics*, p. 20. Hellman, "The Italian Communists, the Women's Question and the Challenge of Feminism," p. 68, notes the party did not challenge family relations and, since they were trying to "mobilize women around issues of war and peace, drew connections which were often retrogressive, [exalting] the feminine role in the most traditional sense."

45. Sharon Wolchik, "Introduction," in Sharon Wolchik and Alfred Meyer (eds.), *Women, State and Party in Eastern Europe* (Durham, NC: Duke University Press, 1985), pp. 9-10. This collection is extremely helpful in understanding the conflicts and pragmatic needs that affect Communist Party policies relating to women.

46. "Idee sulla democrazia cristiana," in Carlo Brizzolari (ed.), *Un archivio della Resistenza in Liguria* (Genoa: Di Stefano, 1974), p. 879.

47. For membership figures, see Elisa Bizzari (ed.), *L'organizzazione del movimento femminile cattolico dal 1943 al 1948* (Quaderni della FIAP, No. 37, Rome, n.d.), p. 11, and Maria Weber, *Il voto delle donne* (Turin: Biblioteca della liberta, 1977), pp. 16-17. Other helpful sources for information on Catholic lay groups are Carla Barlassino Tagliarino and Enrica Andoardi, *Cattolici e "Azzurri"* (Novara: Istituto Storico della Resistenza in Provincia di Novara, 1973), p. 45; Paola Gaiotti de Biase, *Questione femminile e femminismo nella storia della Repubblica*, p. 29; Vittorio E. Giuntella, "I cattolici nella Resistenza," in Traniello and Campanini (eds.), *Dizionario storico del movimento cattolico*, Vol. II, p. 119, and L. Brunelli, et al., *La presenza sociale del PCI e della DC* (Bologna: Il Mulino, 1968), pp. 345-415.

48. Micelli's chronology is backwards, as the suffrage campaign preceded the establishment of CIF. Testimony in Cecilia Dau Novelli, "'Daremo sei millioni di voti': Il Movimento delle donne cattoliche nei primi anni della Repubblica," *Memoria*, N. 21 (1987), p. 49; Antonio Cucchiare affirms the importance of AC groups as a basis for anti-fascism and resistance activity in *I cattolici dal fascismo alla Resistenza* (Rome: Coines Edizioni, 1977), pp. 13-14.

49. Associazione Partigiani Cristiani, *Il contributo dei cattolici alla lotta di Liberazione in Emilia-Romagna* (n.p.: n.p., 1966), p. 394; Brizzolari, *Un archivio della Resistenza*, p. 400; Danilo Veneruso, "La donna dall'antifascismo alla Resistenza," in Benelli, et al., *La donna nella Resistenza in Liguria*, p. 66; and Andrea Damilano (ed.), *Atti e documenti della Democrazia Cristiana, 1943-1967* (Rome: Cinque Lune, 1968), Vol. I, p. 145, and Vol. II, pp. 93, 96.

50. Cingolani Guidi described the sections in an issue of *Azione Femminile*, the paper of the MFDC, cited by Gaiotti De Biase, *La donna nella vita sociale e politica*, p. 118, fn. 115. The party actions are described in Poggi, *L'organizzazione del PCI e della DC*, p. 417, and in Daniela Boccacci,

"Lo spazio delle donne nei congressi politici del 1946," in Gaiotti De Biase, *La donna nella vita sociale e politica,* pp. 287-89. In 1946 Cingolani still supported the separate sections.

51. Gonella is quoted in Gaiotti De Biase, *La donna nella vita sociale e politica,* p. 151, fn. 328.

52. Reprint of "Il programma della D.C. per la nuova Costituzione, 24-27 Aprile 1946, Roma," in Damilano (ed.), *Atti e documenti della Democrazia Cristiana,* I, p. 240.

53. Alcide de Gasperi, "Messagio alle democratiche cristiane," *Azione femminile* 1:1 (25 December 1944), 1:2-4.

54. Weber, *Il voto delle donne,* p. 17 summarizes a 1963 mimeographed study by Lidia Menapace that discusses connections between Catholic organizations, the DC, and women. For Pius XII and the GF, see Brunelli, et al., *La presenza sociale,* p. 395.

55. Damilano, *Atti e documenti,* Vol. I, pp. 236-40, and Partito della Democrazia Cristiana, *La Democrazia Cristiana ha mantenuto gli impegni del 2 giugno! Il programma constituzionale della DC* (Rome, 1946), 16 pp.

56. Poggi, *L'organizzazione del PCI e della DC,* p. 417. The authors also point to the fact that these figures seem very low and that, in fact, membership data for women until 1954 is quite unreliable. Information on women party members can be found in tables in this same volume, pp. 422-24.

57. Menapace cited in Poggi, *L'organizzazione partitica,* p. 418.

58. Damilano, *Atti e documenti,* I, reprints National Council minutes and attendance lists beginning in 1944. Between 1944 and 1959, the same twelve women appear and reappear either on the National Council or as deputies and senators. Additional leadership figures are in Poggi, *L'organizzazione partitica del PCI e ella DC,* p. 511; Karen Beckwith, "Women and Parliamentary Politics in Italy, 1946-1979" in Penniman (ed.), *Italy at the Polls* (1979), pp. 242-43; and Leonilde Iotti, "I diritti della donna alla Costituente," *Donne e politica,* Nos. 5/6 (1971), p. 28.

59. Pieroni Bortolotti, "Le donne della Resistenza antifascista e la questione femminile," p. 113; Casadio and Fenati (eds.), *Le donne ravennati,* p. 113; Paola Gaiotti De Biase, "La donna nella vita sociale e politica della Reppubblica: 1945-48," in volume by same, Vol. III of *Donne e Resistenza in Emilia Romagna,* p. 212, and *Bollettino di Partito: Publicazione mensile della Direzione del PCI* (March 1945, numero straordinario) (Milan: Feltrinelli Reprint, 1966), p. 27.

60. Partito Comunista d'Italia, Rapporto Organizzativo (probably Lombardy, early 1945) located in IFFR, Vol. II, b.8/f.43, 9 pp., p. 7.

61. See, for example, "Risultati e deficienza del nostro lavoro fra le donne," *La nostra lotta* II: 7-8 (April 1944) (Milan: Feltrinelli Reprint, 1966), pp. 15-18; Partito Comunista d'Italia. Ai comitati di settore e di zona (IFFR, Vol. II, b.10/f. 51, 3 pp.), p. 2; Partito Comunista d'Italia. Ai Comitati di settore: Urgente (IFFR, Vol. II, b.4/f.18, 3 pp.), p. 2, and Partito Comunista d'Italia. Comitato di Zona 4 Relazione settimanale (IFFR, Vol. II, b.15/f.88, 5 pp.), p. 2.

62. Partito Comunista d'Italia. Ai triumvirati insurrezionali; Ai comitati federali: Le norme cospirative devono essere applicate. 5 January 1945 (IFFR, Vol. II, b.2/f.8, 5 pp.), p. 3.

63. Documents relating to the negotiations are in ISML, Fondo CLNAI, b.18/f.7. Also see Documenti ufficiali del Comitato di Liberazione Nazionale per l'Alta Italia, p. 48.

64. Brizzolari, *Un archivio della Resistenza,* p. 403. Documents in this volume include minutes from CLN meetings in Liguria from September 1944 to January 1945, which illustrate a similar position.

65. See memos of 11 April 1945 by the PSIUP, Milan, and 12 April by the DC (ISML, Fondo CLNAI, b.18/f.7).

66. *Bollettino,* No. 5, Della Democrazia Cristiana Alta Italia, Milan, 12 February 1945 in Brizzolari, *Un archivio della Resistenza,* p. 845.

67. On the founding of UDI, see "Costituzione dell'Unione Donne Italiane," in *Posta della settimana: Documenti e orientamenti,* II: 13-15 (Rome: UDI, November 1963), pp. 6-10; *Bollettino di Partito: Publicazione mensile della Direzione del PCI per tutte le Federazione,* I:2 (September 1944) (Milan: Feltrinelli Reprint, 1966), pp. 27-28; Maria Michetti, Margherita Repetto, and Luciana Viviani (eds.), *UDI: Laboratorio di politica delle donne* (Rome: Cooperativa libera stampa, 1984), pp. 1-24, which includes reprints of founding documents, pp. 17-24, and Lia Randi, "L'UDI e lo

sviluppo del processo di emancipazione femminile dopo 1945," in Casadio and Fenati, *Le donne ravennati*, p. 174.

68. "Costituiamo l'Unione delle Donne Italiane," *Noi Donne*, No. 4 (19 October 1944), p. 2.

69. "Per la conquista del diritto di voto alle donne," 25 October 1944 in *Posta della settimana*, pp. 10-11; "Le donne italiane hanno diritto al voto" (Pamphlet by the committee, UDI Files, Rome), 13 pp.

70. Alessandro Albertazzi and Angiola Maria Stagni, "Il primo anno di vita del Centro Italiano Femminile in Emilia Romagna," in Gaiotti De Biase (ed.), *La donna nella vita sociale e politica*, pp. 243-44.

71. Valmarana cited in Brunelli, *La presenza sociale del PCI e della DC*, p. 432 from a 1945 speech. See pages 431-42 for description of founding, structure, and program of CIF.

72. *Noi Donne* 2:4 (1 April 1945), p. 3. Each issue of the journal included a section on local activity and organization under the heading "Life of the Movement."

73. *Noi Donne* 2:7 (May 1945), p. 3, and No. 3 (15 September 1945), p. 3 (they dropped year volume after June); Unione delle Donne Italiane, Preparazione del Congresso Nazionale e dei Congressi Provinciale (Rome: UDI, 1945?), p. 5, and Unione delle Donne Italiane, Programma approvato dal primo congresso nazionale, Florence, October 1945.

74. Federici cited in Gaiotti De Biase, "La donna nella vita sociale e politica," p. 123, fn. 154. Interview with Guarini is in Lia Barone, "Fra tradizione e innovazione il lungo e travagliato processo di emancipazione della donna a Parma (1943-1948)," in Pieroni Bortolotti, *Le donne della Resistenza antifascista*, p. 241.

75. Partito Comunista Italiano, *L'emancipazione della donna, problem nazionale* (Rome: Societa Editrice L'Unitá, 1945), pp. 10-11. Minutes from UDI meeting of 6 June 1945, including Rodano's comment, are reprinted in Michetti et al. (eds.), UDI: *Laboratorio*, pp. 25-26.

76. ISML, Fondo CLN Lombardia, b.92/f.1 contains minutes of meetings in 1945-46.

77. Tromboni, "Le donne di Bondeno," in Vaccari (ed.), *La donna nel ventennio fascista*, p. 329.

78. Palumbo quoted in Alloisio and Ajo, *La donna nel socialismo italiano*, p. 70.

79. Silvana Martignoni, "Movimento autonomo delle donne: Le sue radici nella Resistenza," in Gaiotti De Biase (ed.), *La donna nella vita sociale e politica*, p. 212, and Casadio and Fenate, *Le donne ravennati*, p. 113. PCI figures discussed earlier in this chapter reveal this as well.

80. Reggio's directorate is described in Guerrino Franzini, *Storia della Resistenza Reggiana* (Reggio Emilia: A.N.P.I., 1966), pp. 206-10. The more general party mixing is confirmed in Rapporto dei GDD all'UDI (Milan, 15 April 1945), p. 11; testimony of Diana Franceschi of Bologna in "I Gruppi di Difesa della Donna nella Resistenza," *Donne e Politica*, Nos. 5-6 (1971), p. 26; Mafai, *L'apprendistato della politica*, pp. 54-55; Pieroni Bortolotti, "Le donne della Resistenza antifascista," in her edited volume with same title, pp. 87-88, and Spano and Camarlinghi, *La questione femminile nella politica del PCI*, pp. 86-87.

81. Margherita Repetto Alaia, "The Union of Italian Women: Women's Liberation and the Italian Worker's Movement, 1945-82" (Unpublished paper presented at the Berkshire Conference on Women's History, Smith College, 1-3 June 1984), pp. 2-3; Letter from Repetto Alaia to the author, 5 February 1982, and documents on CIF organizing and membership in Bizzarri, *L'organizzazione del movimento cattolico femminile*, pp. 92-94.

82. Gobetti, *Diario partigiano*, pp. 216-18.

83. Interview between Beltrami and Franceschino, Trieste, September 1977; author's interview with Floreanini, Milan, 14 October 1981, and Gaiotti De Biase, "La donna nella vita sociale e politica," in her edited volume with same title, pp. 65-68.

# Chapter 5

1. Carlo Smuraglia, "Introduzione," in Marco Fini (ed.), *1945-1975 Italia: Fascismo, antifascismo, Resistenza, rinnovamento* (Milan: Feltrinelli, 1975), p. 11 raises this question and concludes that the Resistance was successful militarily and in its fundamental objective of defeating fascism but that it was much less effective in transforming the state.

2. Rapporto dei GDD all'UDI, 15 April 1945, 15 pp.

3. Lia Barone, "Fra tradizione e innovazione," pp. 233, 242, fn. 15. The study for Brescia is Rolando Anni, Delfina Lusiardi, Gianni Sciola, and Maria Rosa Zamboni, *I gesti e i sentimenti: Le donne nella Resistenza bresciana* (Brescia: Comune di Brescia, 1989), pp. 7-13.

4. Cited in "I gruppi di difesa della donna," *Donna e Politica*, Nos. 5/6 (1971), p. 23, which consists of various interviews including Vecchio and Franceschi, pp. 25-26.

5. Rapporto dei "Gruppi di difesa della donna," reprinted in Franceschi and Gaeta, *L'altra metá della Resistenza*, pp. 81-82.

6. Report of the Central Sector, GDD, Milan, 14 April 1945 (ISML, Fondo CLNAI, b.18/f.7).

7. Report of the Forces of the GDD by Sector and Zone (Milan and Province), March 1945 (ISML, Fondo CLNAI, b.18/f.7), 2 pp.

8. Relazione parziale sulla attivitá delle compagne svolta per la costituzione dei "Gruppi di difesa della donna" nella cittá di Ravenna e dintorni, reprinted in Casadio and Fenati, *Le donne Ravennati*, pp. 140-41.

9. Danilo Veneruso, "La donna dall'antifascismo alla Resistenza," and G. Petti Balbi, "La donna nelle compagne e in montagna," in G. Benelli, et al., *La donna nella Resistenza in Liguria*, pp. 62-63 and 176-77, respectively, address the issue of rural women. For Luciano Bergonzini's discussion, see *La Resistenza a Bologna*, V, pp. 36-39.

10. Bergonzoni testimony in L. Bergonzini (ed.), *La Resistenza a Bologna*, V, pp. 693-96.

11. Report from the National Secretary, GDD, Milan, 19 March 1945, "Direttive per il lavoro di svolgere fra le contadine" (ISML, Fondo CLNAI, b.18/f.7), 2 pp.

12. Report to GDD National Committee and CLN Lombardy from the Provincial Committee, GDD Milan, November 1944 (ISML, Fondo CLNAI, b.18/f.7), 2 pp.

13. Marisa Rodano, "Un difficile processo di emancipazione nella Resistenza Italiana," *Donne e politica* 5:5 (December 1974), pp. 40-47.

14. Mafai, *L'apprendistato della politica*, p. 35.

15. In *Donne e Resistenza: Atti del Convegno, Pisa* (Comune de Pisa, April 1979), p. 130.

16. Rossi in Pieroni Bortolotti, *Donne e Resistenza in Emilia Romagna*, Vol. II, pp. 56, 84.

17. Borellini in *Donne Emiliane nella Resistenza*, p. 17.

18. In Giudetta Serra (ed.), *Compagne*, I, p. 125.

19. Gobetti, *Diario partigiano*, p. 57.

20. Interviews with Giorgina Levi in Scroppo, *Donna, privato e politico*, p. 68, with Carmen Nonotti Margaro in Serra, *Compagne*, II, p. 613, and Bertini in Pieroni Bortolotti, *Donne e Resistenza in Emilia Romagna*, Vol. II, p. 30.

21. In Bergonzini, *La Resistenza a Bologna*, Vol. III, p. 341.

22. *Attivitá dell'Unione Donne Italiane*. Sezione Provinciale di Pisa (Pisa, 1945), p. 11.

23. From transcribed testimony by Giuliana Beltrami taken in 1978.

24. *Noi Donne*, No. 1 (May 1944), p. 1.

25. GDD Provincial Committee, Milan, Report to UDI, 1945 (UDI Files, Rome). The various local papers include *La difesa della lavoratrice* (Defense of the Working Woman, Piedmont), *La voce delle donne* (Woman's Voice, Bologna and a Swiss edition), and *Donne in lotta* (Women in Struggle, Liguria).

26. "Madri e spose," Comitato Bolognese dei GDD (n.d.), 1 p; and "Donne Modenesi," I Gruppi di difesa della donna (n.d.), 1 p. A variety of these broadsides are in the Milan archives, and some have been reprinted in works on the Resistance.

27. *Noi Donne-Ligure* (Numero Straordinario, November 1944), p. 4.

28. *La voce delle donne* 1:1 (20 December 1944), reprinted in Bergonzini, *La Resistenza a Bologna*, II, p. 924.

29. "Le donne Salernitane per la ricostruzione e la democrazia" (14 October 1945, 1st Congresso Provinciale dell'Unione Donne Italiane, Relazioni sull'attivitá svolta, Salerno), p. 5; GDD, Comitato di Bergamo, "La donna e il fascismo," in *La Donna nella Resistenza* (n.p., n.d., but probably 1945, mimeographed pamphlet in UDI Files, Rome), p. 3, and *La Rinascita: Organo del Comitato Provinciale di Bologna. Fronte della Gioventú* 1:1 (22 July 1944), in Bergonzini, II, p. 748.

30. "Che cosa vogliamo?," *Noi Donne* (August 1944, reprint), p. 13.

31. Floreanini, from her speech in *Donne e Resistenza. Atti di Convegno, Pisa*, p. 53 and the author's interview with her; Beltrami, "La donna e la Resistenza," in *La donna in cinquant'anni*, p. 16. Paola Gaiotti De Biase also concludes that "what emerges clearly from the Resistance is the stimulus for women to be 'protagonists,' [though] this impulse does not become the sign of a refutation of the traditional family dimension." *Questione femminile e femminismo nella storia della Repubblica* (Brescia: Morcelliana, 1979), p. 28.

32. In "I Gruppi di Difesa della Donna," *Donna e Politica*, 5/6 (1971), p. 26.

33. Testimony in Paterlini, II, p. 472.

34. These ideas appear again and again in the words of Nilde Jotti, "Una metá dell'esercito," in *Donne emiliane nella Resistenza*, p. 3; *La Resistenza nelle campagne modenese*, p. 14; G. Floreanini, *Donne e Resistenza. Atti di Convegno, Pisa*, p. 53; Marisa Rodano, *Donne e Politica*, 5:5 (1974), p. 44, and Rina Picolato as National Secretary of GDD in speech of April 1945 in Milan printed in *L'Unità* (29 April 1945) 2:6-7.

35. Obici comment is in a response to a questionnaire used by Gaiotti de Biase, *La donna nella vita sociale e politica*, p. 104, fn. 9, while Minelli's testimony is on p. 148, fn. 307.

36. For women's political participation, see *I Deputati e senatori del primo parlemento repubblicano* (Rome: La Navicella, 1949); Spano and Camarlinghi, *La questione femminile*, pp. 150-53; Leonilde Iotti, "I diritti della donna alla Costituente," *Donna e politica*, Nos. 5/6 (1971), p. 28; Mafai, *L'apprendistato della politica*, p. 177; and Karen Beckwith, "Women and Parliamentary Politics in Italy, 1946-1979," in Harold Penniman (ed.), *Italy at the Polls* (Washington, 1981), p. 243.

37. "Le donne hanno diritto al lavoro," *Noi Donne*, No. 1 (31 September 1945) (Reprint), p. 3.

38. *Noi Donne* 1:7 (1 December 1944), p. 6, and 2:4 (1 April 1945) (Reprint), p. 3.

39. A good example of this argument is found in "La donna e la nuova vita," *L'Nuova Realtá*, No. 1 (27 February 1945), pp. 1-2.

40. This is from a variety of newspapers and from a national conference of Catholic Action in late 1945 cited by Gaiotti De Biase, *La donna nella vita sociale e politica*, p. 128, fn. 175.

41. In Turin, for example, in the spring of 1945, such a change in designation was proposed. *La difesa della lavoratrice* 2 (1945), pp. 1-2.

42. UDI, Preparazione del Congresso, 1945, pp. 6-9; UDI, "Materiali di propaganda per il referendum istituzionale" (9 April 1946), in Repetto, et al., *UDI: Laboratorio di politica*, pp. 45-46.

43. "Appello alle donne italiane del Comitato d'iniziativo dell'UDI," *Noi Donne* (Special Edition, 10 October 1944) in Repetto, et al., *UDI: Laboratorio della politica*, p. 23; exactly the same wording appeared in PCI, *Bollettino di Partito*, No. 2 (September 1944) (Feltrinelli Reprint), p. 28.

44. *Noi Donne* (Liguria), No. 1 (January 1945), pp. 1-2; *La voce delle donne* 2:3 (15 March 1945), in Bergonzini (ed.), *La Resistenza a Bologna*, II, p. 941.

45. *Noi Donne* 1:1 (July 1944) (Reprint), p. 2.

46. Interview in *Noi Donne*, No. 2 (31 August 1945) (Reprint), p. 2. A year earlier UDI had prepared a list of requests that were to be presented to the National CLN; among things on the list were the requests for an extraordinary tax on luxury items, like coffee, to provide help for infants and that UDI have a representative on the government committee that was distributing American goods. UDI Memo, 23 October 1994, National Archive ACS; CCLN UDI B. 3.

47. The lire had been valued at 50 to the dollar in 1944; by 1946 a devaluation established a rate of 225 to 1. At the same time, it has been estimated that in 1945 national income was about half of its prewar value. For this information, see: John Harper, *America and the Reconstruction of Italy, 1945-48* (Cambridge University Press, 1986), especially pp. 25, 61-62, and Jon Cohen, "Economic Growth," in Edward Tannenbaum and Emiliana Noether (eds.), *Modern Italy* (New York University Press, 1974), pp. 171-97.

48. UDI, "Progetto di volantino presentato al Comitato direttivo del 9.4.1946," in Repetto, et al. (eds.), *UDI: Laboratorio di politica*, p. 45.

49. *La Compagna* (Piedmont) (1 September 1944) 1:1-2, and (Lombardy) 1:2 (8 September 1944); MFGL broadside (n.d.) reprinted in Commissione Femminile ANPI, "Donne piemontesi nella lotta di liberazione," p. 33.

50. "Il problema delle casalinghe," *La Nuova Realtá* 1:1 (February 27, 1945), 3:2-4.

51. *Il pensiero femminile* (March 8, 1945), pp. 5-10.

52. *Compagna* 2:2 (March 1, 1945) in Arbizzani (ed.), *La stampa periodica clandestina*, p. 882.

53. I Congresso Nazionale della D.C., Il programma della D.C. per la nuova Costituzione, 24-27 April 1946, in Damilano (ed.), I, p. 236.

54. Gobetti, *Diario partigiano*, p. 67.

55. Rosetta Longo, "Per la nostra dignitá di donne," *Noi Donne* 2:7 (31 May 1945), p. 3.

56. *Noi Donne* 2:6 (15 May 1945), p. 1.

57. 15 May 1945, p. 9; 2:8 (25 June 1945), p. 11.

58. Rita Montagnana, "Nostro contributo all rinascita nazionale," *Noi Donne* 4 (31 September 1945) (Reprint), p. 1.

59. Repetto, et al., *UDI: Laboratorio di politica*, p. 13.

60. Interviews by Olga Prati, "Le donne ravennati nell'antifascismo e nella Resistenza," in Casadio and Fenati (eds.), *Le donne Ravennati*, p. 104. Lenzi's comments from a questionnaire that Gaiotti De Biase used for *La donna nella vita sociale e politica*, cited in fn. 9, p. 104.

61. Petti Balbi, "La donna nelle campagne e in montagna," in Benelli (eds.), *La Donna nella Resistenza*, p. 180.

62. Testimony in Bruzzone and Farina (eds.), *La Resistenza taciuta*, p. 144.

63. Sonya O. Rose, *Limited Livelihoods* (Berkeley, CA: University of California Press, 1992), pp. 11, 13. These words are a part of her definition of the term "gender."

# Chapter 6

1. Gina Borellini, "Discorso d'apertura," Convegno "Donne e Resistenza," 13-15 May 1977 (Unpublished paper, UDI Archives, Rome); Nilde Jotti, "Una metá dell'esercito," in *Donne emiliane nella Resistenza*, Special Edition, *Quaderni de "La Lotta,"* No. 3 (Bologna, 1964), p. 4; Aida Tiso, *I comunisti el la questione femminile*, p. 62, and Daniela Colombo, et al., "The Response of Public Authorities in Italy to the Needs Expressed by Women," in Kate Young (ed.), *Women and Economic Development* (London: Berg Publishers, 1988), p. 74.

2. Conti cited in Carla Ravaioli, *La donna contro se stessa* (Bari: Laterza, 1969), p. 32; Maria Vittoria Ballestrero, *Dall'tutela alla parità: Legislazione italiana sul lavoro della donna* (Bologna: Il Mulino, 1979), p. 112; Marisa Rodano, "Un difficile processo di emancipazione," pp. 41-43.

3. This paper was printed posthumously. Franca Pieroni Bortolotti, "L'altra Italia della Resistenza," *Donne e politica* 16:6 (Nov.-Dec. 1985), p. 37.

4. Italy. ISTAT, *Sommario di statistiche storiche dell'Italia, 1861-1965* (Rome, 1968), Table 93, p. 119; Donald Sassoon, *Contemporary Italy: Politics, Economy and Society Since 1945* (London: Longman, 1986), p. 25.

5. These employment percentages actually decreased slightly by 1961. See Bandettini, "The Employment of Women in Italy," pp. 371, 374; Associazione per lo sviluppo dell'industria nell'mezzogiorno, *Un quarto secolo nelle statistiche nord-sud, 1951-1976* (Rome: Svimez, 1978), Tables 19 & 20, pp. 61, 63, and Centro Studi CISL, *Donna, lavoro, sindacato* (Florence: Editore Centro Studi CISL, 1977), pp. 78-83.

6. The particular features of the 1948-51 period are discussed by Antonio Santini, "Cicli economici e fluttuazioni demografiche: Nuzialitá e natalitá in Italy, 1863-1964," *Quaderni storici* 17 (May/August 1971), pp. 554-60. For the statistics which follow, see *Un secolo di statistiche*, pp. 26-38; ISTAT, *Sommario di statistiche, 1861-1965*, pp. 22-23, 52, and Associazione per lo sviluppo, *Un quarto secolo nelle statistiche*, pp. 44-49, 135-37.

7. Simonetta Ulivieri, "La donna nella scuola dall'unitá d'Italia a oggi: Leggi, pregiudizi, lotte e prospettive," *Nuova DWF*, No. 4 (July-Sept. 1977), pp. 82-102; Marisa Ferrari Occhionero, "La partecipazione femminile nell'universitá Italiana," *Sociologia* 9:3 (1975), pp. 60, 72, and Carla Ravaioli, *La donna contro se stessa* (Bari: Ed. Laterza, 1969), pp. 15, fn. 6, 17, fn. 9, and Repubblica Italiano. ISTAT, *Annuario Statistico dell'Istruzione italiana, 1948-49* (Rome, 1951), Table 171, p. 225.

8. Barkan, *Visions of Emancipation*, p. 34.

9. Lesley Caldwell, "Church, State and Family: The Women's Movement in Italy," in Annette Kuhn and AnnMarie Wolpe (eds.), *Feminism and Materialism* (London: Routledge and Kegan Paul,

1978), p. 75. Attempts to reform the workplace are detailed by Maria Vittoria Ballestrero, *Dalla tutela alla paritá: Legislazione italiana sul lavoro delle donne* (Bologna: Il Mulino, 1979).

10. Party membership figures can be found in Poggi (ed.), *L'organizzazione del PCI e della DC,* pp. 356-57, 419; Weber, *Il voto delle donne,* p. 66, and Alida Castelli and Nino Magna, "Chi é la militante comunista," *Donne e politica* 15:1 (Jan.-Feb. 1985), p. 15.

11. Poggi, *L'organizzazione partitica,* pp. 490, 511; Beckwith, "Feminism and Leftist Politics in Italy," p. 24.

12. Beckwith, "Women and Parliamentary Politics in Italy," p. 243. Ravaioli, *La donna contra se stessa* notes the absence of women (in 1968) in the cabinet, the judicial system, and in party National Directorates, while neither the CGIL nor CISL (the two major labor organizations) had a woman on its national executive group, and of 8,055 mayors, only 81 were female, pp. 27-28.

13. Repetto Alaia, "The Union of Italian Women," p. 6; Repetto, et al., *UDI: Laboratorio di politica,* pp. 58-59, and Hellman, *Journeys Among Women,* pp. 61-63 discuss this phase of UDI's history.

14. Agendas and programs of the organizations, and how they referred to each other, illustrate this point. See "Congressi: Le parole d'ordine," in Mirella Alloisio (ed.), *L'Udissea; Storia lunga trent'anni di una associazione femminile* (UDI: Special Issue of *Noi Donne,* 1975), p. 37; Repetto, et al. (eds.), *UDI: Laboratorio della politica,* pp. 178, 213, and Marisa Rodano, "In quanto donna: L'UDI al 1952-1964," in Anna Maria Crispino (ed.), *Esperienza storica femminile nell'etá moderna e contemporanea* (Rome: LaGoccia, 1988), pp. 177-95.

15. Women who participated in the Resistance and have written about the experience agree on the notion of women as "protagonists." See Paola Gaiotti de Biase, *Questione femminile e femminismo nella storia della Repubblica* (Brescia: Morcelliana, 1979), p. 28, and M. Rodano, "Un difficile processo di emancipazione nella Resistenza," p. 44.

16. Beckwith, "Women and Parliamentary Politics," pp. 249-51.

17. Quoted in Beckwith, Ibid., p. 250, fn. 53.

18. Interview with Anita Pasquali in Laura Lilli and Chiara Valentini (eds.), *Care compagne* (Rome: Riuniti, 1979), pp. 196-97; Giuliana Dal Pozzo's comments are in the same, p. 226.

19. Ingrao testimony in Gerosa (ed.), *Le compagne,* pp. 169-85.

20. Yasmine Ergas, "Las mujeres italianas en los años setenta, *debate feminista* 1:2 (September 1990), pp. 42-58.

21. In Marina Addis Saba, "Rappresentanza e non-questione femminile alla Consulta Nazionale," *Storia e problemi contemporanei* 2:4 (July-Dec. 1989), pp. 30, 32.

22. The DOXA poll, much like the U.S. Gallup Poll, emerged at the end of the war and was produced by a private institute. The first ten years of the polls, with questions and results, have been collected and reproduced by Pierpaolo Luzzatto Fegiz (ed.), *Il volto sconosciuto dell Italia: Dieci anni di sondaggi DOXA* (Milan: Editore Giuffre, 1956). This particular poll appears on pages 339-40.

23. Ada Gobetti, "Panorama della stampa femminile," in *Le donne e la cultura* (Rome: Edizione "Noi Donne," 1953), p. 15. This volume contains the proceedings of a conference held in 1953. In the same volume, Dina Jovine, "Divulgazione della cultura fra le donne," p. 76.

24. See, respectively, *Grazia,* 8 July 1950, p. 16, and 25 November 1950, p. 17; *Gioia* is quoted in Maria Antonietta Macciocchi, "Un avvenimento nuovo nella vita culturale italiana," in *Le donne e la cultura,* p. 146.

25. Mariella Loriga, who directed the nursery/day care center at Olivetti/Ivrea in the 1950s, remembers this. See Loriga, "Ricordi di Ivrea," *Memoria,* No. 6 (1982), p. 15.

26. Leslie Wahl Rabine, "A Feminist Politics of Non-Identity," *Feminist Studies* 14:1 (Spring 1988), p. 25.

27. Rhyme quoted in Sandra M. Gilbert, "Soldier's Heart: Literary Men, Literary Women and the Great War," in Marilyn Boxer and Jean Quataert (eds.), *Connecting Spheres* (New York: Oxford, 1987), p. 234.

28. Anna Bravo, "Italian Women in the Nazi Camps: Aspects of Identity in Their Accounts," *Oral History* 13:1 (1985), pp. 20-27.

29. Bruzzone, "Women in the Italian Resistance," p. 281.

# Bibliography

## I. Archival Material

Although numerous repositories in the United States and Italy contain material on the Resistance, the extent of documentation relating specifically to women varies. For example, the Charles Delzell collection in the Hoover Institution Archives includes records of the various centers of Resistance command (such as the Committee of National Liberation for Northern Italy, CLNAI, and the Corps of Volunteers for Freedom, CVL) as well as copies of numerous newspapers published by Resistance units and organizations. Material on women is scattered throughout the collection. Holdings on the Resistance in Europe at the National Archives in Washington, DC are extensive, and fortunately there is a guide to this material: David Ellwood and James Miller, *Preliminary General Guide to American Documentation of European Resistance Movements in World War II* (Turin: University Institute of European Studies, 1974). Of particular interest for Italy are the records of the Allied Control Commission, Patriots Branch, and the records for Italy of the Supreme Headquarters Allied Expeditionary Force (SHAEF), which between them contain more than 6,000 cubic feet of documents. None of this material is organized with specific regard to women's participation, and actual references to women are few and far between, as one might expect, since the concerns of both groups were military conditions, overall questions of command and direction, and the general political situation.

Sources in Italy are much more extensive and contain substantial information relating to women. It is important to understand that in the decades following the war, many Italians considered the Resistance epoch a major turning point in their history, one which would set the course for future developments, as well as a unique series of events that in many ways sets them apart from the other nations of Western Europe. Understanding their Fascist past, explaining its origins, and applauding the regime's demise (or in most recent history perhaps seeing it in a more positive light?) have preoccupied many Italian scholars and citizens alike. This resulted in the desire to document the Resistance movement as fully as possible. National and local government agencies, the political parties, and private organizations have, as a result, developed numerous archives of appropriate material. Here, too, we are fortunate to have several helpful guides: Laura Conti (ed.), *La Resistenza in Italia* (Milan: Istituto Feltrinelli, 1961); Istituto Nazionale per la storia del movimento di Liberazione in Italia, *Guida agli archivi della Resistenza* (Milan, 1974); and *Catalogo della stampa periodica, 1900-1975* (Milan, 1977).

In most of the major urban centers of provinces that were key sites in the Resistance struggle, there is an Institute for the History of the Resistance (e.g., in Florence, Genoa, Milan, Modena, Turin, and Trieste). Fortunately for the researcher, most material in these local archives is duplicated and located centrally at the National Institute for the History of the Liberation Movement (ISML) in Milan. Records are organized by command groups or by regions (for example, Fondo CLNAI or Committee of National Liberation, CLN, Lombardy, Fondo Liguria, and Emilia Romagna) and within these often by political parties (e.g., PCI records) or groups like the GDD. Certainly the correspondence among all these groups is helpful in understanding the institutional and structural place of women in the Resistance. The ISML also has both originals and copies of most of the newspapers and broadsides published by the various women's units.

Adding to the wealth of material and often providing a slightly different dimension and emphasis are the collections at various private research centers. Certainly the Fondo Resistenza of the Feltrinelli Institute in Milan is one of the most helpful and easily used archives. It has separate volumes of documents under the heading "Women" as well as most of the newspapers published during the Resistance, many of which duplicate those at the ISML. Among the private collections in Rome are those of the Gramsci Institute, the UDI Archives, the Sturzo Institute, and the library of ANPI (National Association of Italian Partisans). The holdings of the Gramsci Institute include archives for the PCI from 1921 to 1939 and from 1943 to 1945, an archive of the Resistance, and papers of party leaders such as Palmiro Togliatti. The Gramsci Institute is undoubtedly one of the best organized and most systematic research centers in Italy. At the time of my research, UDI headquarters in Rome was the source of extremely valuable materials, though these were not organized or catalogued and therefore somewhat difficult to use. Recently, with the demise of UDI as a central, national institution, its records have been moved and reorganized in a more formal archive in Rome. Various UDI records from 1944 and 1945 are also located at the Central State Archive in Rome under the heading "Comitato Centrale di Liberazione Nazionale" (Central Committee of National Liberation). Finally, the ANPI library in Rome is a major source for published primary materials, diaries, memoirs, conference proceedings, and generally hard-to-locate materials. Since the Resistance is their sole focus, the staff there are extremely helpful and supportive, though I would add this was generally true for personnel at each of the research centers mentioned.

## II. Published Primary Material

In keeping with the desire to document and publicize the events of the Resistance, the Italians have collected and printed much primary material. For example, immediately following the end of the war, the secretary of the CLNAI in Milan published *Documenti ufficiali del Comitato di Liberazione nazionale per l'alta Italia*; in 1947 the CLN in Genoa published *Documenti del C.L.N. per la Liguria*; and some years later G. Rochat edited *Atti del comando generale del corpo volontari della libertá* (Milan: Franco Angeli Editore, 1972). The records of the Constituent Assembly and of its various committees and drafts of the proposed constitution are also available in printed form, as are the results of the first national elections for the new Republican government, e.g., *I deputati e senatori del primo parlamento repubblicano* (Rome: La Navicella, 1949). Other useful collections of documents are Luciano Bergonzini, *La Resistenza a Bologna: Testimonianze e documenti,* 3 Vols. (Bologna: Istituto per la Storia, 1967); Giuseppe Bonfanti, *La Resistenza: Documenti e testimonianze di storia contemporanea* (Brescia: La Scuola, 1976); and Sandro Contini Bonacossi and Licia Ragghianti Collobi, *Una lotta nel suo corso: Lettere e documenti politici e militari della Resistenza e della Liberazione* (Venice: Neri Pozza Editore, 1954).

As one might expect, the political parties also have gathered and printed a wide variety of primary material documenting their histories for the period. Typical of these sources are Pietro Secchia, *Il partito comunisti italiano e la guerra di liberazione, 1943-45: Ricordi, documenti inediti e testimonianze* (Milan: Feltrinelli, 1973), and Andrea Damilano, *Atti e documenti della Democrazia Cristiana, 1943-1967,* 2 Vols. (Rome: Edizione Cinque Lune, 1968).

The women's organizations as well have produced volumes recording their activities and development. The women's movement of the DC (MFDC) edited *Donne cristiane nella Resistenza: Tesitmonianze e documentazione sul contributo femminile alla lotta partigiana in Lombardia* (Milan: Molinari, 1956), while more recently Maria Michetti, Margherita Repetto, and Luciana Viviani have put together a most useful volume of documents detailing UDI's history, *UDI: Laboratorio di politica delle donne* (Rome: Cooperativa libera stampa, 1984). Published collections of this sort, of course, have the problem of conscious selectivity, and one must be aware of what might be omitted as well as what is printed and then attempt to fill in the gaps by referring to the primary archival records. This problem is less pronounced for recent UDI publications, as, beginning in the 1960s, that organization underwent a great deal of autocriticism that involved looking at problems regarding its relations with the PCI and other political parties, its lack of autonomy in the decades following World War

II, how its policies and programs were determined, and the degree to which it was able to appeal to Italian women from all social strata and political and religious traditions. Generally, this willingness to admit lack of harmony, unevenness of development, and historical contradictions adds important material and perspective to the study of women and the Resistance.

Moving beyond the published institutional and political records, countless personal autobiographies, memoirs, and diaries of participants in the Resistance are indeed some of the most positive sources for research on the topic. However, here, too, one must be keenly aware of the advantages and drawbacks in such sources, even though they provide an invaluable personal dimension to the sought-after history. To use these materials, recent publications that describe salient features of, and provide hints for the analysis of, women's autobiographies and other personal documents are most helpful. Among the many collections of criticism are Shari Benstock (ed.), *The Private Self: Theory and Practice of Autobiographical Writings* (Chapel Hill: University of North Carolina Press, 1988); Bella Brodski and Celeste Schenck (eds.), *Life/Lines: Theorizing Women's Autobiography* (Ithaca: Cornell University Press, 1988); Estelle Jelinek, *The Tradition of Women's Autobiography: From Antiquity to the Present* (New York: G. K. Hall, 1986); and Sidonie Smith, *Subjectivity, Identity and the Body: Autobiographical Practices in the 20th Century* (Bloomington: Indiana University Press, 1993). Among the helpful points made in these collections are that autobiographies must be treated carefully because they are based on memory and often written to justify and explain rather than simply to record one's activities and that there are gender-specific problems in autobiographical writing because women often write the story of women as expected of them or, if recording non-traditional experiences, often adopt the public posture of men. At the same time, as I pointed out in my conclusion, it is important that we listen to the writer's own words and perspective, even though these might seem to contradict other historical records.

For the materials on the Resistance, one must consider whether the author was a well-known public figure, the degree to which she was involved in the political debates of the time, and ultimately what her purpose might be in leaving such a record. Among the prominent political women who have published their memoirs are: Bianca Ceva, *Cinque anni di storia italiana, 1940-45* (Milan: Edizione di Comunita, 1964); Rina Chiarini, *Una donna della Resistenza* (Florence: Parenti, 1955) and with Remo Scappini, *Ricordi della Resistenza* (Comune di Empoli: Comitato Unitario Antifascista Empolese, 1974); Ada Gobetti, *Diario partigiano* (Novara: Einaudi, 1956); Joyce Lussu, *Portrait* (Bologna: Transeuropa, 1988); Lina Merlin, *La mia vita* (Florence: Giuti, 1989); Teresa Noce, *Rivoluzionari professionale* (Milan: Bompiano, 1977) and *Vivere in piedi* (Milan: Mazzotta, 1978); and Camilla Ravera, *Diario di trent' anni, 1913-1943* (Rome: Riuniti, 1973). All of these women were activists prior to the Resistance, spent time in prison or exile, and had long-established connections with either the Pd'A, the PSI, or the PCI, all of which factors give a particular slant to the writing.

The advantage of the writings of lesser-known women is that the emphasis is more on recording specific events and personal reactions than on interpretation and rewriting the history from a particular political perspective. Among these sources are Cesarina Bracco, *La staffetta garibaldina* (Provincia di Vercelli: Borgosesia, 1976); Iste Cagossi, *Da piccola italiane a partigiana combattente* (Modena: S.T.E.M.-Mucchi, 1976); Elsa Oliva, *Ragazza partigiana* (Novara: Istituto per la Storia della Resistenza in Provincia di Novara, 1969); Ines Pisoni, *Mi chiamero serena* (Ravenna: Edizione del Girasole, 1978); and Giovanna Zangrandi, *I giorni veri, 1943-45* (Milan: Mondadori, 1963).

Finally, contemporary Italian women scholars and activists concerned with preserving women's experience during the Resistance, particularly the history of unknown women, have conducted interviews and produced several extremely useful oral histories. Among the most valuable are Anna Maria Bruzzone and Rachele Farina, *La Resistenza taciuta* (Milan: La Pietra, 1976); Mirella Alloisio, Carla Capponi, Benedetta Galassi Beria, and Milla Pastorino, *Mille volte no: Dai no di ieri ai no di oggi* (Rome: Riuniti, 1975); G. Franco Casadio and Jone Fenati, *Le donne ravennati nell-antifascismo e nella Resistenza* (Ravenna: Edizioni del Girasole, 1977); Lydia Franceschi, Isotta Gaeta, et al., *L'altra metá della Resistenza* (Milan: Mazzotta, 1978); Bianca Giudetti Scrra, *Compagne: Testimonianze di partecipazione politica femminile,* 2 Vols. (Turin: Einaudi, 1977); Luisa Sturani, *Antologia della Resistenza* (Turin: Centro del Libro Popolare, 1951); and Erica Scroppo, *Donna, privato e politica* (Milan: Mazzotta, 1979).

### III. Secondary Sources

#### A. Italian

Not only have Italian scholars and political figures been interested in preserving the primary materials of the Resistance but have published countless volumes that serve to tell the story of the Resistance in a more comprehensive form. These works are often printed collections of the proceedings of conferences held to commemorate the events and actors of the Resistance, some are simply chronological narratives of those years, and others focus on specific topics. Frequently, the more general histories of the Resistance say little about women, except perhaps to point to the "heroines" or applaud the efforts of the *staffette,* thus presenting a "distorted view of women's role in the Resistance as either revolutionary heroine or housewife-mother" [Lia Barone, "Fra tradizione e innovazione," in F. Pieroni Bortolotti (ed.), *Le donne della Resistenza antifascista* (Milan: Vangelista, 1978), p. 232].

Nevertheless, some works, often because of their focus, are of special value to the history of women in the period. Among them are: Luigi Arbizzani (ed.), *La stampa periodica clandestina dal luglio 1943 all'aprile 1945 nel Bolognese*

(Bologna: Istituto per la Storia, 1969); Franco Antonicelli (ed.), *Trent'anni di storia italiana, 1915-1945: Dall'antifascismo alla Resistenza* (Turin: Einaudi Editore, 1961); Giorgio Bocca, *Storia dell'Italia partigiana* (Bari: Laterza, 1966); Carlo Brizzolari, *Un Archivio della Resistenza in Liguria* (Genoa: Di Stefano Editore, 1974); Luciano Brunelli, et al. (eds.), *La presenza sociale del PCI e della DC* (Bologna: Il Mulino, 1968); Franco Fucci, *Spie per la Libertá: I servizi segreti della resistenza Italiana* (Milan: Mursia, 1983); Roberto Finzi, *L'unitá operaia contro il fascismo: Gli scioperi del marzo '43* (Bologna: Consorzio Provinciale Pubblica Lettura, 1974); Giorgio Gimelli (ed.), *Cronache militari della Resistenza in Liguria,* 2 Vols. (Liguria: Istituto Storico della Resistenza, 1969); Gianfranco Poggi (ed.), *L'organizzazione partitica del PCI e della DC* (Bologna: Il Mulino, 1968); and Francesco Traniello and Giorgio Campanini (eds.), *Dizionario storico del movimento cattolico in Italia, 1860-1980,* 2 Vols. (Turin: Marietti, 1981).

In recent years, Italian women have criticized historians of the Resistance for omitting or ignoring women's contributions. The effect of this criticism is evident in the fact that the most recently published works attempt to provide a more gender-balanced picture. Claudio Pavone, *Una guerra civile: Saggio storico sulla moralitá nella Resistenza* (Turin: Bollati Boringhieri Editore, 1991) is one such work as the author focuses on the varied popular responses and emotions of the men and women who lived through the war years. It also goes without saying that the volumes that focus on workers and strikes or the clandestine press are more likely to include material on women than those that deal strictly with the organized military or power struggles among the political parties.

In Italy, as elsewhere in Western Europe and in the United States, the upheavals of 1968 marked the beginning of a more autonomous feminist movement. A component of this most recent women's activism was an interest in uncovering women's history and the eventual publication of a number of general works on women's experience in the twentieth century. Michela De Giorgio's *Le italiane dall'unitá a oggi: Modelli culturali e comportamenti sociali* (Rome-Bari: Laterza, 1992) is a most welcome social and cultural history of Italian women since the late nineteenth century. Works such as this are important to the placing of women's participation in the Resistance in a broader context. Among the publications focusing primarily on women and politics are Mirella Alloisio and Marta Ajo, *La donna nel socialismo Italiano: tra cronaca e storia, 1892-1978* (Cosenza: Lerici, 1978); Franca Pieroni Bortolotti, *Socialismo e questione femminile in Italia, 1982-1922* (Milan: Mazzotta, 1974); Annarita Buttafuoco (ed.), *Sul movimento politico delle donne: Scritti inediti* (Rome: Cooperativa Utopia, 1987); Aurelia Camparini's chapters on women's organizations in Volumes 3 and 4 of *Storia del movimento operaio del socialismo e delle lotte sociali in Piemonte,* edited by Aldo Agosti and Gian Mario Bravo (Bari: De Donato, 1979-81); Francesco Maria Cecchini (ed.), *Il femminismo cristiano: Le questione femminile nella prima democrazia cristiana, 1898-1912* (Rome: Riuniti, 1979); Marina

Ceratto, *Il 'Chi é?' delle donne Italiane, 1945-1981* (Milan: Mondadori, 1982); Anna Maria Crispino (ed.), *Esperienza storica femminile nell'etá moderna e contemporanea* (Rome: UDI, Circolo "LaGoccia," 1988); Paola Gaiotti De Biase, *Le origini del movimento cattolico femminile* (Brescia: Morcelliana, 1963); and by the same author and publisher, *Questione femminile e femminismo nella storia della Repubblica* (1979); Laura Lilli and Chiara Valentini (eds.), *Care compagne: Il femminismo nel PCI e nelle organizzazione di massa* (Rome: Riuniti, 1979); Miriam Mafai, *L'apprendistato della politica: Le donne italiane nel dopoguerra* (Rome: Riuniti, 1979); Lidia Menapace (ed.), *Per un movimento politico di liberazione della donna: Saggi e documenti* (Verona: Bertani Editore, 1972); Nadia Spano and Fiamma Camarlinghi, *La questione femminile nella politica del PCI, 1921-1963* (Rome: Editore Donne e Politica, 1972); Aida Tiso, *I comunisti e la questione femminile* (Rome: Riuniti, 1976); Maria Weber, *Il voto delle donne* (Turin: Biblioteca della Libertá, 1977).

Other general works that detail the history of women's work and education, and laws pertaining to women, are Maria Vittoria Ballestrero, *Dalle tutela all parità: Legislazione italiana sul lavoro delle donne* (Bologna: Il Mulino, 1979); Annamaria Galoppini, *Il lungo viaggio verso la parità: I diritti civili e politici delle donne dall'Unitá ad oggi* (Bologna: Zanichelli, 1980); and two invaluable articles, that by Marisa Ferrari Occhionero, "La partecipazione femminile nell'università Italiana," *Sociologia* 9:3 (1975), pp. 59-75, and Simonetta Ulivieri, "La donna nella scuola dall'Unitá d'Italia a oggi," in *Nuova DWF*, No. 4 (July-Sept. 1977), pp. 82-102.

Assessing the significance of and categorizing the works specifically devoted to women and the Resistance is difficult for a variety of reasons. First, most focus on a specific province and particularly on the areas in which women organized most visibly; second, many are narrative or descriptive with little analysis or general historic context; and third, since many of the works are the printed results of commemorative conferences, they include a range of articles that are quite uneven in quality. Most have as their goals an attempt to correct traditional historiography by illustrating the importance of women's contributions to the Resistance and an assessment of whether or not the Resistance was an emancipatory experience for women.

The broadest general account is that of Giuliana Beltrami and Mirella Alloisio in *Volontarie della libertá* (Milan: Mazzota, 1981). This work's greatest strengths are the presentation of new material derived from the authors' extensive interviews and its coverage of all the regions of Italy, arranged by such topics as women's strikes and demonstrations, women in the political parties, and, of course, GDD organization for each area. A second general work is the collection of essays, reprints of documents, broadsides, and newspaper articles edited by Ferdinando Etnasi, *Donne Italiane nella Resistenza* (n.p.: Editrice "Il Calendario," 1966). There is little narrative content in this volume, and what does appear lacks gender-specific analysis, stressing instead women's heroism and contributions to the overall effort. Recently, Anna Bravo and Anna Maria Bruzzone have published *In guerra senza armi: Storie di donne, 1940-45* (Bari: Laterza, 1995). Although they include some partisans, the story they tell is primarily that of "ordinary" women in the Piemonte who had no defined political or military role.

Regional studies of women abound and vary in quality. Though often limited by their geographical focus and lack of comparisons, some are particularly useful. One of the better collections is the three-volume series *Donne e Resistenza in Emilia Romagna* (Milan: Vangelista, 1978), which stems from a conference organized by the Women's Commission of the Committee to Commemorate the Thirtieth Anniversary of the Resistance in Emilia-Romagna, held in Bologna in May 1977. Each volume focuses on a specific period and includes a lengthy introductory essay by the author/editor plus additional shorter and more limited topical chapters by various contributors.

The first volume, *La donna nel ventennio fascista, 1919-1943*, edited by Ilva Vaccari, is one of the best available Italian works on women under fascism, but it also contains a helpful essay by Delfina Tromboni, "Le donne di Bondeno dal fascismo alla Resistenza," which covers the period from 1919 to 1945. Volume 2, by Franca Pieroni Bortolotti, *Le donne della Resistenza antifascista e la questione femminile in Emilia Romagna, 1943-1945,* is an essential piece for the region but also of wider significance because it is more speculative and interpretive than many, thus pointing to a wider conceptual framework for understanding women's experience during the Resistance. Finally, the third volume, by Paola Gaiotti De Biase, *La donna nella vita sociale e politica della Repubblica,* serves as a bridge carrying Resistance experiences and themes into the postwar era. Two of its articles are particularly helpful: Silvana Martignoni, "Movimento autonomo delle donne: Le sue radici nella Resistenza," and Alessandro Albertazzi and Angiola Maria Stagni, "Il primo anno di vita del Centro Italiano Femminile in Emilia Romagna," one of the few histories of the origins of CIF. Complementing these volumes is another collection, "Donne Emiliane nella Resistenza," a special edition of *Quaderno de "La Lotta,"* No. 3 (Bologna, September 1964). This work includes articles with a somewhat unusual focus, such as that of Paris Tassinari, "Settemila a fianco dei 'ribelli' di Bulow," which deals with resistance in the workplace, as well as remembrances and commentaries by Resistance leaders, such as Gina Borellini, and interviews with ten ex-partisans.

A second regional study of considerable usefulness is the collection of papers presented at another commemorative conference held in 1976 in Liguria. Edited by G. Benelli, and others, and entitled *La donna nella Resistenza in Liguria* (Florence: La Nuova Italia Editrice, 1979), it includes articles dealing with women's resistance in the city, the countryside, and the mountains, in the factories, and in the schools, plus a listing of the women in the area who were engaged in resistance activity. The women of Reggio Emilia have also been the focus of study by Avvenire Paterlini, whose work *Partigiane e Patriote della provincia di*

*Reggio nell' Emilia* (Reggio Emilia: Editore Libreria Rinascita, 1977) was also based on extensive interviews, which in turn enabled the author to list the participants along with some data on their lives and excerpts from their personal testimonies. The list of these regional studies would be much too long to cite, as at some point in the last twenty years or so most provinces or even communes, particularly in the area north of Rome, have held commemorative meetings and published the results. Conference sponsors range from UDI and ANPI to local government agencies and institutes for the history of the Liberation Movement, and representative localities include Mantua, Siena, and Modena (all in 1965); Ferrara and Turin (no dates given); Tuscany (in both 1974 and 1978); Bologna (1975); Pisa (1978); Ancona (1987); and Brescia (1989). The utility of these publications varies, as they are often more rhetorical than factual, their purpose more patriotic than scholarly, but because they usually include personal remembrances, they add to the breadth of experiences one should consider. It is important to note that the area of Rome has not been studied in comparable detail, though this can no doubt be explained by the peculiar features of Roman resistance (i.e., much less formal military organization and the involvement of Allied forces) and the fact that Rome was "liberated" a year before the other regions discussed.

Two other types of work add another dimension to these chronicles of regional activity. The first is biographies of important female figures, though surprisingly these are few in number and do not match the contribution of the many autobiographies, diaries, and memoirs. One of the few examples is Mario Lizzero's *Virginia Tonelli: "Luisa" Partigiana,* No. 1 of the *Quaderni della Resistenza,* published in 1972 by the Regional Committee of ANPI in Friuli-Venezia Giulia. This work is especially helpful because the area in which Tonelli operated has often been overlooked in general studies. It would appear that the whole range of biography of Italian women could be fruitfully studied, and detailed portraits of major female figures such as Noce, Ravera, Merlin, and Jotti are certainly needed.

Finally, *Partigiane delle libertá* (Rome: Sezione controle stampa e propaganda, 1973), editied by the PCI, typifies new feminist perspectives on the Resistance. Instead of providing great factual detail or historical methodology, it attempts to assess the impact of women's activism in those years on postwar events and contemporary Italian history. Representative of the articles included is Adriana Seroni's "Protagoniste della lotta per un societá nuova."

This same sort of feminist politics appears in a number of journal articles and special editions, many of which focus on women's rights and women's organizations as they emerged in the twentieth century. This political perspective is extremely important to a non-Italian historian, as many of the writers were themselves participants and their experiences, combined with political and feminist consciousness, express one reality of women's history in Italy. Several of these works are of special note: Giuliana Ascoli's "L'UDI tra emancipazione e liberazione, 1943-64," *Problemi del socialismo* 17:4 (Oct.-Dec. 1976), more valuable in its historical detail than most; Silvana Casmirri, "L'Unione Donne Italiane, 1944-48," a special edition of *Quaderni della FIAP*, No. 7 (April 1978); and Volumes II, Nos. 5/6 (1971) and V, No. 5 (1974) of the PCI journal, *Donne e politica,* which includes several articles on the GDD by organizers such as Stella Vecchio and Diana Franceschi, the early history of the PCI and the "Woman Question" by Camilla Ravera and Aurelia Camparini, and the process of emancipation and women's rights in the new constitution and post-war republic by political activists Leonilde Jotti and Marisa Rodano. Women's experiences in the PSI have also been documented, and a mimeographed collection of articles published by the party, *La donna in cinquant'anni di lotte socialiste, 1924-74* (Milan: Circolo De Amicis, 30 November 1974) includes Elvira Badaracco, "La donna e il fascismo" and Giuliana Beltrami and Anna Granata, "La donna e la Resistenza," as well as interviews and commentaries by figures such as Senator Pina Palumbo and ex-partisan Maria Beltrami.

Several other articles should be added to this listing because of their somewhat different topical focus. The variety of Catholic women's experiences are the subject of Elissa Bizzari, "L'organizzazione del movimento femminile Cattolico dal 1943 al 1948," another special edition of *Quaderni della FIAP*, No. 37 (n.d.); and of Cecilia Dau Novelli, "'Daremo sei millioni di voti': Il Movimento delle donne Cattoliche nei primi anni della Repubblica," *Memoria* 21:3 (1987).

Finally, the following provide provocative challenges to the methods, interpretations, and theory of Italian historiography of the Fascist and Resistance periods: Marina Addis Saba (ed.), *La corporazione delle donne: Ricerche e studi sui modelli femminili nel ventennio fascista* (Florence: Vallecchi, 1988); Giovanni De Luna, *Donne in oggetto: L'antifascismo nella societa italiana, 1922-39* (Turin: Bollati Boringhieri, 1995); Maria Fraddosio, "Le donne e il fascismo: Ricerche e problemi di interpretazione," *Storia contemporanea* 17:1 (February 1986); and a special edition of *Storia e problemi contemporanei,* Vol. 2, No. 4, entitled "Resistenza femminismo," published in 1989.

### III. Secondary Sources (cont'd)

#### B. English

Valuable material on the Resistance is interwoven into a number of excellent studies in English on the history of Italy in the twentieth century. Works on fascism and antifascism, the histories of institutions, politics and political parties, diplomatic relations, and the social and economic developments of this period all provide essential material context and conceptual frameworks. The existing literature on fascism is far too vast to cite, but helpful starting places are Borden Painter's essay, "Renzo De Felice and the Historiography of Italian Fascism," *American Historical Review* 95:2 (1990); and Alexander De Grand's *Italian*

*Fascism: Its Origins and Development* (University of Nebraska, 1982), which is a comprehensive summary of the phenomenon, especially useful for those without a great deal of knowledge of the period. Also helpful are three recent works, typical of contemporary interest in social and popular cultural history: Victoria de Grazia, *The Culture of Consent: Mass Organization of Leisure in Fascist Italy* (Cambridge University Press, 1981); Tracy H. Koon, *Believe, Obey, Fight: Political Socialization of Youth in Fascist Italy, 1922-1943* (Chapel Hill: University of North Carolina Press, 1985); and Alice Kelikian, *Town and Country under Fascism: The Transformation of Brescia, 1915-1926* (New York: Oxford University Press, 1987). We now are also most fortunate to have Victoria de Grazia's fine study, *How Fascism Ruled Women. Italy, 1922-45* (Berkeley: University of California Press, 1992), and that of Perry R. Willson, *The Clockwork Factory: Women and Work in Fascist Italy* (Oxford: The Clarendon Press, 1993). A final helpful resource is Philip V. Cannistraro (ed.), *Historical Dictionary of Fascist Italy* (Westport, CT: Greenwood Press, 1982).

Revisions in historical assessments of Fascist Italy have produced studies that are concerned not only with regional and gender variations and experiences of daily life but also with new ways of looking at the degree to which the population supported or opposed fascism. These new approaches recognize that there was no universal support for the regime, or later for the partisans, and that consent and dissent must be placed on an ever-shifting continuum. These perspectives can be found in David Forgacs (ed.), *Rethinking Fascism: Capitalism, Populism and Culture* (London: Lawrence and Wishart, 1986); Luisa Passerini, "Work Ideology and Working Class Attitudes to Fascism," in Paul Thompson and Natasha Burchardt (eds.), *Our Common History* (London: Pluto Press, 1982); and, more recently, Passerini's *Fascism in Popular Memory: The Cultural Experience of the Turin Working Class* (Cambridge: Cambridge University Press, 1987).

The acknowledged authority in the study of antifascism is Charles Delzell. Not only did he collect most of the materials that constitute the Hoover Institution archive on the subject but has also written a number of essential works, most importantly: "Catholics in the Italian Armed Resistance, 1943-45," *Italian Quarterly* 24:91 (Winter 1983); "The Italian Anti-Fascist Emigration, 1922-43," *Journal of Central European Affairs* 12:1 (April 1952); "Literature on Resistance to Fascism in Italy," *Journal of Modern History* 47:1 (March 1975); and *Mussolini's Enemies: The Italian Anti-Fascist Resistance* (Princeton University Press, 1961). These works are significant for providing the connections among the individuals and movements opposed to fascism after the mid-twenties and the later organizations and participants of the armed Resistance. Along the same lines, Frank Rosengarten's *The Italian Anti-Fascist Press 1919-1945* (Cleveland: Case Western Reserve University, 1968) is an important resource.

To date, there are few general studies or specialized monographs in English on any aspect of Italian women's history, and the whole area begs for new research and analysis. There are no works on women and the Resistance, though modest and recent beginnings can be found in selected chapters of Judith Adler Hellman, *Journeys Among Women* (New York: Oxford University Press, 1987) and Shelley Saywell, *Women in War* (Ontario, Canada: Penguin Books, 1985); in Anna Maria Bruzzone's brief article "Women in the Italian Resistance" in Thompson and Burchardt, *Our Common History* (previously cited); and in the author's own essay, "Women Partisans," in Volume 2 of Helen Tierney (ed.), *The Women's Studies Encyclopedia* (Westport, CT: Greenwood Press, 1991).

## IV. Other Italian Women's History Sources (English)

The following list of publications includes works that provide either general background information or quite specific coverage of aspects of the period from the Fascist era to the Resistance and into the first decades of the postwar Republic.

### A. Books

Baranski, Zygmunt G., and Shirley Vinall, eds. *Women and Italy: Essays on Gender, Culture and History*. New York: St. Martin's Press, 1991. None of the essays in this collection discuss the Resistance era, but several focus on Fascist film, literature, and propaganda.

Barkan, Joanne. *Visions of Emancipation: The Italian Workers' Movement since 1945*. New York: Praeger, 1984. Though the subject is workers' organizations and emancipation, a great deal of the information deals with women.

Bettio, Francesca. *The Sexual Division of Labour*. London: Oxford University Press, 1988. This unusual study uses the Italian case to assess certain economic and statistical models used to explain women's work patterns.

Birnbaum, Lucia Chiavola. *Liberazione della donna: Feminism in Italy*. Middletown, CT: Wesleyan University Press, 1986. This volume covers the period from World War I to the present, though emphasis is on the years since 1968. Birnbaum's focus is on changes in attitude, ideas, and collective consciousness, particularly in the form she refers to as "unedited Marxism and Catholicism."

Gabaccia, Donna, ed. *From the Other Side: Women, Gender and Immigrant Life in the U.S.* Bloomington: Indiana University Press, 1994. This, as well as numerous other studies of immigration by the author, considers gender differences in the immigrant experience and connects pre- and post-emigration histories.

Gibson, Mary. *Prostitution and the State in Italy, 1860-1915*. New Brunswick, NJ: Rutgers University Press, 1986.

Horn, David G. *Social Bodies: Science, Reproduction and Italian Modernity*. Princeton University Press, 1994.

Katzenstein, Mary F., and Carol M. Mueller, eds. *The Women's Movements of the U.S. and Western Europe*. Philadelphia: Temple University Press, 1987. Contains three chapters dealing with Italian women.

Meyer, Donald. *Sex and Power: The Rise of Women in America, Russia, Sweden and Italy*. Middletown, CT: Wesleyan University Press, 1987. Meyer discusses some aspects of women's material conditions in the nineteenth and twentieth centuries but focuses more on ideology and images.

Pickering-Iazzi, Robin, ed. *Mothers of Invention: Women, Italian Fascism, and Culture.* Minneapolis: University of Minnesota Press, 1995.

Slaughter, Jane, and Robert Kern, eds. *European Women on the Left.* Westport, CT: Greenwood Press, 1981. Includes articles on Anna Kuliscioff and Angelica Balabanoff as well as Italian Communist women in prison under fascism.

**B. Articles/Book Chapters**

Archibugi, Franco. "Recent Trends of Women's Work in Italy." *International Labor Review* 81 (1960): 285-318.

Bandettini, Pierfrancesco. "The Employment of Women in Italy, 1881-1951." *Comparative Studies in Society and History* 2 (1959-60): 369-74.

Beckwith, Karen. "Feminism and Leftist Politics in Italy: The Case of UDI-PCI Relations." In *Women and Politics in Western Europe*, edited by Sylvia Bashevkin. London: Frank Cass, 1985.

_____. "Women and Parliamentary Politics in Italy." *Italy at the Polls, 1979,* edited by Howard Penniman. Washington, DC: American Enterprise Institute for Public Policy Research, 1981.

Buttafuoco, Annarita. "Italy: The Feminist Challenge." In *The Politics of Eurocommunism*, edited by Carl Boggs and David Plotke. Boston: South End Press, 1980.

Caldwell, Lesley. "Church, State and Family: The Women's Movement in Italy." In *Feminism and Materialism,* edited by Annette Kuhn and Ann Marie Wolpe. London: Routledge and Kegan Paul, 1978.

_____. "Reproducers of the Nation: Women and the Family in Fascist Policy." In *Rethinking Fascism: Capitalism, Populism and Culture*, edited by David Forgacs. London: Lawrence and Wishart, 1986.

Colombo, Daniela. "The Italian Feminist Movement." *Women's Studies International Quarterly* 4:4 (1981): 461-69.

De Grand, Alexander. "Women in Fascist Italy." *The Historical Journal* 19:4 (December 1976): 947-68.

Del Boca, Daniela. "Women in a Changing Workplace: The Case of Italy." In *Feminization of the Labour Force: Paradoxes and Promises,* edited by Jane Jenson, Elisabeth Hagen, and Ceallaigh Ready. Cambridge: Polity Press, 1988.

Ergas, Yasmine. "1968-79, Feminism and the Italian Party System." *Comparative Politics* 14:3 (1982): 253-79.

Gaiotti De Biase, Paola. "The Impact of Women's Political and Social Activity in Postwar Italy." In *The Formation of the Italian Republic,* edited by Frank J. Coppa and Margherita Repetto-Alaia. New York: Peter Lang, 1993.

Gellott, Laura, and Michael Phayer. "Dissenting Voices: Catholic Women in Opposition to Fascism." *Journal of Contemporary History* 22 (January 1987): 91-114.

Hellman, Judith Adler. "The Italian Communists, the Woman Question and the Challenge of Feminism." *Studies in Political Economy* 13 (1983): 57-82.

Koonz, Claudia. "The Fascist Solution to the Woman Question in Italy and Germany." In *Becoming Visible*. 2d ed, edited by Renate Bridenthal, et al. Boston: Houghton Mifflin, 1987.

Lavigna, Claire. "The Marxist Ambivalence Toward Women: Between Socialism and Feminism in the PSI." In *Socialist Women*, edited by Marilyn Boxer and Jean Quataert. New York: Elsevier, 1978.

Noether, Emiliana. "Italian Women and Fascism: A Reevaluation." *Italian Quarterly* 23 (Fall 1982): 69-80.

# Index